FROM MICROSOFT TO MALAWI

Learning on the F
Peace Corps \

Michael L. Buckler

Hamilton Books
A member of
The Rowman & Littlefield Publishing Group
Lanham · Boulder · New York · Toronto · Plymouth, UK

I dedicate this book to the Boys:
Myson Jambo, Gift Chimimba and Alfred Piyo.

According to a Chinese proverb, "When
planning for a year, plant corn. When planning for
a decade, plant trees. When planning for life, train
and educate people."

May the proceeds from this book pay for the
Boys to attend college in Malawi, so they can
realize their dreams, just as I have.

Thank you, dear sons.

Your American Father

Dear Mike,

You are completing what will probably be one of the most difficult years of your life. Preparing for change is always difficult.... I wish I could give you a road map of what to do and how to act, but I cannot.... No one [can] give you simple answers to tell you what is right.

Mike, we are all humans. The world is not perfect.... Our job is not to condemn or correct others. We cannot set up rules for others.... Rules and laws are not the way for mature adults. No one can write rules that will make people good.

Love,

Dad

— Letter from Lew Buckler, Spring 1996

What do poor people in Malawi have to offer us? Most people think nothing. I disagree. I love the amalgam of sights, smells, voices, and cultures that make Malawi such a paradoxical place. Simultaneously uplifting and depressing, welcoming and foreboding, liberating and oppressive, cruel yet undeniably vivacious, occasionally commonsensical yet vexingly illogical, Malawi gets in your blood, inhabits your dreams, and dares you to be smitten by its charms. No matter where you go, it never leaves you.

I wasn't always this way. Before joining the frontlines of the war on global poverty, I grew up in small-town America and did everything expected of me — church choir, Little League, Boy Scouts, good grades, prestigious schools, top jobs, and holy matrimony. But something was wrong: I was living everyone else's American dream. So, I walked away, determined to fulfill my destiny, my way. I haven't looked back.

Peace Corps Malawi was my calling. Without running water or electricity, I slept in a dilapidated brick house on the outskirts of a rural village, devoting two years of my life to gritty introspection, personal enlightenment and international development. I spoke local languages, cooked on open fires, drank from a nearby well, bathed out of a bucket, and shit in a hole in the ground. I was white, famous, and celibate — well, mostly celibate.

I tried my best to help. I taught at an underserved school alongside Malawian colleagues. I opened my home and heart to three of my Malawian students, whom I now consider sons. I hobnobbed with crooked politicians and starry-eyed development workers – watching aid money well spent and grossly wasted. Every day brought a blank slate of astonishment and toil, as I labored from the grassroots in nowhere Africa.

Welcomed as a Western sage, I was humbled by the wisdom of the plainspoken and powerless. Whether international aid has improved their lives is a matter of heated debate, but no one is asking them. The dominant voices are wealthy donors, government officials and international economists, not the intended recipients living in places you've never seen or heard of. But they, too, have insights and opinions that need to be considered. Indeed, they have as much to teach us as we have to teach them.

This is what I learned.

I

CHIPMUNKS & LIONS

*Have you ever wondered what someone was doing at a particular mo-
ment? If only you could tune your TV to a station showing that person
going about daily life. Many of you want to follow my Peace Corps service
this way (especially Mom and Dad), but my words alone must suffice to
satisfy your curiosity and convey what you might see on the screen if you
visited the Mike Channel.*

— Letter Home, May 2007

Light seeps into the room from the cracked window, gingerly at first, and then more assertively with the rising sun. I cannot escape it, so I groggily rouse my aching body from bed, feeling the effects of yesterday's bicycle ride, lactic rust ringing in shredded, driftwood legs. With a moan and slow roll, I part the cracked drapes of mosquito netting canopied above and fantasize about turning back the clock, falling backwards onto my foam mattress and squeezing out a few extra minutes of sleep. Yet, I know there are rewards for standing and starting the day.

On a table just across the room are the ingredients of a familiar morning treat — hot water (kept overnight in a Thermos) and instant coffee. Together with a sprinkle of powdered milk, they form the ultimate morning elixir, instantly transforming me from grumpy zombie to enthused jitterbug. I mix the concoction, pausing to take a deep sniff of its chicory aroma. A year ago, I would have scoffed at the thought of drinking this crap, but now it's all I've got — a relationship of convenience, a dependency of desperation.

Unfortunately, this morning there is no time to savor the drinking experience. Immediately after the first sip, my stomach growls and churns like a meat grinder, and I scurry from my room, through the backdoor and into the yard. Coolly scrambling past neighbors and their livestock, nodding apologetically for not stopping to chat, I lunge inside the *chimbudzi,* a cramped, brick outhouse with a rectangular bull's-eye hole in the floor. Crisis averted, at least for now.

Thankfully, Alfred, Gift and Myson (the "Boys") miss the bathroom ruckus. My Malawian students and housemates, they rise quietly at 3 or 4 a.m. each morning to study in a nearby classroom under solar lighting. Gift is always the first to stir from the communal bed: a creaky reed mat and blanket unrolled across a cement floor. With a shake and a rebuke, he spurs the other two to rise and seize a harsh but precious opportunity to shine in school and escape the village.

As full-fledged members of the Buckler family, the Boys have a room in my standard-issue teacher house. Theirs is square like the other three: ten feet by ten feet. Yet, unlike my tidy den, organized with bookshelves and food containers, and swept daily to remove dust and ant colonies, theirs is a mess — a rat's den of papers, shoes, skin grease, trinkets, candies and exercise books, with school schedules, sepia 4x6 inch photographs, and inspirational quotes adorning the bare, whitewash walls.

School clothes, however, are sacred cows, set apart from the ordinary clutter. Each boy has one outfit to last the entire week: perfectly polished leather shoes are parked in rows on the floor like luxury cars; and draped above them, on the backs of chairs, are folded blue trousers and white shirts, showing the wear and tear of time and wash cycles in the river. No one is particularly fond of the uniform, but wearing anything else (except on Wednesday, the school's casual dress day) draws the ire of the Headmaster.

Eager for the school day to begin, the Boys return promptly at 6 a.m. to bathe and dress. Hearing their banter, I return from the chimbudzi to find them preparing for a special event. Today is a school variety show, a showcase of songs, dramas and comedies performed by students, and as school leaders, the Boys will attend as organizers and entertainers. As I listen to their entries, I beam with pride, as a father should, at the depth of their talents. In addition to possessing strong minds, all three sing beautifully — like most Malawians, they seem to possess a gift for music.

* * * *

By Malawian standards, the Boys are not only my housemates, but my sons. Given that two years of celibacy is an insufferable grind, and Malawian women are gorgeous, I could have made a few rug rats of my own. But instead of impregnating a villager, and playing Russian roulette with the HIV virus, I simply invite three students to live with me. It's de facto adoption — village style.

Alfred, Gift and Myson are proven "good kids" between the ages of eighteen and twenty who deserve a helping hand. For each, living in my home means extra study time to prepare for the college entrance examination and the end of long, arduous commutes to and from school. Over several months of cohabitation, maybe I can do for them what I cannot do during forty-minute teaching blocks in the classroom for the hundreds of other underprivileged and deserving students. In short, it's an experiment.

And, to be clear, it isn't altruism or pity. Well, not entirely. I'm lonely and occupying an entire teacher house by myself seems wasteful. The late Paul Tsongas (U.S. Senator and 1992 Democratic Presidential Candidate) lived with students as a Peace Corps teacher in Ethiopia and later recounted it as one of the best decisions of his life (I'm sure it beat running for President). Based on my experience, I have to agree with Paul.

The Boys, friends since primary school, enthusiastically accepted the cohabitation invitation, dramatically enriching my life. Now, they make me laugh, cook my dinners, tidy the yard and common areas, and generally fill my house (if not life) with a lively, warm humanism. No longer am I living like an island castaway, eating and sleeping in solitary confinement, envious of my colleagues and their familial support structures. In short, I am finally "at home," and the feeling is mutual.

And each of my sons has amazing tales to tell. Gathering for meals, or just lounging around the house, we chronicle our lives. They learn too much about English slang and other peculiarities of America, about the skyscrapers and TV dinners, about the poverty in Appalachia and the opulence of Park Avenue, and about the truths and fictions of homosexuality and masturbation, both Malawian taboos. And I listen intently as they describe village gossip, becoming a trusted insider and learning that Malawian life is not an innocent Peanuts comic strip (as it first appeared to me) but a torrid, Jane Austen novel full of scandal, debauchery and mayhem.

Our relationship is like Alvin and the Chipmunks, a popular cartoon from my childhood. The basic plot, as I recall: precocious, charismatic Alvin leads Simon, the bespectacled student, and Theodore, the caring, sensitive chipmunk, in and out of endless escapades, as their father shakes his head in dismay. My Malawian triumvirate is just as good-natured and rambunctious as the Chipmunks, bee-bopping through the fields of Africa, stirring up amusement and occasional trouble. And I, like the cartoon father, watch over them with disbelief and profound gratitude.

Alfred (a.k.a. Alvin) Piyo is a love child. His parents met as young farm workers in Northern Malawi. As they picked tobacco, a valuable cash crop, under the hot sun, hormones raged, loins ached, and inhibitions melted. Nine months later, Alfred arrived. But adolescent romances always come to an end, and before long Alfred's mother (with little Alfred in tow) returned to her family in Southern Malawi. To this day, Alfred's father remains in the north, a veritable stranger. In my opinion, he's missing out.

He doesn't know that his son is flighty, impulsive and spontaneous. Alfred doesn't walk so much as bounce along like Tigger with a sprightly unmistakable gait, as if choreographing his steps to a spunky Caribbean rhythm. Daffy and unpredictable, things just seem to slip his mind, but on the bright side, he is always happy. For weeks he asks me the meaning of his Western first name. I never produce a full answer, but his face beams with pride when I tell him about Alfred the Great. Guess what he calls himself now?

Alfred is also very musical. He used to play guitar in a village band — a troupe that jams with drums, various bean-filled shakers, and three-string guitars made from recycled oil drums. Yet, unbeknownst to him, his favorite guitar was emblazoned with the name and logo of a mega corporation — Exxon Mobil, a perfect marriage of Malawian resourcefulness and American brand penetration. Fascinated by my "modern" guitar, a wooden traveler's model, Alfred often asks, "Mr. Buckler, will you play us happy sound?" I always oblige. My favorite, and his, is the G-Major chord.

Major chords help Alfred forget the past. His life was tough from the beginning and never got easier. Fatherless and poor, he lived with his mother and her family until she died, probably from HIV. Hurt, undisciplined, unwanted and motherless, he left the family compound to live with an uncle in the city. But the uncle was selfish and resentful, sometimes making dinner only for himself and eating openly under Alfred's hungry gaze. His family failing him, Alfred turned to a local gang for companionship and support.

The gang was trouble. It routinely committed petty thefts at stores and warehouses, and its favorite target was Southern Bottlers, a massive beer and soda factory. Craving sugar over alcohol, each member would steal a full crate of soda bottles, drink five or six, and pour the remainder over their bodies, ritualistically cleansing their sins in a baptism of acidic, sugary syrup. Sometimes, he reports, body parts would become glued together, temporarily immobilizing the perpetrators.

Alfred abandoned his life of crime when he narrowly escaped a police raid that netted several members of his gang. Hearing about the close call, his mother's family sent for him, imploring his immediate return to the village. Alfred initially refused, a city man shunning country life, but things changed when his family turned to a traditional healer (i.e., medicine man) for help. Unsuspecting Alfred drank the medicine man's concoction (of who knows what) and before long his "heart longed for the village," where he remains today, living in my house with his compadres.

Gift (a.k.a. Simon) Chimimba is solemn and driven. More aloof and enigmatic than the others, he devotes his energies not to socializing, but farming and preparing for the college entrance examination. Forced to fend for himself since boyhood, bouncing between households, Gift operates with an acute sense of independence and drive, products of his singular struggle for survival in one of the world's harshest environments. Of the three, he has the best chance of succeeding academically.

Both of Gift's parents have passed away, casualties of the HIV pandemic. Yet, instead of abstaining from risky behaviors, like unprotected sex, he succumbed at the end of primary school, carelessly impregnating a fellow student. His child, I am told, lives with her mother in a nearby village, lacking the attention and financial support of a real paternal caregiver and role model. She is a "gift" like her father, but nevertheless a reminder of how desperately villagers need health education. Gift doesn't volunteer this personal information; he doesn't like to talk about it. The others tell me.

The others also notice that, despite his checkered past, Gift blossoms with us. He bests shyness to become a proactive, outspoken school leader, overcoming a tendency to follow the wrong crowd and please the cool kids. Oozing with potential, yet prone to bouts of stubbornness and rebellion, he works hard to achieve his goal of becoming a nurse, earning high academic marks and an invitation to a Peace Corps Camp for promising students. At the camp, he thrives under the tutelage of positive role models and is asked to return the following year as a Junior Counselor.

Lastly, Myson (a.k.a. Theodore) Jambo is affable and easygoing. His father, the headmaster at a local primary school, has the financial resources to provide basic necessities for his family, pay school fees for Myson (the oldest son), and invite me over for chicken dinners. That modicum of stability and status feeds Myson's congeniality and optimism. He's a talker, and that mouth, framed by a large, picturesque smile and powered by a generous spirit, might take him places. Of all my Malawian students, he behaves the most like an American.

In fact, Myson likes to fantasize about finding an American wife. After meeting several Peace Corps Volunteers, he concludes that American women are the most beautiful creatures on Earth, and once I inform him that in America, black men can marry women of other races, he is determined to realize his dream. Every morning as he bathes from a bucket, he pays tribute to American ladies in song:

"I want an American girl. You are so beautiful, my American girl," he sings.

Splish. Splash.

"No you don't," I retort, creating a dueling duet, "She will tell you to cook, and she won't eat your favorite Malawian foods. You will be very unhappy."

Splash.

"I don't care," he answers, "just give me an American, American girl…oh baby, oh baby."

Myson is also our domestic sign maker, and every week he posts new creations on the wall. We have signs banishing females (except Peace Corps women), welcoming guests, and listing duties and responsibilities of household members (after Alfred forgot to cook dinner one night). On the signs, I'm delighted to read that the Boys are responsible for doing pretty much everything, from fetching water to cooking meals. Unless all three are "on a journey," which is a rarity, my only job seems to be staying out of the way. All the signs proudly declare our shared identity in large letters — "The Buckler Family."

* * * *

Having refined their vocal act for the variety show, the Boys rush off to school, reaching their desks in the nick of time. The day proceeds uneventfully, but in the waning hours, students struggle — giddy with emotion, their minds are elsewhere. After a student leader rings the final bell (by striking an old car rim hung from a tree), they rush to the library building, and the variety show begins. Villagers are starved for entertainment, so special events like variety shows and discos ("dances" in the USA) are spirited, riotous affairs that give kids (and sometimes teachers) a valuable creative outlet.

Reviews of the show are mixed. The crowd grows impatient when a trio of nervous young girls limps through a minor-keyed, dirge of a church song, swaying stiffly in unison to an adagio beat. But things heat up when two students (a popular campus comedy duo) perform an original spoof about old, senile Malawian men. Dressed in ragged sports jackets and holding canes, they walk like hunchbacks and speak with toothless gums, as the crowd erupts in laughter. But the Boys receive the most applause of all after they take the stage and, with perfect pitch, belt out a harmonious a cappella song.

I'm there as a spectator, seated in a chair of honor (along with my fellow teachers) facing the crowded room of students. The day is hot and sunny, a rarity during the rainy season, and my body is weak, its resources spent from fighting the latest influenza virus. Just as I drift into an impromptu nap, Gift takes the floor with a speech that shakes me awake:

> Since he came here in 2006, our Peace Corps Volunteer is producing delicious fruits. As we can say — a new broom sweeps clean. Some of the things which are happening because of this hero are: providing our school with four computers which is not a joke. Furthermore

we're expecting more from this man. But I would like to appeal to my fellow students to handle those items with care and also we must work extra harder. Lastly I beg almighty God to bless this hero, not forgetting our teachers.

Wow! A bit obsequious, but someone was actually noticing, let alone appreciating. Speechless and embarrassed, I bow my head and focus on the floor, trying to avoid the awkwardness of accolades. Yet, the kind words serve as needed reminders that my impact on this school and the surrounding villages is probably far grander and more penetrating that I can possibly know. I'll carefully file them away in a safe place and revisit them for inspiration on the low, "what the hell am I doing here" days to come.

* * * *

Gift's public tribute to me was touching, but he would have called me a "new miracle worker" instead of a "new broom" if he had known how difficult it was to procure those computers. It all started during my first year of service when Peace Corps generously donated them in Lilongwe (Malawi's capital), subject to the condition that I ferry them to my school. I needed a free delivery service, and the Member of Parliament (MP) for my area — Patricia Kaliati — promised to provide it. Accompanied by Mr. Zimbota (our Headmaster) and Stephen Rawls (a fellow Peace Corps Volunteer who also needed help transporting donated computers to a school), I went to Lilongwe to call her bluff.

MP Patricia Kaliati has quite a reputation. As our democratically elected representative, and Minister of Information and Civic Education, she stands out in the raucous world of Malawian politics as a bully with dramatic stage presence and flair, the female Bill O'Reilly. No stranger to controversy, Kaliati was once accused in the newspapers of trying to kill her husband's lover (a charge she vehemently denies). It is also rumored that despite her modest government salary, her children attend elite boarding schools in Great Britain, fueling speculation that she is swimming in corruption.

Indeed, corruption got her canned as Minister of Tourism. In that position, she accepted a foreign company's proposal to convert a large portion of the Nyika Plateau, a pristine natural area for the public, into an elite, private hunting ground. It was akin to inviting Wal-Mart to build a warehouse super-store smack dab in the middle of Yosemite National Park. Her decision was controversial from the onset, but after it was revealed that she was flown by the company in question to the United Arab Emirates, and lavished with gifts, the deal imploded. The President, who campaigned on an anti-corruption agenda, moved her to another cabinet position.

After taking a gimpy, smog-belching bus from the heart of Lilongwe, Stephen, Mr. Zimbota and I arrived in MP Kaliati's neighborhood in a driving rain.

Dodging streams of water that smelled of stale sewage, Mr. Zimbota guided us down the paved streets, past countless lots lacking numbers or mailboxes, to the foot of her property. From the outside, her digs looked just like all the others — an expansive lot made impervious to the greater world by a tall brick fence with a single portal of entry or exit — a hefty, steel gate.

I knocked on the gate, expecting the grandeur of her property to match her reputation. Yet, when the guard answered and motioned us inside the fence, the scene was surprisingly austere, notable not for what it possessed, but what it lacked. The grounds were quintessentially Malawian — maize gardens, goats and chickens ambling about with scruffy mutts occasionally giving chase, and a large clothesline bowing under the weight of freshly washed laundry. Aside from a guard stand, there were three modest buildings — a main house, a guest house and staff quarters.

Frankly, it was a bit disappointing. Missing in action were the luxuries enjoyed by the white aid workers living down the street — large, noisy generators that spring to life seconds after a blackout, air conditioners, manicured flower beds and Labrador Retrievers that bear a striking resemblance to Cameron, my former dog. A gleaming black Mercedes sedan parked in Kaliati's driveway, and a machine-gun wielding army soldier, were the only hints of opulence or prestige. Surely she had a couple million dollars buried somewhere in the backyard, set aside for a rainy day.

"Are we in the right place?" I asked Mr. Zimbota.

"Yes, I recognize car and dogs," he replied.

"I expected to see more stuff," I said, as the guard waved us toward the house.

"Maybe she keeps that inside. Let's enter."

After passing through the front door, we were received with signature Malawian hospitality. Although MP Kaliati was elsewhere, and purportedly doing her best to rush home, her family was present and congenial, if not curious. After learning the nationality of Stephen and me, two of her daughters peppered me with flirtatious questions.

"Where are you from?" they asked.

"Stephen and I are from America," I responded, "We are Peace Corps Volunteers."

"Oh, we love America," they exclaimed, "Will you take us there?"

"Well, you might be able to study there," I suggested.

"I don't want to study. Are there any other ways of going?" the eldest one inquired, batting her eyes.

Oblivious to his sister's salacious overtures, the baby of the family diffused the sexual tension. A ten-year-old boy conditioned to believe that all Americans were proficient in kung fu, he channeled his hyperactivity into challenging Stephen and me to bouts of play-fighting in a makeshift gladiator ring in the center of the living room. He had no idea that Stephen is a black belt in karate, and, thankfully, Stephen didn't show him.

Between awkward questions and drop kicks, I inventoried the room, investigating the lifestyle of a Malawian Member of Parliament, savoring the surrealism. Plush, worn couches lined the walls. Hung high above them along the ceiling line were fancy, framed pictures of revered elders, a crown molding of visages. An old computer sat in the corner, near a dated stereo system and a satellite-fed television, all rendered inoperable by yet another power outage. A few stained ceiling tiles drooped like overcooked macaroni.

"May I use the bathroom?" I inquired.

"Yes, it is over there," said Kaliati's eldest daughter, pointing down the hall, "Would you like me to show you?"

"Oh, no thank you. I can see it from here," I replied, leaping off the couch and trying not to blush.

Like the rest of the house, the bathroom was nothing special. A flush toilet sat in one corner, a dingy sink in the other, a cracked tile floor separating the two. The door didn't lock, and the sink didn't have a hot-water tap. A naked light bulb hung by a wire from the ceiling begging for a shade to soften its glare. Are you telling me that a Member of Parliament cannot afford a lamp shade? As I finished my business, a car pulled into the driveway.

Seconds later, doors opened and voices filled the foyer. It was Kaliati alright, home from a long day of agonizing Parliamentarian debate. She looked like a two-hundred pound tropical fruit in her African-print blouse, ankle-length skirt and headgear. But instead of coming to greet us in the living room, she stormed off in a different direction.

"Where is she going?" I asked Mr. Zimbota.

"Don't worry," he replied, "She will see us soon," an amorphous time descriptor that could mean anywhere from five minutes or three hours.

"I hope so," I added, "It's getting late."

Before long, a house worker appeared and thanked us for waiting. She then led us down a hallway and into a bedroom.

Sprawled across an expansive mattress in the dark, like Cleopatra patronizing her subjects, was our queen. A sole candle illuminated her shapely body, which was adorned with dangling gold earrings, drawn-in eyebrows, and chemically whitened skin (a fad among wealthy women in Malawi). In the shadows, her personal accoutrements lay scattered this way and that — trunks of knick-knacks, racks of shoes, and bottles of wine. There was barely enough floor space for our chairs.

Joining her in bed were two cell phones. Resting nearby like toy poodles, they rang incessantly, prolonging and interrupting our unconventional bedroom meeting. She answered each ring (sometimes two at a time) and lectured callers with an angry, self-aggrandizing tone, shouting into phones not held, per se, but delicately perched on the side of her lying head. It was an impressive feat of balance.

"I have a terrible headache," she explained.

"I'm sorry," I replied.

"I don't know why all these people are bothering me."

"Don't worry about it," I assured her, "Thank you for meeting with us on such short notice."

Between calls, we described the purpose of our visit, competing for her exhausted and phone-weary attention.

"Peace Corps is an aid agency within the U.S. Government," I started to explain.

"I know Peace Corps," she interjected, "Volunteers like you have been in Malawi since the 1960s. Now continue."

"Well, Peace Corps replaced its computers and made the old ones available for Volunteers to assist their communities," I said.

"Ah, hah," she commented, "very interesting."

"Stephen and I are both teachers. We were fortunate to get some computers for our schools. But we need your help getting them there."

"You want me to take computers to Stephen's school, too?" she asked incredulously, probably thinking, "He's not my constituent."

"Yes," I responded, "His school is on the way, a few hundred yards off the paved road."

"Ok," she schemed, staring at me with the let's-make-a-deal look of a used car salesman, "Why don't you give a computer to my Ministry?"

Here we go. Her bald attempt to better the government at the expense of poor village students was shameless and brilliant. After exchanging looks of disbelief with Stephen and Mr. Zimbota, I gathered my composure and answered her question. Tempted to grant her unsavory request, I swung the other way and took my chances with the truth.

"I'm sorry, but the computers are entrusted to us for the benefit of villagers, not government agencies," I politely explained.

"Wrong answer!" she shook her head.

"Also, as Peace Corps Volunteers, we cannot participate in political activities. Giving your Ministry a computer would violate that rule."

"Just one computer, that's all I'm asking for. You can spare one. I know you can," she pushed.

"I'm sorry," I repeated, "We really can't."

Lioness Kaliati uttered a low growl of disappointment and turned her head away, as our unfulfilled transport request hung precariously in the stiff evening air. So much for the truth — I guess it doesn't always set you free.

To say that she was disinterested in the rest of our conversation would be an understatement. When she wasn't talking on the phone, we described the situation at my school, speaking in taglines to capture her attention, like guests debating on a cable TV show. "Have big plans...trying to build boarding facility for girls...fieldtrips to Mulanje Mountain...developing student-run businesses... blah, blah, blah." The Lioness registered nary a glimmer of recognition.

After ninety minutes of intermittent phone conversations (by the MP) and lobbying (by us), the candles and participants had reached the ends of their respective wicks. It was late, and we had no idea where we would sleep or how we would get there. Malawians are adamant about the dangers of travelling at night, and I didn't want to try my luck wandering around an unfamiliar section of Lilongwe at the witching hour. We also didn't know whether the computers would be delivered to our schools. Yet, after receiving dozens of calls that evening, the MP made a few of her own.

Hanging up the phone, she resolved the uncertainty. She said that a van would come the following day to transport "all" of the computers to our schools, and that given the late hour, we would be her house guests for the night. As we thanked her profusely for helping us and exited her bedroom, the MP offered two parting gifts — a bottle of red wine and a lighthearted invitation for Stephen to stay the night with her. I quickly accepted the former and playfully tried to accept the latter on Stephen's behalf, despite his protestations.

As it turns out, a bit of immodesty may have served him well. Barely discernible in the dark, the "guest quarters" were a hard tile floor, reed mats and blankets. No mattresses, no mosquito nets, no soap by the sink in the corner. As the mosquitoes gaily buzzed around our weary heads in anticipation of the bloodletting to come, Stephen and I donned iPods and imagined ourselves in better places, as Mr. Zimbota coped by humming village rhythms from his youth. Luckily, we quickly succumbed to exhaustion and enjoyed a decent, albeit stiff, night's sleep.

In the morning, the Lioness found us in a familiar spot. We were watching satellite television in her living room (mostly Nigerian soap operas and professional wrestling from the States), not a bad way to pass time as the political prisoner of a Member of Parliament. Our jailer entered the room just as a wrestling warrior leaped from a tall ladder onto his dazed, incapacitated opponent.

"What a strange uniquely American juxtaposition," I thought, "steroid-fueled behemoths pummeling each other in bikini briefs and bookish Peace Corps Volunteers begging for some community assistance."

"Ahem," the MP signaled, as all the heads in the room swung around to her.

"Yes," we nodded, "Do you have good news for us?"

"No," she explained in a causal and unapologetic tone, "There's a transport problem, so the computers will be moved tomorrow, not today."

Reactions in the room were decidedly mixed. Her family looked delighted, especially the suggestive eldest daughter, and Mr. Zimbota didn't seem to mind, as usual. But I hid my crushing disappointment beneath a stoic face and blaring television, calmly feigning apathy, but wanting to scream. The MP graciously offered us her home for the duration of the delay, with full access to her staff and the contents of her pantry, but Stephen and I already had other plans.

Unbeknownst to the MP and Mr. Zimbota, we had plotted an escape. Celeste, a quirky but lovable middle-aged American woman from North Dakota, lived down the road. By day she toiled as a budget specialist at the Ministry of Finance, a high-level aid worker provided by the U.S. Department of Treasury. But in her free time, she was a fun-loving, party-hopping biker chick (Harley Davidsons only), routinely welcoming bedraggled Peace Corps Volunteers into her home for heavenly respites.

To execute the plan, Stephen and I slinked away from the MP's house under the auspices of doing work at the Peace Corps office. With baited breath, I frantically dialed Celeste's phone, knowing that she was at work.

"Come on, please be there," I pleaded.

I was hoping that she would answer and say, "You want to stay over? I would love to see you," which she did after the third ring.

"Yes, we would love to see you, too," I answered with a sigh of relief.

"Great, I'll grab you in a few hours," she assured us.

"Boy, do we have stories to tell you!"

"Wonderful," she replied, "Peace Corps Volunteers have the best stories."

That afternoon she retrieved Stephen and me from the Peace Corps office in her car, completing the rescue mission.

Passing through the front door of Celeste's posh compound was like entering the pearly gates. It was otherworldly and unabashedly civilized. Celeste's hospitality was legendary and seemingly endless — large meals (prepared American-style), chocolate-chip cookies, bottomless red wine, margaritas, hot showers, firm mattresses, movies, clean dogs, Western magazines, the Internet…a divine taste of America. And unlike Kaliati, Celeste had door locks, hot water taps and guest beds. Thank GOD for Celeste!

Back at Celeste's place, we decompressed. Over liberal helpings of wine and cookies, we reported on the intervening months since our last visit, including the unfolding Kaliati computer saga. Celeste listened to our tales of Peace Corps service with rapt attention and, like a doctor treating a sick patient, ordered us to eat more food and drink more wine.

"I wish that we could stay here permanently," I said, rubbing my full belly.

"Well, you can stay for a few days," Celeste responded.

"No, we cannot," Stephen interjected.

"Why?" she asked.

"Because we are taking the computers to our villages tomorrow," he explained.

"Then come and stay the next time you are in Lilongwe," she offered.

"Oh, don't worry," I said, "We'll be here."

The next morning we awoke refreshed and thankful, savoring our final moments in paradise and cherishing the soothing sound of a percolating coffeemaker.

As "good" Volunteers, we arrived at the Peace Corps office early, heeding the admonishment of Mr. Zimbota (who stayed another night at the MP's) that the vehicle was coming at 7:30 a.m. sharp. True to form, that is to say, fashionably late, the "vehicle" arrived not at 7 a.m. or 8 a.m. or even 11 a.m., but no earlier than 1 p.m., and the sight of it caused me to gasp. Instead of an empty van, as promised, the MP had provided a dual-cab pickup truck with a squat cargo bed. Matters worsened when a cadre of her supporters, joining us on the journey, emerged from the passenger compartment like clowns at the circus. "Are they all coming along to Blantyre?" I asked, irritation oozing from my lips, already knowing the answer.

Where on earth we were going to squeeze the computers was very much in doubt. After managing to maneuver some of them (but only four of Stephen's) into nooks and crannies of the truck bed, we repeated the space game, with people this time, and lost. In a rare display of selfishness and disrespect, the Malawian passengers scurried to take every available seat in the vehicle, vanquishing Stephen and me to endure the two-hundred mile journey in an open truck bed, contorting our bodies into whatever space we could find among our electronic cargo. All I could do was laugh — it was easier than crying.

And, in the end, it was all worth it. After Steven and I survived the bouncy, wind-whipped torture ride, the computers reached and improved our schools. At my school, the Boys helped assemble one in the corner of a lockable storage room (powered by a solar system), and after receiving lessons from me, most of the teachers used it to write end-of-term examinations, promising harbingers of hope and testaments to the power of community development through computing. And once the teachers understood how to operate a computer, they helped the students.

For example, after a geography lesson, Mr. Nyambalo, a young and ambitious teacher, used the computer to show his students a video on volcanic activity.

"Wow, look, look at screen," they shouted in amazement.

"You see," Mr. Nyambalo said to me, "The computers are wonderful gift from you. Many students shall be assisted."

"Thanks," I replied, "But when I'm gone, you must continue using them to teach students. I don't want them to sit in the staff room, used only by the teachers."

"No, that will never happen," he assured me, "You have my word."

And I did.

II

LIVE FROM MARS

We deploy to our respective schools next week. It will be our first tastes of true freedom since we arrived in Malawi, but it will require us to use our new language and cultural skills to find safe food, clean water, and trusted friends. Surviving in an unfamiliar place won't be easy, but I'm excited to get settled and put my training into practice.

— Letter Home, December 2006

Imagine that you are the first human being to land on Mars. What would you do? Perhaps your first order of business would be to find a Martian leader and ask some questions. Start with the essentials: What can I eat and drink? Where can I sleep? Then, turn to the secondary stuff: How am supposed to dress and act? What's the layout of this place? How's the weather? Once I get settled, can you put me to work? Incidentally, none of this information was contained in NASA's Martian guide book.

A Martian leader finds you and pats you on the back.

"Don't worry," she chuckles, "everything will be fine."

"I'm not worried," you reply, "I just need some answers."

"I understand. I will provide the answers you seek."

"Thank you. You are my Martian teacher."

"Yes," she adds, "but I'm not the only one."

"What do you mean?"

"Every Martian you meet will teach you something," she explains.

"Martians are friendly?"

"Of course," she laughs, "Martians are rich in friends, but poor in other ways."

"Poor? You mean you don't fly around in saucers?"

"Oh, no," she explains, "We can barely feed ourselves."

"Wow. I'm learning already," I say.

"Before long, you'll know all about Mars," she winks, "Just be patient."

That's pretty much how things go down when I land at my school in Khwalala Village.

* * * *

The warped front door squeaks open, causing my jaw to drop. At first glance, my standard teacher house has one story, four rooms, a corrugated steel roof, and a small, exterior courtyard off the rear separating the main living area from a pair of additional rooms — one for bathing and the other for cooking. It also comes with a toilet — an outhouse located in the backyard, a short walk from the courtyard. Headmaster Zimbota, my new boss, proudly hands me the keys like I'm a contestant who has just won the mansion of his dreams on an American game show.

"Welcome to your new house," he announces.

"Thank you," I reply softly, trying to reconcile my luxurious living in America with present conditions.

"We want you being comfortable," he says, "If you need anything, I live next door."

"What about food?" I ask, as my stomach growls.

"For now," he explains, "You eat meals with me and my family."

Only five minutes since our introduction, I'm already smitten by this angel. In his mid-forties, Mr. Zimbota is a sweet gentleman who loves to smile and laugh. One of many children born into a village family in an adjoining district, he excelled academically and earned a teaching certification. After paying his dues as a teacher for many years, he was promoted to Headmaster. With a paltry but stable government income, he supports not only his wife and three young daughters, but an entire extended family. In Malawi, when you make good, you give back.

Yet, he is not giving back to me at the moment. My heart sinks as I look around the teacher house, trying to hide my disappointment. A genuine fixer-upper, it's an aging structure with no furniture or hint of charm. Several of its windowpanes are missing or cracked, and someone has recently patched crater-sized holes in its floor with cement and coated its walls with chalky lime paint — nothing more than lipstick on a pig.

"Is there a bed?" I wonder aloud.

"Oh, yes," Mr. Zimbota replies, as two of his daughters squeeze though the door with a squeaky mess of metal supports and springs that resembles a flabby trampoline.

"Oh, dear," I laugh, recounting the tribulations of my first day, a quixotic time when all things (even struggles of impoverished living) are new and somehow charming.

Little did I know, to survive here, laughter would become my best medicine.

****

I live in Khwalala Village. It isn't bad as villages go: poor for sure, but beautiful and only forty-five miles from the City of Blantyre, Malawi's commercial epicenter. Lying in an arid, high valley and offering unobstructed views in every direction, the surrounding landscape reminds me of New Mexico, minus the snow-capped peaks and Mexican food.

On the southern tip of the Great Rift Valley, Khwalala sits at circle center on a panoramic clock face of mountains. Who better to keep time? Mulanje Mountain, a ten-thousand-foot geological marvel, looms at five o'clock, standing guard like a sphinx. In its shadow, Palombe Mountain sits at four o'clock, a silhouette of sunrises, across from its counterpoint, Chiradzulu Mountain, at nine o'clock, which captures the shadows of mauve, ambient sunsets. Off in the northern sky, all alone, is Zomba Plateau at one o'clock, sculpted like a boat hull and cropped like a flattop haircut.

Not to be outdone by its towering alpine neighbors, the Mombezi River snakes around Khwalala like a fat, slithering boa. Flowing year-round (even during the dry seasons), it is a wellspring of life, gracefully entertaining an endless cycle of clothes washing, bathing, and riverbank gardening. Though not the cleanest water source on the planet, naked children often play in its chocolaty currents. On a warm day, they call to me as I cross a crumbling bridge, en route to the nearby trading center of Milepa.

"*Mikolo, Mikolo*," they scream, unable to pronounce my English name, followed by "*Moni*," a *Chichewa* greeting meaning "Hello."

"Hello, hello," I wave and smile.

"Sweetie, sweetie, sweetie," they say after getting my attention, a desperate plea for hard candy from a local grocery.

"*Ndilibe sweetie, pepani* (I don't have any, sorry)," I reply, "*Mwina pa tsogolo* (Maybe later)."

"*Tiwonana* (Goodbye)," they answer, quickly returning to their river games.

They seem so happy that I want to jump off my bike and join them. And I probably would (at my peril) if the water weren't so brown from dirt.

In Khwalala, dirt abounds, in wet and dry varieties. With homemade, twiggy brooms in hand, women circumnavigate their barren compounds performing dusty sweeping rituals to remove "litter" — whether organic or inorganic — anything that's not dirt. "We don't like our yards to look bushy," Mr. Zimbota explains. Fields cleared for crop production are idle dirt piles during the dry seasons and frothy mud bogs during the rains. Without trees to act as wind breaks, air gusts howl ferociously, rattling homes and spewing dust.

Dirt is also the building material of choice. Rich-red earthen bricks invigorate the faces of churches, school buildings, homes, and groceries. Making bricks from local soil, in metal molds and wood-fired pyramidal ovens, is an annual rite. Wealthy and poor use the same bricks to build, but cement and corrugated-steel sheets differentiate the haves and have nots, the poor settling for mud-filled walls and grass-thatched roofs. Hence, the average life expectancy of a village home, of the poor variety, is about ten years.

Like dirt, creatures are ubiquitous in Khwalala, especially in and around my house. Geckos dance across walls, eating unsuspecting insects and depositing unsightly piles of lizard poop. Swarms of mosquitoes patrol the airspace in swirling squadrons, trying to penetrate my protective bed netting. A gorgeous fluorescent green and yellow snake slithers through a slimy drainage hole and into my courtyard, causing me to jump out of my britches. An adolescent spitting cobra makes a similar appearance next to a school classroom. I hate snakes. And I'm not alone — Malawians hate them, too.

Whether it's Biblical or superstitious is unclear, but the hatred unleashes itself at school when students discover a massive black mamba hiding in some tall grass. Alerted by a chorus of screams and shouts, I watch the students reach for sticks to strike the serpent, which immediately senses the precariousness of its situation and attempts to flee alongside a low retaining wall. That the black mamba is the world's fastest snake is of no consequence, as it doesn't have time to escape the hunters' repeated blows. The carnage is brief, and after the students deliver the lethal strike, they proudly parade the carcass around campus. One of the world's most fearsome snakes is reduced to a limp trophy.

I understand their rage. Though respectful of most beasts, I draw the line at bats, roaches and mice — all irritating creatures of the night. Bats chirp loudly after sundown, hunting for insects, and nest beneath my roof line, making a scratching sound when they move. Roaches, on the other hand, are innocuous but creepy, and mice doggedly try to eat my foodstuffs, which are vulnerable to attack in the absence of cabinets and refrigerators. At night, I sometimes wake to the noisy antics of these unwelcome houseguests and groggily stalk the house with a long, pointy stick, looking for perpetrators. Most of the offenders — whether bats, roaches or mice — flee or die a quick death.

The "domesticated animals," however, might be worse. Western supermarkets advertise "free range" as a specialty category of meat, but in Malawi, everything is free range and ravenously hungry, including cattle, goats, chickens, ducks, turkeys, and the occasional pig. And each leaves a path of destruction in its wake. Cows, for instance, are quite valuable, and need to be walked regularly, so every village allows its herds to amble around, eating grasses and plopping fist-sized piles of steaming turds on the roads and soccer grounds. Likewise, goats decimate everything edible, from crops and trees to flower beds. It's infuriating, but I try to be understanding — after all, if I were a cow in Malawi, I would poop on the soccer pitch, too, and if I were a goat, I would eat the trees.

Every bit as critical to survival as bricks and animals are heavy steel bicycles. Roving packs of farmers mount them at the witching hour, carrying crops on five-hour treks to markets in Blantyre. In their wake, tinsmiths leave unencumbered but return with rickety stacks of fifty-gallon oil drums, toxic scrap metal for village-made buckets, watering cans and cooking pots. Once bakery trucks deliver fresh bread stocks to regional trading centers, bikes emerge draped with scones and bread loafs, like shaggy, yeast-puffed show dogs. Others shoulder the inelegant chore of carting a bellowing goat, lashed sideways across skeletal, horizontal rear racks, en route to a market slaughter. Poor, poor goat.

* * * *

On a warm, windy day, as I watch bikes pass, going from one unfamiliar place to another, I turn to Mr. Zimbota.

"Where is everything?"

"What?" he asks, clearly confused by the question.

"Where are the hangouts?" I try again, getting at where people congregate in the course of their daily lives.

"Oh," he smiles, "I was waiting for you to ask that. Take a seat."

I oblige. The inquiry prompts a cartography lesson, featuring a hand-drawn map showing every nearby market, school, health center, grain mill and tea shack. The aerial view of the region reveals that Khwalala sits at the junction of four roads. In three directions, the roads are gullied vehicle graveyards that ride like rumble strips from the cockpit of a car or seat of a bicycle. The fourth, a partially graded road, blazes the best way out of Khwalala Village to the greater world — up a ten-mile-long hill.

Mr. Zimbota's map shows that one of the bad roads leads to the post office in Milepa. Every week the postmaster rides his bicycle from Milepa to a regional post office to exchange incoming and outgoing mail. On those days, I camp at his doorstep, knowing that letters from home feel like starter gifts on Christmas Eve and that packages inspire the same wonderment as a wrapped present on Christmas morning.

"What do you have in there for us?" the curious assistant postmaster loves to ask when I receive a package.

"Oh, you don't want any of my American stuff," I laugh, inching toward the door, clutching the corrugated postal cardboard like it's my first-born child. "I'll let you know if there's anything good."

"Sure, sure, sure," she jokes as I make my escape, "Maybe you give me something next week."

"Maybe," I lie, strapping the package to my bike for the ride home.

She probably suspects the truth: the boxes addressed to me are packed to the gills with all sorts of exotic items — news from home, books, beef jerky, food spices, chocolate, and energy bars. Some friends and family even send wind-up flashlights and books of poetry. Always, their unwavering support is inexpressibly appreciated and jealously guarded.

Back at my house in Khwalala, stashing the spoils of another bumper postal package, I take a second look at Mr. Zimbota's map. Something is missing, but I cannot place my finger on it. Out of the corner of my eye, a woman walks by with a heavy bundle of bound branches perched on her head, straining to look at me without dropping her cranial cargo. Suddenly, it comes to me — the map doesn't show forests or other natural areas.

"Mr. Zimbota," I call, walking toward school, "Where are the trees?"

"What?" he says from his office.

"The trees!" I repeat, reaching his doorstep.

"Most have been cut down to make firewood or clear fields for corn farming," he explains.

"When did that happen?" I wonder.

"It gets worse each year," he explains, pointing in all directions, "When I was boy, most of this place was beautiful forest."

Not so any more. Spared the ax, a smattering of tropical fruit trees variegates rows of corn stalks and handmade soil ridges (plow animals are nonexistent). On the perimeters of fields and homes, small lots of eucalyptus, a water-hogging fuel wood introduced by the British, grow skinny and straight toward the heavens, awaiting an ashy fate. Yet, the only "wild" areas lie on non-arable lands that grow little more than thickets of endemic bushy species whose imposing thorns puncture bicycle tires. Most places aren't so lucky. Suitable for agriculture, they get cleared and planted with corn.

Consequently, meals in Malawi are pretty basic, and revolve around one type of plant — corn (a.k.a. "maize" in Malawi). Almost every Malawian meal has some form of it. Cornmeal porridge is a common breakfast food. As snacks, Malawians eat popcorn, or corn that has been boiled or roasted. For lunch and dinner, families typically prepare *nsima* (the staple food), a whitish glob of boiled corn flour reminiscent of grainy, dried out mashed potatoes, which is eaten in small handfuls with greens such as pumpkin leaves or cabbage. In short, corn is king, and probably always will be.

Still, despite the abundance of corn and *nsima*, there are patent signs of desperation in Khwalala Village. Much of the arable land is clayey and difficult to farm, schools burst with students but lack teachers, health centers are few and distant, roads are lousy (especially during the rainy season), infant mortality is high, and HIV infects about fourteen percent of the population. Here, near the crossroads of several political districts, skirting the hinterlands of myriad jurisdictions, problems are known to everyone but owned by no one. In short, this place is a perfect Peace Corps site.

"What are you thinking?" Mr. Zimbota inquires, finding me lost in thought.

"I want to help this place" I say, scanning the horizon, "but where do I begin?"

"Where do you want to begin?" he asks.

"Well, the people have chopped down all of the trees to plant corn," I say, "Let's replant some trees."

"It's a welcome move," he agrees, "but we should plant fruit trees, most especially mango and banana, not thorny species."

"What about baobab?"

Baobobs, mangoes or papayas — I don't care. Regardless of which trees the community decides to plant, more are desperately needed.

"I'll apply for funding to start a tree-planting project," I say, oozing with excitement, finally "doing something productive."

"When will we know whether project is allowed?" Mr. Zimbota asks.

"I'm not sure," I reply, "I need to do some research and get back to you."

"Good luck," he says, hopeful but not expectant.

"Thanks, I'll probably need it."

It is my first community project.

* * * *

But I'm forgetting something, and I know it. Maybe something about the trees....

"Oh!" I remember.

"What is it?" Mr. Zimbota asks.

"When should we plant the trees?"

"You mean, what time of year?" he inquires.

"Yes," I reply.

"Well," he explains, "Anytime is fine, but rainy season is best."

"Rainy season?"

"Yes," he continues, "It's part of weather cycle."

"What weather cycle?"

Mr. Zimbota explains that Malawi has three seasons. Let's call them Wet Hot, Dry Cold and Dry Hot. During Wet Hot, from November to March, storms bombard the land, flooding roads and irrigating fields. Things dry out during Dry Cold, lasting from April to July, but nippy temperatures cause shivering in most places. Dry Hot arrives in August, as the sun moves closer to the Southern Hemisphere, and lasts until October, ending with the first big rain. That's the weather cycle.

During Wet Hot, watching thunderheads roll across the valley is a favorite pastime. There isn't much else to do. Every day they visit, leaving standing water in their wake that struggles in vain to move somewhere, anywhere, but finds little solace. We live in the *dambo* ("swamp" in *Chichewa*), surrounded by thick soil rich in nutrients but poor in drainage. After a deluge, moving around the *dambo* is a chore and game of chance, as puddles hide the true depths of ruts and gullies, and roads are slick and muddy.

I once made the mistake of riding on those roads. It was raining, but I was bored and certain that my Peace Corps-issue mountain bike was up to the challenge. Needless to say, I was wrong.

"Where are you going?" Mr. Zimbota asked.

"Oh, just to Milepa," I replied, "I want some exercise."

"Wait," Mr. Zimbota, "It is going to rain."

"I know," I said, hastily setting off on my journey, "but I have ridden in the rain before in America."

"You do not understand," he tried to warn me, "This is Africa. You need to be careful about...."

But I was off.

I rode to Milepa without incident, as a light rain tickled my face, cooling my flushed skin. On the return trip, a heavy rain fell, soaking my clothes but not affecting my bike. About halfway back, however, the rain stopped and everything changed. Thick clods of African soil quickly leapt from the road onto my face and tangled my knobby tires, grinding the bike to an abrupt halt. What once was a coveted transportation steed had been reduced by a little water and dirt into a useless hunk of heavy metal, which I had to pick up and carry home, slipping and sliding the entire way on brown slime.

"Mr. Buckler is here," the Boys announced, watching me enter the school grounds, "He carries his bike."

"Let's greet him," Mr. Zimbota said, walking from his house to the school's well, where I had stopped to catch my breath.

"How are you doing?" he asked me, smiling at my predicament.

"Just look at me. I'm exhausted and covered in mud," I replied, "My bike is ruined. I understand why people use this stuff to make bricks. I collected enough mud from my ride to build an entire house."

The Boys were laughing. They started to take my bike away, a customary way of greeting a visitor, hoping to get indoors before more rain fell.

"Before going home, clean Mr. Buckler's bicycle," Mr. Zimbota told them, pointing toward the well.

Turning to me he said, "I tried to tell you not to go, but you didn't listen."

"Sorry," I replied, "I'll listen next time. But I don't understand what happened. I see people riding in the rain all the time. Why did I get stuck out there?"

"Oh," he laughed, "Riding in rain is fine because rain washes mud off road. But when rain stops, mud stays on road."

"Thanks," I said, "that makes sense."

"Yes," he smiled, as if to say, "Most things do, silly American."

"I won't make the same mistake twice," I vowed, "I'll remember this lesson. But, I won't stop riding altogether, dammit!"

No way — I'm too stubborn for that. It would kill me to give up riding during this verdantly beautiful time when roads and trails metamorphosize from unmistakable lines of dust, crisscrossing like wires on a circuit board, into hidden grass-covered passageways, enveloped in tall corn and interspersed with thick-leafed Burley tobacco, a lucrative cash crop. Hard at work in this veritable rainforest, barefoot villagers spend most of their time in the fields — planting, weeding or harvesting. Students, supporting their families, are routinely absent from class. I ride past them, smile and wave.

They wave back, returning the gesture or perhaps swatting at mosquitoes dancing to and fro around their bodies. Replicating by the thousands, every puddle an aqueous breeding ground, mosquitoes feast voraciously on the plentiful food supply of people and their livestock. I drift asleep every night to the disconcerting hum of microscopic wings buzzing within inches of my head, trying to breach my protective netting, and when I schlep to the outhouse, I'm greeted by squadrons of the winged predators, rising like smoke from the filthy depths, making me feel like a bee keeper pulling his trousers down to squat over a hive. My feet and ankles resemble the arms of a heroin junkie.

Of course, the rainy season is about more than bicycle mishaps, lush greenery, and mosquitoes. Off in the distance, when the clouds part, thin rivers run down the face of Mulanje Mountain, like a child's tears. In addition to mangoes, several seasonal treats make brief appearances to lift your stir-crazy spirits — green maize (freshly harvested corn), pumpkins, and avocados. During storm breaks, everyone emerges from homes to dance and play in the freshness that follows a cleansing rain. As a white-hot sun dries the roads, life returns to normal, at least until the next deluge, when the cycle repeats itself.

With the arrival of the Cold Dry season, days are crisp and arid. Before long, damp roads are dehydrated and dusty once again, and when farmers swing their hoes in the fields, the soil snaps and cracks like a brittle saltine biscuit. The mornings smell like burnt toast as villagers burn anything to stay warm, and some days it's too smoky to see Mulanje Mountain standing guard in the distance. Intimidating, yet comforting, it yearns to say, "If you're cold down there, imagine how cold I am up here!" Even at high noon, the hottest part of the day, I cycle in pants and a long-sleeve shirt to stave off goose pimples, and the nights are even chillier, requiring the cozy company of two blankets.

Yet, before slipping into bed, I must shower. Practicing a daily rite of masochism, I fill a bucket with fresh water, wrap my naked body in a towel, and skulk to the bathing room of my house. There I wash from head to toe, one cup of cold water at a time, too lazy to heat the water first and too numb to really care. I am virtually hypothermic by the end, but it beats bathing in the morning, as the Boys do, when temperatures are much colder. On the bright side, cold weather is conducive to sound sleeping, but only if you are toasty warm under the covers.

"Sir, do you have other blanket?" the Boys ask with chattering teeth, "We share small one."

"I think so," I say, entering their room and seeing them cuddling for heat like newborn puppies.

"Here, take one of mine," I offer, "I'll use my sleeping bag."

"Thank you, sir."

"See you in the morning."

And the morning brings more scenery changes. Browner corn stalks line the roadway, sagging despondently in the afternoon sun. Tomato plants take their places, thriving in the dry milieu, much less water hungry than the vegetables (e.g., greens, cabbage, eggplants) grown in irrigated plots along the riverbanks. With the corn-growing season behind them, old friends enjoy long, impromptu conversations on the porches of crumbling brick houses. Beautiful small bird varieties dance from tree to tree, their brilliant plumages of yellow, orange, blue, and red glistening in the midday sun.

The warm weather returns with the Dry Hot season. Not marking the end of a long cold spell, like springtime back home, it is a comforting renewal nevertheless, a reminder of the resilience of life and a harbinger of better days ahead. Temperatures rise as the sun strengthens, and trees sprout flowers and leaf buds. Haze, smoke, and dust linger in the air as villagers continue cremating their parched fields, an easy way to remove remnants of last year's harvest and prepare for the imminent arrival of another growing season.

Energized by the sun, villages bustle with daily life. Women draw water from wells, goats fettered to roadside stakes plead for freedom, and young boys train their sling shots on field mice (a village delicacy) or play sandlot soccer with makeshift balls constructed with string and bundled, plastic bags. Men mold bricks from topsoil and fire them in large pyramidal ovens. Planting and harvesting seasons behind them, students are back in school, trying to prepare for the college entrance examination coming in the fall.

By the end of Dry Hot, the rain is sorely missed, a long lost friend. Mother Earth is desperately parched, her pleas silent but undeniable in the growing fissures dotting her dark, thick soil. Lizards dance in and out of these cracks, thankful for new hiding places, and ants swell from the depths, a collective as always, searching for moisture and sustenance. Everyone is running low on food and water, sparking spates of rationing and theft.

"Myson, you look tired today," I say, "Are you alright?"

"Oh, yes sir, I am just so fine," he responds.

"Then why are you walking around like an elephant?" I ask.

"Sir, I did not eat all day. Hunger is beating me."

"You didn't eat any breakfast or lunch?" I wonder, surprised by the late hour.

"No, sir," he explains, "There is no food in the market."

"Take this banana. You need to eat something."

It's gone in five seconds.

* * * *

Speaking of the Boys and food, after leaving Mr. Zimbota's lesson on Malawian weather, I enter my house to a concert of juvenile banter.

"What do we need from the market?" I shout, as the air goes silent.

"Greens and soap, sir," Alfred responds after a few seconds, giggling as usual.

"We don't need corn because my family gave us bag," Myson adds.

"Mr. Buckler loves avocado," Gift reminds us, "We can find them today."

Markets are sensory star bursts. They offer countless sights, sounds, smells, wonders, scams, deals, and stuff to buy, sell, trade or even give away. All things under the sun are displayed in rows of makeshift stands, lashed together with pliable, young trees and erected in the dirt alongside rutted gullies that double as footpaths and drainage ditches. Scattered among the aisles are meat, produce, cell phones, shoes, clothing, DVDs, hardware (e.g., nails), cookery, and sporting equipment. Then, there are the people.

Malawian men peruse the market for new threads. Thanks to generous clothing donation programs from the United States, they leave proudly sporting a golf shirt from McDonald's or a second-hand suit for church — the same one your Uncle Ted wore for fifty years. When not working in the fields, they prefer to look "sharp," wearing crisp, clean business causal or formal attire for even the most trivial occasions, like classroom teaching or trips to town. Shoes, however, are the ultimate fashion accessory, and the newer and shiner they are, the better. In Malawi, clothes really do make the man.

Most of the market merchants are local women, a hopeful sign for aid workers trying to promote entrepreneurship and gender equality. They favor traditional dress, covering their legs at all times so as not to arouse the prurient attentions of men (the hips and upper legs are erogenous zones). Their outfits are hand-sewn from brightly colored and intricately patterned traditional fabrics called *zitenje* (*chitenje* in singular), manufactured in Malawi or nearby countries like Tanzania or Zambia. Similar in concept to saris in India, *zitenje* have countless uses in addition to making clothes, such as strapping children to backs of mothers (the preferred method of carrying) and cleaning up spills.

Both sexes wear hats of one sort or another. Even in the furnace of summer, women don vivid head wraps, and men opt for second-hand baseball lids. On the hottest days, some people actually endure the discomfort of woven winter hats.

"Why are people wearing those hats while I'm sweating my butt off?" I ask Mr. Zimbota, as he chuckles and looks at my hair.

"What?" I inquire self-consciously.

"Africans wear them to protect head from sun."

"But, they don't protect their skin with suntan lotion," I observe, "What's the real story?"

"Well," Mr. Zimbota confesses, "they don't want hair to turn red. They don't want to look like you."

But they look like me already. To be more precise, the people at the market remind me of how I used to look and dress. They make me nostalgic for my formative decade.

Village markets are time machines from the 1980s. Boys pass in faded Def Leopard shirts and acid-washed jeans. The top Hollywood celebrities are Arnold Schwarzenegger and Chuck Norris, whose explosion-filled action flicks are hot tickets in ragtag theaters, and Walter Payton and Erik Dickerson (or at least their jerseys) still grace the gridiron, competing for football rushing titles. Lastly, there is no mental health system to speak of in Malawi, so mentally ill people loiter in the open, sometimes naked, just like the 80's when President Reagan cut social services funding. Khwalala Market is no exception.

Located a short walk from my school, it convenes on Tuesday and Friday mornings around nine o'clock. Each week, I try to arrive early, during breaks in my teaching schedule, fearing that the good stuff (e.g., fresh greens and mangoes) will be gone by noon. The Boys come, too. Entering the fray, they flank me like Secret Service agents protecting the President, carrying my plastic shopping bags, and shooing away hordes of star-struck onlookers. Whether running around to investigate the "real" prices of items, or taking time to explain an intriguing cultural nuance, they make market shopping a family experience.

And, by now, they know that I cherish the opportunity to see her, my Malawian Madonna. Tucked away, in a little cul-de-sac of produce, among snake oil salesmen and hucksters, her transcendent smile and effusive warmth attract customers like moths to a beacon of light. Seeing her and exchanging greetings becomes a ritual of replenishment and an infusion of encouragement — her bright smile (stark white on ebony skin) an island of equipoise and grace. She, strikingly beautiful in her forties, with the hands of a worker and the heart of a saint, insists on giving me free vegetables. I stand smitten every time.

I come as often as possible. Our interactions, always warm and cheerful, follow a now-familiar script performed in *Chichewa*, her language. It goes something like this: an effusive vocal greeting; the snug embrace of our bitonal hands (hugging would be culturally inappropriate); me offering to buy tomatoes or onions followed by her adamant refusal of payment; me feigning disbelief then sincerely thanking her; her heaping vegetables into a plastic bag as I present a token of appreciation, often a chocolate bar; and a bittersweet parting with promises of future meetings. It happens like clockwork.

I don't know why she is so kind to me. Perhaps it's a reward for speaking *Chichewa* or showing my face in the dust bowls of African commerce. Maybe she has never been shown respect before by anyone, much less a white man. Or, perhaps it's something different — a pact between us that transcends race and culture, a mutual realization that we need each another in this world to be fully human and that by reaching out to others, we achieve our fullest potential for ourselves and society. What better way to celebrate this reality than by practicing random acts of kindness?

A few steps from my Malawian Madonna are the groceries. On their porches, tailors (always men) work next to loitering friends and sleeping dogs, using antique foot-powered sewing machines. Inside these brick and mud shacks, shelves line the walls from floor to ceiling, displaying an array of knickknacks and food stuffs, a veritable pegboard of options — batteries, eggs, thread, bicycle oil, candles, powdered milk, exercise books, pens, kerosene, mobile phone units, cooking salt, hard candy, packets of soybean pieces, soda pop — anything that can be found in Blantyre. And the best part is that you can buy one of anything: a scoop of this, a dash of that, and a pinch of something else. Taking in the spectacle, I wonder how the owners keep everything straight.

Grocery owners are like family because I visit them every day. Mr. Kenneth, who owns the closest one, has a resplendent selection of goods and always gives me good prices, despite the grief it earns him from his wife (a heavy woman with an attitude and a bushy afro). A sweet, young Catholic couple with small children runs another grocery. When it's closed (especially on Sundays), they let me sneak around the fence to their adjoining family compound to buy goods on the sly. Still, I find the cheapest prices and the best service across the market, where I am the only customer spoiled with the luxuries of hot hand-washing water for hygiene and a gleaming metal plate on which to eat bread.

The commitment to hygiene and dishware are significant perks because this grocery (like many others) doubles as a tea room. Thanks to the Brits, Malawi has a healthy tea industry, and while the best stuff leaves the country bound for America and the UK, dregs remain behind to energize the masses. As convenient way points within webs of rural trade routes, tea rooms replenish the energy stores of entrepreneurial men hauling goods long distances (thirty to seventy miles) on the frames of rickety, overloaded bicycles.

And tearooms are cheap — the admission price is merely a gauntlet of greetings. Yet, be forewarned that each person between you and the door expects a separate and personally-tailored exchange. Nothing less is acceptable in Malawi.

"Hello," I say with a handshake, "How are the kids?"

"*Mikolo, Mikolo,*" they mutter, taking turns to shake my hand.

"And you there, it has been awhile," I continue with the next person, and so on.

Finally inside, I plop my hungry body on a wooden bench. Though tongue-tired and cotton-mouthed, I greet the other customers and butter up the owner with brief conversation, good faith attempts to follow the requisite courtesies. Resting my elbows on the tall counter separating customer from vendor, I wait my turn to order, glancing at the handwritten menu of prices and cup sizes, virtually identical to all the other tearoom menus I've seen (*yaing'ono* = small, *yaikulu* = large, and *medium* = medium). In the corner, a homemade teapot steams itself over a red-hot bed of coals, making me salivate.

Tearooms offer one of my guilty pleasures — milky black tea served piping hot and supersaturated with sugar. On many an afternoon, I assuage my hunger with fat chunks of fresh, white bread, painstakingly dipped in this delectable nectar. Sometimes I read a book and pretend to be at a Starbucks, but it's hard to pull off the fantasy with tea-scalded skin on the roof of my mouth and village children staring at me with rapt attention from the exterior windows. After finishing my tea and bread, I stand against the weight of the carbohydrate gut bomb and reach for the door, just before the onset of food coma.

Similar to tea, alcohol is readily available, even in the village. Consumption of the alluring sauce seems inelastic, making alcohol a thriving business, a kissing cousin of gasoline. Bars and taverns, and the geysers of happy juice flowing within them, abound everywhere, amidst wealth and destitution, without regard for color, religion, region, or government policy. Most people like to let loose and party from time to time.

"We're worried about you. Is everything alright?" my parents ask during our weekly phone calls.

"I'm fine," I assure them.

"Just don't get malaria," they explain, "We watched a television report about how malaria is the biggest killer in Africa."

"You know the greatest threat to my health and wellbeing isn't malaria, a deadly animal or a hideous disease."

"What is it?" they inquire.

"A person doing something stupid under the influence of alcohol, just like in the States."

Malawi offers many varieties of alcohol, all of which have been tried by Peace Corps Volunteers. *Kachasu*, the cheapest and most dangerous, is Malawian moonshine distilled from corn and millet. Sometimes containing traces of industrial solvents, it can cause blindness. Yet, it is the drink of choice for the throngs of washed-up villagers accustomed to drinking all day at the market and then staggering home. I sometimes see them lying awkwardly in roadside ditches, next to their contorted bicycles. Most Malawians either abstain from drinking altogether or drink to excess — there is scant middle ground.

One of my teaching colleagues does the latter. A raging *kachasu* alcoholic, he frequently misses school with hangovers and comes drunk to extracurricular events. His bloodshot eyes, sickly body, and demented demeanor tell the sad story. Occasionally, his colleagues confront him about it, but when they do, the response is pathetic.

"I have faced many problems in life," he mutters, wiping tears from his eyes.

"Yes, but drinking is causing you more problems," I say, "You should try to quit."

"No," he growls, "I don't drink that much. I am fine."

"It is pitiful," the other teachers sigh, not knowing how to help their friend, "He was very smart man, but he cannot stop drinking."

"Was a very smart man?" I inquire.

"Yes," they explain, "drinking has damaged his brain."

Unfortunately, too many schools have at least one teacher like him.

Moving on from *kachasu*, other alcoholic drinks are markedly safer and tastier. Malawi boasts the only brewery in Africa for Carlsberg, a good Danish beer that comes in several varieties. For lovers of hard liquor, there is Malawi Gin, Malawi Vodka and Powers Cane Spirits, all locally manufactured and distributed. At the highest level, the *crème de le crème* of alcohol in Malawi, are the imports — the wines from South Africa and liquors from the West that lubricate wealthy, mostly white aid workers and their dependents — elite Malawians operating in the highest levels of business and government.

Like alcohol, soda pop is ubiquitous. The same facility that brews Carlsberg also manufactures Coca Cola products and distributes them in classic glass bottles. Many Malawians love sugar in tea, soda pop or straight from the source — raw sugar cane. And travelers often comment that the soda pop in Malawi tastes better than in the States because it is made using raw sugar, not processed corn syrup. For alcohol drinkers, soda pop acts as a decent cocktail mixer to cut the pungent taste of Malawian hard liquor. But, unfortunately, it doesn't alleviate the nasty hangover. Trust me.

* * * *

Located just down the road from the weekly market and groceries is Khwalala Community Day Secondary School (C.D.S.S.), the government-sponsored institution where I teach. Its grounds are a hodgepodge of new and old buildings, reminiscent of a gentrification experiment on an American Indian reservation. During a campus tour, Mr. Zimbota explains.

"These are school blocks where pupils learn. Behind them are some outhouses."

"Where do the teachers work?" I ask.

"This small building is staff room where teachers meet and prepare lessons. My office is right next door."

"What's that?" I inquire, pointing to another large building across a quadrangle, a padlocked bunker with wire grates over the windows.

"Oh, yes, that is library."

"With all that security, you must have gold-plated books," I quip.

"No, no" he laughs, "but if we are not careful, students steal books."

"What about the remaining buildings?" I inquire, pointing to new construction.

"They are not ready yet."

There are several, including two school blocks with solar panels, a science laboratory and a library, and two garish, McMansion teacher houses. Campus is more a construction site than a learning environment, with sand piles, cement bags, and building supplies strewn every which way, adding decorative touches to the barren milieu. Every day chiseled, sinewy men converge to earn an honest wage, making a racket and remarkable progress given their primitive tools — shovels, machetes, wheelbarrows and muscle.

The workers are paid by the African Development Bank (ADB), an arm of the World Bank. Like a white knight, the ADB has promised to fund campus renovations at select schools like ours. Khwalala C.D.S.S. is among the chosen thanks to the sway of our powerful Member of Parliament, Patricia Kaliati. Earlier in their careers, she and Mr. Zimbota were teaching colleagues.

"We are blessed to have a new school," Mr. Zimbota smiles.

"When will we be able to use it?" I inquire, knowing that I have been placed at Khwalala C.D.S.S. to help the school manage its new resources, especially the science laboratory.

"Hmm, I'm not sure," he answers.

"When did they break ground?"

Momentarily lost in thought, Mr. Zimbota responds, "about three years ago."

"And how long was the project supposed to take?"

"Ah, about two years," he thinks.

"How many more years until it's finished?" I ask rhetorically.

He has no idea.

Neither does the ADB project foreman. A sweet, middle-aged man from Blantyre, he'll reside here nonchalantly implementing construction plans as long as he and his men are getting paid. A few days after my conversation with Mr. Zimbota, the foreman announces his intention to cut down three mature trees standing on school grounds. According to the plans, they are located on the edge of a proposed driveway that will allow vehicles to drive to the doorsteps of the new teacher houses, a rather infrequent occurrence in a place with no cars. After hearing the news, I find the foreman.

"There are very few tall trees around here," I implore him, "why are you cutting down those three?"

"I'm sorry," he replies, "it's in plans."

"Well, can you divert the road a few feet to miss the trees?"

"No, the plans show straight road, so trees must come down."

Mr. Zimbota shakes his head incredulously and laughs. Every day he learns so much about Americans and their idiosyncrasies.

"Why do you care so much about trees," he asks.

Carefully weighing my response, I say, "Because trees make America beautiful and rich. And your government says that Malawi needs more trees. I'm just following its policy."

"I'll speak with ADB manager on his next inspection visit," he offers, "maybe he will agree with you."

"Thank you."

Long story short — Mr. Zimbota speaks with the manager and after some behind-the-scenes negotiations, undertaken without me, the ADB relents. The trees are spared, at least for the moment. Emboldened by my environmental victory, I decide that the timing is good for the tree-planting project that Mr. Zimbota and I discussed. So, I write a proposal for a "campus beautification" project with intention of submitting it to VAC, a governing council of Peace Corps Volunteers that funds Volunteer activities.

Meeting with the teachers, I ask, "What do we need for the tree-planting project?"

Responding in lockstep, faithful to the synchronized clockwork of Malawian collaboration, they suggest, "Seeds and plastic tubes to grow our own seedlings, but that will take several months."

"Are there any alternatives?" I inquire.

"Maybe we should buy some seedlings that we can plant right away," they explain, "There are nurseries near here."

"Anything else?" I inquire.

"Yes, but we have plenty of water right here on campus."

There are several sources of water in Malawi. Sadly, many rivers and lakes are polluted, tapped by multitudes for daily needs. Others, like the pristine streams cascading down Mulanje Mountain, are inaccessible. Yet, natural, clean, underground aquifers exist at various depths below Malawian cities and villages. To access them, people dig a shallow well or install a pumping system called a borehole. In the absence of sewer lines and water treatment plants, boreholes are reliable sources of clean water for everyday needs, and, like most schools, Khwalala C.D.S.S. has one smack dab in the center of campus.

Like icebergs, boreholes are deceptively unassuming on the surface. A stout metal lever connected to a spigot, they resemble half of a schoolyard seesaw. But below ground they reach deep into the earth with a succession of suction-sealed pipes, interconnected like drinking straws, to suck water to the surface, where village women wait to fill plastic buckets. The pumping motion resembles the pivoting arm of a car jack, and it doesn't take much effort for an adult to fill a twenty-liter bucket in one to two minutes. Indeed, for young girls, filling a bucket without assistance is a rite of passage.

Each day I carry empty buckets to the school's borehole. Most of the time I have company — women and girls from surrounding villages waiting in line, some of whom walk from miles away, and occasionally an embarrassed husband if his wife is ill. The chatting women greet me warmly and, with signature Malawian hospitality, defer to me as a man and visitor by cleaning my buckets by hand (ironically, by scrubbing them with dirt) and filling them with water. Girls often carry the filled buckets on their heads to my house, over-spilling water glistening on their kinky curls and running down their faces like sweat. I am forever grateful for their kindness, and embarrassed by their sacrifice.

At home, treatment is an optional final step. Water for bathing, hand rinsing, and clothes washing is left untreated. All of my drinking water, on the other hand, is mixed with chlorine and filtered for parasites. I keep Nalgene bottles full of treated drinking water around the house and carry them everywhere. Bar none, those bottles are the most prized item of envy for village Malawians, which is ironic given how little water they drink in a day. Maybe they know that I am about to put them to work under the hot sun.

The "campus beautification" proposal is approved!

"Congratulations," Mr. Zimbota exclaims, "I doubted you, but you proved me wrong and kept your promise."

"I always try," I say.

"Are you ready to begin?" he asks.

"Let's get started!"

With meager funding (around thirty dollars), we buy thousands of seeds and growing tubes, purchase seedlings from a local nursery, and create the Khwalala C.D.S.S. Wildlife Club. Thirty kids attend the first meeting, including the Boys, where Alfred is elected President and given the task of writing a rudimentary work schedule. In theory, the Club and its mission resonates with the students because as Alfred explains, "Malawians know how to grow stuff." Very true, but now it's time for the hard part — implementation.

The occasion is manual work, and the students hate it. Every Wednesday, the last two periods of the day are devoted to student labor, chain gang style. On these dreaded days, students come to school in casual attire toting hoes and brooms. The girls are supposed to sweep and mop the classrooms, while the boys pull weeds and dig drainage ditches, but everyone just tries to socialize and go unnoticed, including the "student leaders." I wonder where they learn it from.

"Are you going to help?" I ask the Deputy Headmaster, Mr. Namanya, who sits cockeyed in a plastic chair, relaxing his chubby body in the shade and showing no signs of moving.

"My body is very tired from long day of teaching," he explains.

"But you didn't teach three of your classes today," I observe, "Each week at assemblies, you tell the kids to work hard, but you don't follow your own advice. That's negative teaching."

He laughs, "Ha, ha, you are very funny, Mr. Buckler," a typical response to any of my unsolicited critiques.

I wonder what's really going through his mind.

Over the next several months, Mr. Namanya watches as Wildlife Club members painstakingly transform the campus. Some dig planting stations in cement-like soil, breaking the spades of their hoes in the process. Others make compost from organic waste and animal dung. Each week is an ongoing cycle of growing, planting, watching, watering, and weeding. Alfred patrols campus, inspecting the young trees and holding Club members accountable to their watering commitments. Consequently, most of the trees thrive, promising years of delectable fruits if the Club keeps up the good work.

One good thing leads to another. I find a stack of broken desks piled haphazardly in the corner of a classroom, waiting for someone to come along and do something with them. On a whim, in the waning moments of a dull afternoon, I choose some benches from the pile, and during the next manual work session, Wildlife Club members arrange them in a circle around a shade tree near the school's borehole.

"What are you doing?" Mr. Zimbota inquires.

"I'm not really sure," I respond.

He laughs and shakes his head. I cannot surprise him anymore.

A few weeks later, the Boys and I continue the mad science. We blaze paths to and from the benches and accent the project with a ring of flowers. The impact is immediate — students congregate there between classes and, waiting in line for water, village women rest their arthritic bodies under shade, socializing with dignity. To everyone's surprise, the project conceived in five minutes, and implemented in twenty, stands the test of time. In the end, it's one of my most successful projects. I guess you just never know.

III

ROAD RULES

As I was fishing for a ride near Blantyre, a car stopped in front of me. In choreographed unison, its passengers swung open the doors, danced around the vehicle and reentered, playing a game of musical chairs. Each, including the outgoing and incoming drivers, brandished a large, rectangular box of Chibuku, a locally-brewed alcohol that people drink for one reason — rapid intoxication.

— Letter Home, February 2007

"Would you like to attend a Peace Corps workshop with me?" I ask Mr. Zimbota.

A smile leaps off his face, as he contemplates the opportunity to leave Khwalala for a few days.

"Where is it?" he asks.

"Dedza," I reply, a mountain town in Central Malawi.

"What will we discuss?"

"The focus of the workshop is HIV-awareness," I answer.

"Who will be there?"

"Peace Corps Volunteers and their counterparts."

I can tell that he is excited about the subject matter and the participants. That HIV infections are a major problem in southeastern Africa is undeniable, but the Greater Blantyre area, where we live and teach, has one the highest infection rates in Malawi. The reasons are many, but everyone agrees that schools are a good place to dispel myths and promote healthy behaviors. That's what we're trying to do at Khwalala C.D.S.S.

"I would love so much to go," he says.

"Wonderful," I reply.

"How do I prepare?" he asks.

"Just be ready for an honest conversation."

Honesty will be key. I hope that the workshop will discuss why the current strategy for HIV education isn't very effective. It's a course called Life Skills, an important but marginalized class about healthy living that covers not only the pathology of HIV, but touchy feely subjects like self-esteem and personal empowerment. Teaching it is a bit like pulling teeth because the material isn't tested on the college entrance examination. At understaffed schools like mine, dedicated teachers have enough trouble getting students to learn the testable subjects, like English and Mathematics.

The indifference of students is understandable because HIV is a quiet and patient killer. Everyone is at risk, especially children of infected mothers and people who are sexually active. Yet, despite a high infection rate, most Malawians seem healthy, and many HIV-positive people live relatively normal lives. Before becoming symptomatic, they often look and act like everyone else, and after getting sick, they can obtain free drugs to rebuild their immune systems, though there are serious problems getting these medications to patients and ensuring that patients comply with drug-taking protocols.

Within this environment, Mr. Zimbota and I are eager to support a complementary approach to battling HIV: nutrition. Communing with other educators on the front lines, removed from donors and their agendas, we want to suggest the creation of school-based businesses to supply nutrient-rich peanut butter to HIV-positive people. Made from hand by roasting nuts and pounding them into peanut butter paste, we know it's a great source of protein and healthy fats. And, to boost its nutritional value, we add a potent multivitamin — powder made from leaves of a Moringa tree.

* * * *

Yet, before Mr. Zimbota and I can ruminate over policies, we need to get to the workshop. As Mr. Zimbota emerges from his house, packed for our journey, he looks at the sky and nods as if to say, "Don't worry. We will not find rain." But it's the Wet Hot season, when weather is fierce and unpredictable, and for him to be right, we must get a move on. During this time, trip planning is moot, and brief periods of dry weather are travel opportunities to be seized immediately. Our first destination is Blantyre, about thirty-five miles away, and there are a couple of ways to get there — his way and mine.

Option 1 (his way) is walking an hour or cycling about twenty minutes to Milepa, and climbing into a *matola*, a dilapidated pickup truck that, if luck is on your side, might depart within an hour or so. Riding in its bed over the rutted, puddle-speckled road is like surfing in a kiddy pool with twenty-five strangers and their livestock. Option 2 (my way) is riding a bicycle for an hour to the trading center at Providence Industrial Mission (PIM), and boarding a minibus (picture a puffy minivan from the 80s that has been stripped to the bare essentials). I strongly prefer the latter option, which is cheaper, more reliable and, overall, a more pleasant experience. I win out this time.

I wish that we had a third option — Myson driving us. He desperately wants to become a driver, and right now I want to step into his car and be whisked away, impervious to the storms gathering on the horizon. Yet, in Khwalala, cars are few and far between, and well beyond the reach of a village kid like Myson. At best, a few shop owners proudly putter around in broken-down jalopies from the 1970s, mostly for show. A few rungs higher on the socioeconomic ladder, village noblesse make a killing running transport companies that ferry goods (most agricultural products) from village fields to city markets. But when their flat-bed trucks roar past, they never stop for passengers.

Consequently, bikes are the only ticket in town. Spot weld repairs dot their frames like scars, testaments to years of unrelenting abuse. Husbands usually do the driving, while wives and children ride on the back, balancing themselves on stout, iron racks. Preparing for our journey, Mr. Zimbota dusts off his rickety, feminine cruiser (no top bar) and tries to inflate a pesky flat tire, laboriously stroking a homemade village pump until the tire is barely rideable.

"You should fix that sometime," I tease.

"The kids are always breaking it," he laughs.

"Well, buy a new one," I suggest.

"I don't have funds," he replies, lifting a piece of lint off his new designer shirt.

For better or worse, bicycles it is, but I don't mind. Daily recreational cycling is my lifeline. With thousands of rural, dirt roads and very few cars, the conditions are perfect for it, and I routinely manufacture excuses to climb onto the saddle.

When I need a break from my village, I just disappear on two wheels to the homes of nearby Peace Corps Volunteers (twenty to forty miles round trip) for a dose of Americana. When they are elsewhere, I have fitness routes and Malawian friends to visit along the way. Lack of a bicycle spells confinement, geographical claustrophobia and social asphyxiation.

Malawians, by contrast, treat cycling as a tiresome necessity. Bemused by my steady diet of pleasure riding, they see bicycles as purely functional implements to haul goods or carry a sick relative to the health center. Most accoutrements of daily life arrive by bike — matches, bread, soap, tea, kerosene, and even other bicycles. Yet, despite their utilitarian status, bicycles are treasured symbols of status and wealth, painted with personalized *Chichewa* slogans and family names that read like vanity license plates. Men who don't own at least one have trouble finding a wife. I don't want a wife, but I do want to fit in.

So, after a few months living in Khwalala, I buy a local bike. Made in India from heavy steel, it has one gear and handles like a Lincoln Continental. But unlike my Peace Corps mountain bike, it can be fixed by local bike mechanics, who operate impromptu repair shops along the roadsides about every five miles. An endless source of entertainment is watching these mechanical wizards fix problems with their bare hands and an aging, mismatched tool set. The solution always entails heavy hammering and use of the mouth to evaluate, stabilize or clean. Sure enough, the bike emerges good as new each time.

Good as new for riding, that is, not for fitting in. Indeed, there's only one thing that prevents Malawi from being my cycling utopia — exposure. I'm a celebrity, a bona fide spectacle of a person. And like most celebrities, I embrace the perks of fame and detest the annoyances. Buying stuff is a breeze, dinner invitations are plentiful, and I never wait in line for water at the borehole. Yet, every moment of every day I live in a bubble of shouts, stares, whistles, laughs and jeers. Everyone knows my name and movements, but no one really knows me. I just want to blend in and go unnoticed, but no one will let me.

These conditions inspire my alter ego. I don't have a funny hat, or a frumpy, brightly colored truck carrying precious ice cream cargo. There are no orange cream bars or snow cones for sale, pint-sized customers to please, or five-mile-per-hour speed limits to observe. "And how could there be," I realize, "Ice cream has the life span of fruit flies in this sun-baked country." Yet as I ride my bicycle down the dirt roads and narrow paths that crisscross my broad, mountain-strewn valley, people make me feel like the Malawian Ice Cream Man. I just need a cape, a theme song and comic strip. *Ring, ring!*

Cycling causes the air around me to fill with sound. From adjacent fields, hidden behind dense rows of crops, bodiless voices carry crisply in the dry afternoon wind. One child yells to another with spastic urgency, from field to field and on down the line, creating a wave of pandemonium that always stays just ahead of me, no matter how quickly I pedal to catch or overtake it.

"*Azungu awa* (white person there)," they yell, like Captain Ahab spotting

Moby Dick.

"*Mikolo, Mikolo, Mikolo,*" they chant in unison.

"*Mikolo, Mikolo, Mikolo,*" they continue chanting.

"*Mikolo, Mikolo, Mikolo,*" they never stop chanting.

Everyone within earshot has a reaction. A full spectrum of emotions (e.g., elation, surprise, disappointment) come and go like undulating ocean waves crashing and dissipating on a beach. When I feign indifference, riding past gawkers at a blinding clip, a casual giggle or sigh signals resignation and perhaps disapproval. Along the roadside children rush toward me, trying to catch me and sometimes managing to touch me, while their parents sit idly on porches, enjoying the spectacle and not registering my displeasure. Drunks and crazies mumble a greeting or maybe a curse — it is hard to tell.

"Here comes the local legend, in the flesh, riding quickly as usual," my adoring fans must think.

"An opportunity awaits," they surely hope, "to taste some of his ice cream — eye contact, or a moment of mutual recognition. Or, dare we dream, perhaps something more — a wave, a few small bills, a conversation."

"Go away," I want to tell them, "Thank you, but NO ICE CREAM FOR YOU!"

Their "affections" are endearing yet dispiriting. What curiosity seekers don't appreciate are the invisible scars of unwanted attention — the painful pocks of popularity. They cannot hear my inner struggle, my steady voice of reason trying (with varying degrees of success) to contain my frustration. When I tell them to bug off, they don't oblige.

Yet, my heart is not embittered: I want to give my Malawian fans ice cream. I wish they understood that our similarities vastly outweigh our differences and that my presence is really no big deal. But, understanding the enormity and surrealism of my company, I also want to thank them. I appreciate the way they rush to my assistance when something on my bike needs fixing and love moments of perfection amid chaos when I look down from the saddle into the face of a beautiful little girl, smiling and calmly waving her hand in my direction. I know they cherish me in their own way. Mr. Zimbota tells me so.

He tells me so today, as we cycle to PIM, en route to the HIV workshop. Children run to the road to scream and touch me, but they see Mr. Zimbota and freeze, uttering barely a twitter. At most, mothers twist their baby-saddled backs, point and whisper into the ears of newborns, "There is a white man." Ironically, the greatest impediments to our forward progress are not overly enthusiastic strangers competing for my attention, but Mr. Zimbota's many friends, all of whom want us to stop and tell them about our journey. With frequent stops and starts, the one-hour journey to PIM takes about two hours and change.

After leaving our bikes with a friend, we board a minibus to Blantyre. The trip isn't long, but the dirt roads rattle the vehicle like an earthquake, banging every deadened shock and twisting every loose screw. Travelling from village austerity to suburban sprawl to urban chaos, we transverse chasms of wealth and opportunity, graduating from village grass huts to brick and cement palaces, from seventy-dollar bicycles to new BMW sedans. Arriving at the bustling Blantyre Market, we gather our bearings and walk to the M1, the longest road in Malawi, bracing for the two-hundred mile, paved leg of our journey.

* * * *

In many ways, Peace Corps Volunteers in Malawi are safer than they would be in the United States. Sure, we're exposed to some pretty nasty viruses, parasites, and bacteria, and dependable medical care is virtually non-existent in our villages. But, on the other hand, we avoid most of the perils of American life, such as lack of sleep and exercise, perpetual anxiety over the next terrorist attack, large fat-laden meals, and congested freeway commutes.

Long-distance transport (which Mr. Zimbota and I need to reach our workshop) is the major exception. Riding a bike on rural roads through villages doesn't faze a scaredy cat — your grandmother could do it during the dry seasons. But outside the village, it's a different story. All bets are off. There, on the "open road," the scene quickly shifts from the quiet streets of Mayberry to a Machiavellian fusion of wheels, steel, and asphalt. The potential for disaster is grave and ever-present, and surely a frequent cause of insomnia among Peace Corps staff in Malawi and Washington, D.C.

Dangerous paved roads transverse Malawi from north to south, connecting all of its metropolitan areas and extending beyond its borders to Mozambique, Zambia, and Tanzania. Rickety minibuses, overloaded tractor-trailers, private passenger vehicles, and bicycles (and sometimes an oxcart) compete for space in a high-speed game of chicken on these narrow arteries. Throwing inclement weather into the mix (e.g., fog, rain, wind) creates a recipe for disaster. Consequently, in sub-Saharan Africa, traffic deaths are second only to AIDS as the biggest killer of people ages fifteen to forty-four.

Within this environment, Peace Corps Volunteers often get around by hitch hiking. That's right — we entrust our lives and possessions to the kindness of total strangers. Most of us, however, do it sensibly, traveling together in twos and threes when possible (especially women) and avoiding dilapidated vehicles or unscrupulous (sometimes drunk) drivers. Almost every day you will find at least one of us standing along a major road in Malawi. Hard to miss in sandals and t-shirts (the Peace Corps uniform), we're smiling, waving our arms for vehicles to stop, and quietly praying for good luck.

Although public transport options exist, like paying for a passenger bus (even nice ones) or taking a minibus (surest way to die in Malawi), we prefer to hitch. It is a romantic stew of danger and chance, an affirmation that our lives are our own, largely free of the paternalism and protection of the Peace Corps bureaucracy supporting our volunteerism. And on the practical side, we save money by paying our rides nothing, or a fraction of the market rate, for reliable transport. Simply put, hitchin' is best bad option out there.

Yet, even on the best days, hitchin' is a crap shoot. Sometimes you wait ten minutes for a free ride in a comfortable car (new SUV or spacious Mercedes sedan) with interesting passengers. Other times you stand in the rain for two hours, fend off numerous requests from opportunist scoundrels, and jump into the first harmless-looking jalopy to stop. To boost their chances, some Volunteers employ sophisticated techniques like bringing their hands together in a desperate prayer pose (my favorite), making tractor-beam eye contact with a passing driver, or reacting to rejections with dramatic indignation.

Still, whether the hitchin' is rosy or sour, it makes life interesting. I've been in cars with Malawian music stars, Members of Parliament and a Catholic clerical duo, including a nun who passed the time by reading a racy book about sexual positions (complete with pictures!). I've ridden in all sorts of vehicles — tractor trailers, SUVs, delivery trucks, pickup trucks and a biofuel-powered truck — and met a variety of aid workers and businesspeople, learning valuable lessons about the challenges of working in Malawi.

These memories occupy my mind as Mr. Zimbota and I stand outside Blantyre, trying to get a ride to the HIV workshop. Given that it is his first time hitchin', and my first time with a Malawian, the arrangement takes some getting used to.

"Quick, get in the grass," I plea, "and don't stand too close to me."

"Is this good?" Mr. Zimbota asks, taking a few steps away.

"No, no, no," I reply, as confusion fills his face, "Cars won't stop if drivers think that we are together."

"Why are we doing this instead of taking minibus?" he inquires, a fair question.

"Because we are poor and cheap," I answer, "Besides, minibuses are dangerous."

An aid worker driving a fancy truck on steroids sees my hand signal and pulls over.

"Where are you going?" I ask.

"Balaka," he replies in a thick, Germanic accent, "Would you like a lift?"

"Perfect," I reply, "that's where we're going."

Glancing furtively in the direction of Mr. Zimbota's partially hidden black head, which is poking over a grassy knoll like the helmet of a tank commander, I accept the ride and wave Mr. Zimbota forward.

"I'm traveling with a friend," I reveal, "Do you mind if he comes?"

"Hmm…I guess that would be alright," he says, looking duped and skeptical, "Let me move some things to make room."

Mr. Zimbota and I throw our bags in the back of the vehicle and climb into the comfort of leather seats, air conditioning and high-definition stereo sound. We could not have asked for a better hitch, except for the conversation. Some hitches are chatty; some are tight-lipped. Our driver, Hans, a trade specialist from Germany, could pass for a robot. But he redeems himself by driving at light speed, like he's on the Autobahn, tapping his fingers to the beats of booming techno music. Safety is in the eye of the beholder, and having scored this ride, I relinquish control over whatever happens next. In a matter of seconds, I am asleep.

"Wake up, wake up!" Hans says, "We're almost to Balaka."

"Where am I?" I ask, "Washington, D.C.? Portland, Oregon?"

"No, no," he laughs, "See the goat. See the savanna. You're in Malawi."

"Right, of course," I moan and stretch, groggy but increasingly lucid.

In Balaka, a town known for extreme heat and a prominent Catholic mission, Mr. Zimbota and I find our hosts for the evening — Dustin and Cara Pattison, a couple from Portland, Oregon. After visiting Malawi in college and flirting with the idea of joining Peace Corps, they decided to create their own third-world community service project by founding *Bola Moyo* (meaning "I have enough because I am alive") without any of the support that Peace Corps provides, like language and cultural training, health care, and housing. Several months a year they live in Balaka, overseeing a local community center painted with colorful murals, stocked with books, and managed by a small but devoted staff of Malawians. They show it to us on a walking tour.

"So, how is the organization doing?" I ask Cara.

"You know, it's Malawi," she says.

"Yeah, I hear you."

"The community center is growing slowly," she explains, "and every day, thirty or forty little ones come to learn and play."

"Are they happy and healthy?"

"Some are," she replies, "but many are HIV orphans. They have nowhere else to go."

"You're doing God's work."

"We try," she responds.

"Moving the country forward, little by little by little."

"Exactly," she sighs, "We know that given enough time and dedication, worthy projects can flourish here. We've seen it with our own eyes."

Now, so have I.

The following morning, we depart Balaka (hitch hiking once again), and before long, our eyes spy the welcoming site of our destination — the mountain town of Dedza. Chilly, especially in the winter months, its wooded foothills host the Malawi College of Forestry and Wildlife, an outpost where Peace Corps rents space and hosts workshops like ours. After several months in the village, the HIV workshop is a vacation, and a precious opportunity to reunite with faraway Peace Corps friends, who have come from all over the country to be here. Complete with uninterrupted hikes in the woods and three hot meals per day, it's the Peace Corps version of the spa experience.

Yet, far from being all fun and games, the HIV workshop is an ambitious undertaking given the participants and the sensitive subject matter. Notwithstanding their private eccentricities, Malawians are reserved and tight-lipped in public, invariably erring on the side of nondisclosure, a stark contrast to their avant-garde

American colleagues. You can even see these dueling styles reflected in clothing and demeanor: Malawians dress immaculately and sit upright in their Sunday-best suits and dresses, while Peace Corps Volunteers slouch comfortably into their chairs, sporting faded t-shirts and jeans.

"You look very nice today, Mr. Zimbota," I jibe, staring at his suit.

"Nice sandals," he retaliates, "Where is your belt? Every man needs to wear one."

I would wear a belt (or anything for that matter) if it would get the Malawian counterparts talking about topics germane to HIV, like gender roles and sex. Knowing that the workshop would flop without frank, two-way dialogue, I try to break the ice at the beginning of day one by sharing an anecdote about a seemingly innocent encounter that almost went horribly wrong. It happened a month ago, as Alfred and I were enjoying an afternoon walk in Khwalala Village, when a middle-aged Malawian woman, standing on the side of the road, motioned us over. After we exchanged greetings, she tried to sell us some fruits and vegetables and, then, something all together different.

"I'm poor and hungry," she smiled, "please buy some of my things."

"Sorry," we replied, "we don't have any money."

Of course, I had some money, but not a lot. In fact, I had just enough to take Alfred to a grocery and buy him a soda for his birthday.

As we started to move along, she persisted, "You, you," pointing to me, "please come see inside my house."

"This is an odd invitation," I thought, "But Malawians are very friendly, and I don't want to offend her."

"Come, come," she said.

"Perhaps I have stumbled upon a peculiarity of Malawian culture," I reasoned, "This opportunity is too good to pass up."

I cautiously accepted, moving toward her nearby house.

Panicked, Alfred grabbed my arm, "Sir, sir, it not what you think. She want sex with you."

"What?"

"She is prostitute, sir."

"Whoa nelly!" I gasped, retracing my steps and shaking my head.

"Come, come," she persisted, sensing that her cover was blown.

"Um...no...not today," I stammered.

"Don't listen to him," she cajoled, looking at me but pointing at Alfred.

"No thank you, mam. Have a nice day."

She laughed, blushed and bid us farewell. Her friends, other vegetable sellers, congratulated her for trying. Alfred thanked me for listening.

He knew that entering that house could have been disastrous for me, riddled with unintended consequences. The sexes don't mix much in rural Malawi — males hold hands and snuggle together openly (homosexual behavior in the States), but touching or spending alone time with a woman means you are having sex, no questions asked. Within this Victorian environment, I frequently chase brazen girls from the Buckler House, and to honor my dedication to adolescent chastity, Myson posts a sign reading:

"No any girls is allowed to inter without notice to come here or in."

Back at the workshop, my prostitution story places "sex" squarely on the table, ripe for discussion.

"What time of year did prostitute proposition you?" a counterpart asks.

"I don't remember, but why does it matter?"

"Because cold season is time of sex," he answers.

Actually, as the counterparts explain, sex is plentiful year round because men want it and, as sustenance farmers, they enjoy a lot of discretionary time in the afternoons. But sex becomes more frequent from April to July because Malawians believe that getting busy in cold weather will make them warm. Seems like pretty sound reasoning to me. A few sets of jumping jacks also would have done the trick, but that's just the envious muttering of a celibate Peace Corps Volunteer.

Thirsty for more knowledge, Volunteers encourage the revelation of more sizzling cultural insights, and the counterparts respond in kind. We learn that in the village, sex is fast, furious and frequent. It's common for Malawian couples to have sex three times per day. And while Western men struggle to prolong sexual acts as celebrations of mutual enjoyment, Malawian men believe that speedy ejaculation ("premature" in the West) is a sign of manhood. "Wham, bam, thank you, mam" is the drill, so a typical sexual act lasts two or three minutes. Take longer and risk offending your lady.

"That is why Malawians not like to use condoms," a counterpart explains, "Condoms cause sex to take longer."

"Well, that makes sense," Peace Corps Volunteers nod, appreciating the honesty.

It is a moment of shared truth. Let's face it, there are a few universal maxims in life — food is good, war is bad, and condoms suck. Convincing Malawian men, the decision makers, to use condoms is like persuading NASCAR drivers to downsize their car engines from eight cylinders to four. They could still get to the checkered flag, but not as fast. It is a nice thought, but it isn't going to happen any time soon.

The revelations about Malawian sex place the public health response to HIV in perspective. As part of PEPFAR (President's Emergency Plan for AIDS Relief), President Bush directs millions of dollars into desperate African countries, but not without strings — dispensing anti-retroviral drugs is fine, but teaching kids about condoms isn't kosher. Under pressure from the White House, the previous three-pronged approach of ABC — Abstinence, Be Faithful and Condoms — is effectively curtailed to AB. Bush is being sanctimonious, not culturally sensitive, but his policies don't exacerbate the HIV crisis.

Though "C" is an important ally in the fight against HIV, the pandemic rages on due to a failure of "B - Be Faithful," as the tragedy of HIV's disproportionate impact on Africans essentially boils down to a cultural difference. To the dismay of many Peace Corps women, Malawian men like playing the field, often passionately but dishonestly asserting, "Don't worry, baby, you're the only one, I promise." Sounds like a lot of American guys. But as the New York Times reported, the reality is markedly different. Although Africans often have fewer sexual partners over a lifetime than Westerners, Africans tend toward polygamy, whereas Westerners favor monogamy. HIV, it turns out, much prefers the former.

But HIV loathes the next topic discussed at the workshop: cellular phones. All the rage in Malawi, they revolutionize business dealings and personal relationships. For the first time in history, a small-scale Malawian tomato retailer can coordinate with suppliers before cycling thirty miles to fetch a load. Likewise, a student living hundreds of miles from home can ask his family to send school fees without paying ten dollars to board a bus and deliver the message in person. During the HIV workshop, phones ring unabashedly, keeping family members informed and connected.

Fifteen years ago, no one thought companies could make money selling cellular phones and service in places like Malawi. Then Mo Ibrahim (originally from Sudan) proved them wrong. He founded Celtel and made billions of dollars by bringing connectivity to villagers. It was reminiscent of Magic Johnson seizing overlooked business opportunities in South Central Los Angeles, famously commenting that he couldn't believe that he was the first person to figure out that black people want movie theaters that serve grape and strawberry soda. Turns out, Johnson and Ibrahim possessed the golden touch of all successful businesspeople: knowing your clientele.

Cell phones are wildly popular in Malawi because they address one of the biggest disparities: information. Remote Malawian villages (like mine) exist in information vortexes, as means of receiving, compiling or disseminating information are few. Papers are scarce and outdated, as if the printing press hasn't been invented. Information arrives via radio, but stations (and their content) are censored by the government, and according to watchdog groups such as IREX and Reporters Without Borders, Malawi doesn't have a sterling reputation as a protector of media freedoms. Consequently, people are starved for timely, reliable information.

And information deprivation creates an ideal breeding ground for HIV, the workshop agrees. Though accurate public health messages are slowly gaining strength, as non-profit organizations hold trainings and community advocates educate people one at a time, progress is slow and arduous. And there is stiff resistance from within: witch doctors prescribe potions and young-virgin sex cures, church elders preach that prayer alone will impede transmission, and leaders condone sex-based initiation rituals for youngsters. It's easy to understand why people are confused.

But cell phones might be a difference maker, knocking the wind out of HIV transmission just as draining swamps eradicates malaria. Information is power, and we live in an era when it separates haves and have-nots as never before. Cell phones expose isolated communities to the greater world, giving all people the opportunity to live informed and autonomous lives. Possessing an unstoppable momentum, good ideas (e.g., human rights) take root in the human mind and spirit. Looking ahead, the sky is the limit when tech-savvy villagers leapfrog PCs and start using Internet-capable phones and Google searches to learn whatever they want, whenever they want.

* * * *

The HIV workshop ends with a field trip. After driving to a local mission house and receiving a classroom lesson from ANAMED (Action for Natural Medicine), we enjoy a tour of a verdant medicinal garden. Mr. Zimbota takes meticulous notes as we learn about therapeutic plants for HIV and taste-test various roots, flowers and leaves. Eager to apply our learning, he collects seeds to sow in Khwalala and digs up samples of lemongrass and ginger for transplantation. Saying goodbye in the late afternoon, we board vehicles for the return trip to our accommodations at the College of Forestry.

A short time later, the two-vehicle convoy sets off. It rumbles down an elevated, single-lane dirt road, riding into the sunset carefree and confidant. In the lead is a new Peace Corps truck, gracefully navigating the ruts and bumps, its clean white exterior a chromatic contrast to blue sky and surrounding greenery. Following closely behind is a small bus. Loaded five-to-a-row with Peace Corps Volunteers and counterparts (including me and Mr. Zimbota), it is much older, wider and less nimble than its traveling companion. These flaws, in hindsight, would be its undoing.

Unbeknownst to us, roadside vegetation obscures a dangerous imperfection — a devilish crevasse on the left edge of the road. The Peace Corps truck adroitly avoids the hazard, but the bus isn't so lucky. One of its front wheels finds the pitfall and suddenly levitates, nothing supporting it from below, like Wily Coyote about to plummet downward from a high cliff to the canyon floor, having once again succumbed to the cleverness of the Road Runner. And down goes the bus with us inside, careening sideways as it falls.

It all happens in an instant, maybe a second or two, hardly enough time to process. Yet, time passes like a movie in slow motion, as the falling bus twists and starts to roll like a large barrel. Just as we brace for impact, expecting to be flung about like clothes in a dryer (most vehicles in Malawi don't have seatbelts), watching the ground approach the windows of the bus with alarming speed, the rotation stops. Thick roadside mud has grabbed hold of a tire and refused to let go. We are lucky this time — no shattered glass, broken limbs, or gushing bodily fluids. "Whew," everyone sighs.

The still silence that follows is eerie. But it doesn't last long: instead of calmly rejoicing, our Malawian counterparts abandon ship, climbing over each other to escape the contorted cabin, sacrificing their composure for an immediate breath of fresh air. Tempting fate, and the laws of gravity, many of them jump out of windows on the roll-prone side of the bus, destabilizing the vehicle and risking a certain, crushing death. Realizing the counterparts' mistake, Peace Corps Volunteers calmly exit on the other side.

After pausing to appreciate our good fortune, we concoct a blunt but sound plan to salvage the stranded bus. Actually, it's less of a plan than a high-stakes physics experiment with expensive, heavy objects. Putting it into action, we connect the vehicles with a rope — bumper to bumper — and use the muscular, military-issue truck to forcefully extract its disabled brother. Courageous Peace Corps Volunteers and their counterparts man the trenches coaxing the extrication along with raw human strength.

As the sun sets, we repeatedly try and fail, our ropes snapping like fish line under the Herculean stresses. But we continue experimenting and hoping, and after a new rope is fetched and reinforced, it does the trick. The bus starts to move, gradually inching backwards, desperately spinning its wheels and muddying its human helpers. The resurrection is slow but steady and soon the bus is atop the road again, coughing water and debris like a resuscitated drowning victim.

We board and set off amidst cries of joy and calls for celebration. But down the dirt road we drive slowly, like a scolded child avoiding further punishment, and once we reach the turnoff, we gingerly touch the comfort of pavement like an ice skater stepping off the rink to walk on solid ground. For the rest of our journey back to the College of Forestry we sit frazzled but thankful, praising God that the accident wasn't worse and repeating a tried and true rule of the road: expect the unexpected in the quagmire of Malawian transport.

* * * *

The next morning, Mr. Zimbota and I set off. The first leg of our trip to Khwalala Village is a breeze because at Mr. Zimbota's urging, we board a thirty-five-passenger bus with direct service to Blantyre. By "direct," I mean "will stop frequently, at every large market and trading center, but not for individual passengers along the roadside." Mr. Zimbota seems satisfied with his decision to attend the workshop. He sits quietly in his seat, clutching a small teddy bear that he bought for his youngest daughter, Memory. Aptly named, Memory was born after his only son died from malaria. She lives for the family as a remembrance of the fragility and cruelty of life.

"Are you done having children?" I ask.

"Yes," Mr. Zimbota laughs, "We, Africans, say that children are wealth, but they are just too expensive."

"You are very blessed to have three beautiful girls," I say.

"Are you sure?" he wonders aloud, thinking about his dead son.

"Yes, there are many people in America who want children but cannot have them."

"Yes," he concedes, "my wife and I are blessed."

"And all of them are healthy, right?"

"Yes, I think so."

"None have HIV?"

"No, no" he replies assertively, "They have been tested."

"What about you and Mrs. Zimbota?" I ask.

He looks at me but doesn't answer. Having unwittingly broached a topic that is off limits, I turn away and the let the question die. Too scared to know the truth, I change the subject to the current standings of the Malawian soccer league and the national team's landmark win over Egypt. Before long, we arrive in Blantyre, tired but determined to get home.

Yet, after we reach PIM, our resolve wavers. The sun is setting fast, leaving just enough daylight for our journey downward to Khwalala, but on the horizon, ominous thunderhead clouds congregate, poised to strike. Within minutes, the sky opens and unleashes a violent deluge of water and wind, causing trees to bend over backwards and power lines to snap. Villagers sprint to their homes for refuge, but stranded travelers like us huddle together on the porches of groceries. The rain subsides just before sundown, leaving us with a precarious decision — do we stay at PIM or risk a nighttime ride?

"What should we do?" I ask Mr. Zimbota.

"Hmm," he ponders, "I think we can go."

"But the road is in terrible shape, and we won't be able to see anything."

"Don't worry," he responds, "We will reach Khwalala in good time."

We press forward into the night. Riding cold and timid in virtual darkness, we trust Mr. Zimbota's "Malawian night-vision eyes" to guide us home. I wish I had them — the sound of puddle splashes and the tactile buzz of rock hitting tire and reverberating through my handlebars are my only sensory inputs. I'm flying blind, on a wing and a prayer in the dark night of Africa. That is, until the slow-rising moon appears, and its luminance reveals a sparkling dreamland of drenched fields and water-speckled crops.

"Are you still there?" Mr. Zimbota inquires.

"I think so," I reply.

"Follow sounds of my bicycle," he says, "We arrive home soon."

By God's grace, we reach Khwalala safely. Greeting us are the comforts of warm baths and hot food, compliments of his family. Before retiring to bed, we meet on his porch in our pajamas to say goodnight.

"Thank you for leading me home," I say, "You always take care of me."

"Thank you for bringing me to workshop," he replies, "I learn so, so much."

"I'll let you know if there is another one," I promise, "Maybe we can take another trip together."

"Hmm," he responds, looking skeptical and fatigued, "Let's stay in Khwalala for awhile. We need to rest before making another journey like that one."

"Couldn't have said it better myself," I yawn, "Goodnight."

IV

THE SCENIC ROUTE

I am very happy that I decided to leave the rat race behind in the States and follow my heart. Overcoming the fear of charting a different course than my peers, and possibly disappointing my elders, has been extremely liberating.

— Letter Home, April 2007

"What are your life goals?" a family friend asked abruptly. Hardly a fair question for a high school senior, I thought, and a rather serious thing to ask at my parents' cocktail party. But no matter — I'd humor him.

After a moment of reflection, I replied, "I'd like to join the Peace Corps. I want see the world, help people, and serve my country."

"Oh, really?" he chided, like I had a lot of learning to do.

"Yeah," I reiterated, "I really mean it!"

A lifelong America-Comes-First, These-Colors-Don't-Run conservative, he chuckled and wished me good luck. Yet, I wasn't in a laughing mood. The tenor of his statements caught me off guard and made me angry, crystallizing my resolve to achieve my Peace Corps goal. It would take me awhile to get there, but in the end, I had the last laugh.

Many years later, after I returned from Malawi, the same fellow had changed his tune. Recalling my prophetic Peace Corps prediction over drinks at a Christmas gathering, he spoke regretfully of lost opportunities.

"You are my personal hero," he proclaimed

"How so?" I asked, flattered by his choice of words.

"I should have just dropped everything and said 'The hell with it.'"

"What do you mean?"

"I wanted to see the world just like you," he explained, "but I didn't."

"Why not?"

"Dunno," he sighed, "I guess I didn't have the guts."

He's not alone — I wish that I had a dime for every person who has lamented a lost opportunity to do something like Peace Corps.

Things turned out differently for me because I was different, and I knew it. I was adventurous and easily bored by the mundane march of everyday life. Fixated on a beacon call of purpose, I thirsted for new experiences and knowledge and valued nothing more than the personal freedom to pursue my passions. My parents, sincere people with the best loving intentions, tried to smother these impulses with didactic protectiveness. Needless to say, they weren't successful.

But they might have been if it weren't for the influence of other family members, like my unconventional grandmother. Gracky, as I called her, filled my head with visions of treasure and travel during our weekend visits. From the furrows of her organic gardens to the sheets of her goose down bed (during our afternoon naps), she boosted my confidence and emboldened me to question, challenge and lead a deliberate life. She also taught me that I was special and loved — a true original — and that I was the only person who could make my dreams a reality. Peace Corps was one of those dreams.

From Gracky's immediate family, I learned that public service was the highest of callings. My grandfather (Gracky's husband) was a civil rights champion in Baltimore during the 1950s and 60s, serving two terms as Chairman of the Equal Opportunity Commission. Closer to home, around Washington, D.C., I was awed by the devotion of my aunt (Gracky's daughter) to consumer advocacy, and humbled by my father's decades of work as a federal government engineer and community church leader. Doing good felt like a birthright, a natural duty flowing from our many blessings and privileges. And joining Peace Corps to teach poor kids was doing good, or so I thought.

Of course, there were also the Jesuits. Throughout the world, their Catholic schools are thriving, providing some of the best educations to the lowliest of peoples. The Xaverian Brothers ran my high school and walked the walk, so to speak, of principled, thoughtful living. They earned my respect and forged my character through countless hours of patient teaching and virtuosity. They taught me that service to others was not only a graduation requirement, but a lifelong calling. Simply put, without mentors like them, I wouldn't be me.

And, although "being me" meant becoming a Peace Corps Volunteer, it took a little while to materialize. There was college at Cornell University, a glorious blur of electrical engineering masochism, fraternity house jocularity, and insufferable weather. And, during my junior year, at an unremarkable pizza party, I met HER — the kind of "her" who changes your life forever, snatching your heart and occupying a decade of your time and attention. Law school at Duke and marriage followed, as did six years of legal practice. Then, it all came crashing down. The catalyst for a long-sought Peace Corps opportunity was an inauspicious yet ordinary event — a divorce.

* * * *

I never should have cheated on her like that. Taking a human lover would have been kinder.

"You gotta be kidding me," I roared incredulously, staring down at the speaker phone.

"The jury just returned a sixty-million dollar verdict against our client, Microsoft," my colleague reported, "I'm in shock."

With eighty billion dollars in the bank, and a reputation as the biggest bully in the computer industry, Microsoft wore a bull's-eye, we all knew that. But, the technology in dispute in this software patent case wasn't worth a million dollars, and there was no evidence that Microsoft had usurped it from anyone.

The circumstances of the case were fishy from the start. The patent holder was a young entrepreneur who had started a small software company in the 1990s, shortly after graduating from Duke University. For a short time he tried and failed to sell software employing the patented ideas, but the market wasn't receptive, so he steered his company in a different direction. Nearly a decade later, a patent vulture company (a firm that exploits the legal system by dredging up dusty, forgotten patents and filing lawsuits against wealthy companies) presented the patent holder an offer he couldn't refuse — a shot at millions of dollars straight from Microsoft's vault.

I worked on the case from start to finish. Every day I toiled well into the night learning the technology in dispute and refining our side's legal arguments. I attended contentious phone conferences and depositions with the opposing side, wondering why such distinguished attorneys couldn't treat each other cordially. I passionately researched and wrote legal motions that were botched by the court. I traveled to meetings and hearings, culminating in three brutal weeks of trial on the opposite side of the country.

It made no difference. In the end, the judge (a new Bush appointee) struggled with the complex legal concepts, the jury didn't understand the convoluted technology, and our opponents did everything they could to paint Microsoft as a heartless monopolist, which had absolutely nothing to do with the merits of the case, a bit like arguing that a criminal defendant committed rape because he had previously been convicted of credit card fraud. In short, the case was a genuine sham — the justice system had failed.

A law school professor of mine once said, "The law is a jealous mistress." He was right! I gave a year of my life to a factious case that ended not in a victory for justice, but in a business negotiation — a settlement. It was mostly about money — getting it, protecting it, bleeding it from your competitors. Justice was a secondary consideration. Sure, I benefited financially, but at what cost? I had neglected friends and family, and pissed away countless hours of leisure time. Worst of all, I had lost some respect for myself.

And, with all that time spent at the office, things were getting pretty bad at home. It was hard not to take it personally when my wife walked out. After months of dysfunction — weeknights apart, her emerging "friendship" with a work colleague, awkward silences around the house, and dispassionate lovemaking — change was in the air. Just before Thanksgiving 2004, she began living across town with a friend. I stayed and cared for the dogs. Months of separation ensued, as we gave each other time and space.

Sporadic therapy sessions were a convenient, perhaps necessary, ruse. Two emotionally fragile, former lovers meeting under the auspices of reconciliation, but really saying goodbye. I think that she knew it was over from the get-go, the moment she walked out the door of our house. I didn't. I thought it was salvageable. She was right; I was wrong. I respect her for reading the ugly writing on the wall and mustering the strength to walk away. It's often easier to stay. That's what I wanted her to do.

"Do you still love me?" I asked.

Fighting tears, she confessed.

"I love you, Mike, but I'm not 'in love with you.'"

This wasn't a good sign. Ignoring the gravity of her words, I persisted.

"Well, could you be 'in love with me' again? I mean, we have so much invested in each other."

She shifted in her chair — more tears. She knew something I didn't. She had entered a personal pact of determination. She was past the point of no return.

"I don't think so," she wept, "so much has changed since we first met."

She was right, again.

A decade earlier, we had dated in college, fallen madly in love and dreamed big. She was smart, beautiful and athletic, a wistful intoxicant that recast my junior year of college. Fresh from a semester in France, she exuded worldliness and cosmopolitan sophistication — withdrawn, even mildly smug at times, but not unfriendly. Our conversations were earnest and engaging. Before long, I was smitten and knew that I had entered uncharted waters, reaching an unprecedented depth of interconnectedness and devotion to another human being. I was in love.

Confident in our bond, I silenced the internal naysayers and ignored the warning signs. There were personality differences, a mutual lack of life experience, and her unhealthy family situation, but we forged ahead anyway, ambitiously charting a course of graduate schools, careers, and children. Our bodies agreed. Nothing stood in our way because it was all about us and our aloof unity. We bought dogs, pooled money and shared living spaces. We were in our early twenties.

Over time we slowly unwound like a braided rope fraying under the stress of time, weight and neglect. Strapped with her outstanding student loans, we disagreed over how to spend money. She wanted kids; I was noncommittal. When we tried and failed to get pregnant, doctors discovered a testicular problem that made my seed about as potent as dish soap. And after that crazy patent case occupied my attention for too many months, she reached outside our home and circle of friends for fresh sources of stimulation and affirmation, a new and improved support network. It was the beginning of the end.

"What time are you coming home?" I asked, fishing for a dinner date.

"Hmm, probably around 7," she answered, running down the stairs, "I have a busy day at the office."

"Clack, clack, clack," her heels sounded across wood flooring.

"Very well," I shouted, "maybe we can get together for...," as the door slammed and my words trailed off into the silence of an empty house.

I needed to do something for her, something special. I knew it. I felt it. I was desperate. So, at work I called around to grocery stores, trying to find her favorite wines and meats, planning for a rare evening of intimacy and reunion. At 6 p.m., I left the office.

"Where are you headed so early?" a colleague asked.

"Just running home to make dinner for my wife. You should do the same," I cracked.

By 6:30, the house billowed with delectable garlic, onion, and roasted meat aromas. The dogs, happy to see me home so early, prowled the kitchen for scraps and spills. Seven o'clock came and went without fanfare. I called her, but she didn't answer. At 8 p.m., I gave up waiting and decided to eat dinner alone. At 9:30 p.m., she came barreling through the door, martini dancing off her breath.

"The house smells great," she said.

"Thank you for noticing," I sneered, "I came home early to make you dinner. Where have you been?"

"Oh," she answered unapologetically, "I just grabbed an after-work drink with some friends. You know how things come up."

"Well, if you're still hungry, leftovers from dinner are in the refrigerator."

"Thanks, but I already had some happy hour food."

"Ok," I acquiesced, "I'm off to bed, but your father called a few hours ago and would like you to call him back tonight."

I didn't envy her — her father was a piece of work.

He is a child molester. Sometimes I hated him; sometimes I pitied him; eventually I forgave him. But drawing clear lines of right and wrong, I always strove to shield his daughter from the troubles of her past by telling her parents to leave us alone and rebuking them for complicating our lives. Yet, over time, this hardball approach fostered an unhealthy dynamic of protector and victim in the marriage, and resentment grew on both sides. I struggled to understand why she and her mother didn't contact the police and report her father's crimes; she became frustrated with my inability to let go of the past.

Yet, father or no father, by 2004 she and I just weren't dazzling each other anymore. I wanted Africa; she wanted Main Street. When I asked her whether she would drop everything and join Peace Corps, she replied wearily, "Mike, I never want to do that, not now, not in the future." It was obvious: she and I, and our respective families, had grown in different directions, with markedly divergent goals and values. Her mother, who had served in the Peace Corps in Panama, understood my yearning but didn't appreciate the timing. Now deceased, one of the last things she said to me summed it up, "Mike, you need to grow up someday." So, I did. I joined the Peace Corps.

But committing to Peace Corps wasn't easy or simple. Facing the greatest tumult of my life, with so many factors outside my control and a world of artifice crumbling beneath me, I wondered, "What does it all mean? What's the point? What is my role, if any, in this madness? What do I need to be happy?" I tried to shut up and listen, silencing the noisy intrusions of career, money and others' expectations. I knew what I wanted in theory: to live a personally fulfilling, deliberate life dictated by principle and passion, as opposed to fear, and guided by an internal compass, not external pressures. Easier said than done.

Living on the opposite coast, my family was rightfully worried about me. After deciding that I would spend my first Thanksgiving as a separated man in Oregon, I surprised them by coming home. Acting as if I were still three-thousand miles away, I called them just before entering their house. Both parents answered the phone and started to chat, but when they saw me standing in the foyer, they did double takes, as tears filled their eyes. Strangely, as I approached them for a hug, they didn't budge. Instead, they continued speaking to me through the phone receiver, as though I were a phantom that would disappear if they hung up.

Of course, I was an apparition of sorts, a shadow of the past.

After Thanksgiving, I returned to Oregon and meditated daily for enlightenment. The answer arrived quietly, like a snowflake falling in a field on a winter night: fulfill your lifelong dreams now because today is here for the taking, but tomorrow is not guaranteed. I might have wavered if Peace Corps had been merely an unfulfilled whim, or a Quotidian windmill, but I knew it wasn't. Instead, it felt like a calling. Whom or what it was coming from, I didn't really know, but it felt like something bigger than me.

Needless to say, reactions were mixed.

"Mom, dad, I'm applying to Peace Corps. You've heard me talk about it for years, and I'm finally putting my money where my mouth is!"

The line was silent. My mother was the first responder, as usual.

"Michael, you are a young, successful lawyer with so much going for you," she pleaded, "I know the divorce is painful, but you cannot run away. We didn't raise you that way."

"Mom, I'm not joining Peace Corps to escape the divorce," I pleaded defensively.

"Fine, but there are other considerations," she persisted, "What about all those diseases and parasites in foreign countries? Do you want to get sick?"

"I'm not worried about getting sick," I replied, "This is an opportunity to fulfill a dream."

"Your dream is to throw away your education and career?" she asked rhetorically.

"Wait a second, Anne," my father interjected, "Maybe this is for the best."

"Thanks, Dad, I appreciate your optimism."

"Lew, how could you?" my mother screamed.

"What?" he pleaded.

"Suit yourselves, but I'm not going to be a part of this madness!" my mother declared, just before she hung up her line.

To her credit, she eventually came around, on her own time, in her own way.

Dave, a good friend and multiple sclerosis patient, understood immediately. He was also enduring a painful divorce, but unlike mine, his had a beautiful, young son caught in the middle. During weekly after-work bonding sessions over beers, he nudged me toward Africa.

"What's the worst case scenario if you go?" he asked.

"I don't know. You tell me."

"You join the Peace Corps, have a bad experience, and pick up where you left off here," he explained, "but if you don't seize this opportunity, you might regret it for the rest of your life."

"You're right," I supposed, "but, but...."

"No 'buts,'" he interjected, "I believe that almost anything is possible, provided you want it badly enough."

Yet, others were skeptical.

"Have you looked into other options?" a friend challenged me over dinner, "I, like, heard from a guy at work that Peace Corps Volunteers are agents for the CIA. Is that true?"

"Well, I didn't know that, but I can check," I replied worriedly.

"Maybe you can work for a non-governmental organization," she continued, "doing similar work, but without the bureaucracy and agenda of the federal government."

"I don't mind working for the government," I said, "Are there any other reasons to go the NGO route?"

"You'll get better treatment — nice houses, cars and good money," she explained, "I've heard that Peace Corps Volunteers are just dropped in the bush somewhere and told to fend for themselves."

She had me worried. So I decided to do some research before taking the Peace Corps plunge. It would be time well spent.

* * * *

What I learned is that Peace Corps is an amazing operation. By design, it's absurdly ambitious and idealistic. Yet, in the hands of mature and well-trained Volunteers, it is as noble and effective (tangibly and intangibly) as they come — just read the service reports and, more importantly, ask the people of the host countries where Volunteers serve. Though its work is disparaged by many, and admired by many more, Peace Corps is difficult to describe to laypeople lacking first-hand exposure to its charms and challenges.

At the risk of quantifying the unquantifiable, let's examine the numbers. With about eight-thousand Volunteers serving seventy-six countries, the reach of the organization is about half of what it once was, despite overwhelming demand from countries wanting to establish or expand a Peace Corps partnership. Worldwide, Africa is the region with the most Volunteers (thirty-seven percent), and education is the most common service assignment (thirty-five percent). Though the median age is twenty-five, only eleven percent of Volunteers have graduate degrees, and given the physically and emotionally challenging nature of the work, the attrition rate hovers around thirty percent.

In monetary terms, Peace Corps is a downright bargain. Its entire annual cost to taxpayers ($343.5 million in 2009), spread over three-hundred and sixty-five calendar days, is roughly the amount we spent on military operations in Iraq in a single calendar day in 2008-09. Instead of buying and firing a cruise missile to destroy a house, the government can launch eight Volunteers into the field for two years to help build houses. In 2009, the cost of Peace Corps was one ten-thousandths of the federal budget of three trillion dollars and a little over one percent of appropriations for foreign operations.

Diplomatically, Peace Corps complements other facets of America's foreign policy agenda. Unlike the CIA, Armed Forces and State Department (which all play important roles), Peace Corps (in theory) maintains some semblance of institutional independence to assist other nations earnestly, without a self-serving agenda or quid pro quo. Host countries welcome Peace Corps because this no-strings-attached service is admired as a noble practice. As the grassroots faces of this movement, Peace Corps Volunteers are the international aid equivalent of elite Special Forces in the military (minus the guns, of course).

Additionally, Peace Corps partnerships with foreign countries can have profoundly symbolic geopolitical overtones. Over the years, Volunteers have served in Russia, Afghanistan, Pakistan, India, China, Zimbabwe, Venezuela, and Chile, to name a few. Cambodia (former U.S. bombing ground) welcomed its first batch of Volunteers in April 2007. A movement to introduce Peace Corps to Vietnam has been in the works for some time, championed by Senator Chris Dodd (former Peace Corps Volunteer) with strong support from Senators John Kerry and Chuck Hagel (both Vietnam vets).

Yet, for all its strengths, Peace Corps is not without blemishes. Over the years Volunteers have been approached (and perhaps used) to gather intelligence, a clear abuse of power and violation of government policy. Also, the organization tends to rest on its laurels and reminisce fondly about the grandeur of President Kennedy (the eventual creator, not architect, of Peace Corps) and a harmonious state of world affairs that never really existed. Peace Corps also oversimplifies the nature of its work. Its mission in the greater world, I have learned, is just as gray, murky and ineffectual at times as the military's.

After exhausting the Peace Corps literature, I decided that my research was incomplete. So, on a brisk summer evening, I joined a herd of Returned Volunteers at a happy hour in Portland, listening as they reminisced about Peace Corps over deli sandwiches and hoppy microbrews. To my surprise, I immediately felt at home among passionate and interesting souls, especially alums from Africa. Lips loosened by alcohol, they revealed the hidden realities of Peace Corps service.

"Zambia, where I served, is a Petri dish for international development," Sarah said, scowling and rubbing her arm tattoos.

"How so?" I asked.

"Hundreds of millions of dollars enter annually. But during my two years, very little, if any, of it reached my village."

"Did you help your village as a Peace Corps Volunteer?"

"I tried," she squawked, "You should go there and see for yourself."

"Well, that's not going to happen anytime soon, so what would I find if I did go?"

"You'd see the community center that wouldn't be there without Peace Corps, and you'd hear local people speak positively about Americans."

"That would be enlightening," I conceded, "I gather that you're a pretty big fan of Peace Corps?"

"Well," Sarah explained, "none of the villagers I worked with will be strapping explosives to their bodies and looking for Americans to kill anytime soon."

"Sorry for Sarah's tirade," Rachel interjected, fiddling with her Blackberry, "She is devotedly loyal to the cause."

"And what about you? What are your feelings?"

"I think Peace Corps is great," she began, "but it's not infallible."

"How can it improve?" I asked.

"It needs to do a better job of recruiting mature, focused people who are dedicated to development work. Peace Corps recruiters should be more forthcoming with Volunteers."

"About what?"

"About tempering expectations and understanding the significant physical and emotional hardships."

"What hardships?"

"Well, for example," she answered, "an isolated school in the African bush is an abrupt wakeup call for dreamers bent on saving the world. It's tough living."

"Fair enough," I commented, wondering whether I fell into the "dreamer" category, "Which bush were you in?"

"Mozambique."

"The best way to entice stronger applicants of any age is to sweeten service and post-service benefits," Roger, a heavyset investment advisor, chimed in.

"What benefits?"

"Applicants with specialized skills like nursing or accounting should be placed in higher-level positions and given the freedom to practice their trades."

"What about post-service perks?" I asked.

"Oh, yeah," he added, "Peace Corps should increase the six-thousand dollar readjustment allowance that Volunteers receive after service and expand loan forgiveness programs."

"This conversation makes me yearn for Tanzania," added Kari, a local yoga teacher.

"How?" I wondered.

"I loved my service there, living in the bush without running water or electricity. I would do it all over again without any additional incentives or perks."

"There is nothing you would change?"

"Well, after serving, not nearly enough Volunteers stay in their host countries and continue working. It's a shame given their language and cultural skills, work experience, and overall understanding of a host country."

"What do you propose doing?"

"Peace Corps Volunteers should be the first people hired at government agencies or non-governmental organizations that dispense international aid."

"But what does Peace Corps really do?" I wondered aloud, "I'm trying to decide whether I should sign up and give up my cushy life for a couple of years."

"That's a hard question," Sarah replied.

"Peace Corps is many things to many people," Roger explained, "But in this era, it's a boutique gem of U.S. foreign policy, bursting with unfulfilled potential."

"Gem? What do you mean?"

"With additional funds and good leadership," Rachel elaborated, "Peace Corps could retool, expand and continue its longstanding mission of doing what no one else does."

"What's that?" I asked, still trying to get a sense of this amorphous organization.

"Nothing less," Kari answered, "than assisting the poorest people in the poorest places by living and working with them to achieve their goals for progress."

The group was momentarily silent and withdrawn, lost in thought and memory, reminiscing…until Kari woke up.

"The bottom line is that Peace Corps is the best thing I've ever done," she said.

The rest nodded in agreement. And I nodded with them, gushing with expectation.

* * * *

This was my shot. Peace Corps wasn't my only option, but it was the only option I wanted. I was relatively young and healthy. I didn't need to make money for the next two years, and the partners at my law firm were openly supportive, even envious, of my decision to leave, knowing that I had marketable skills and could resume a career when I returned. Also, no family hang-ups stood in my way. My parents were aging and retired but still quite self-sufficient, and my dear, independent aunt continued working like a dog at her public interest organization, showing no signs of slowing down. I knew that a dream delayed might be a dream denied. I was tired of delaying dreams.

By late 2005, everything fell into place. After getting divorced officially (by judicial fiat), I completed the time-consuming Peace Corps application process. This entailed a personal interview with a recruiter, mountains of forms, and several exhaustive medical examinations. Over several months, I mailed in the required materials and waited impatiently to hear something, anything, about where Peace Corps would send me. Information arrived in bits and pieces: Teacher…Africa… Southern Africa. Finally, three months before shipping out, I received the long-awaited answer: Malawi!

Before I left, my ex-wife invited me to lunch twice. I should have known better, but I happily accepted both times, yearning for a platonic resurrection of our lost intimacy, blissfully unaware of what was coming. The first time, over deli sandwiches and lemon-infused water, she told me that she was moving in with her boyfriend, a mutual friend who (unbeknownst to me) had recently left his wife. A glutton for punishment, I foolishly attended the second lunch a few months later, a picnic at a farmer's market, where she revealed that she was pregnant. As bright sun shone on her beaming face, it was clear that she had what she wanted, and I was happy for her. Yet, the news stung to the core.

Needless to say, that double doozie was like a knockout punch. With weak knees and a spinning head, I shuddered at the thought of another lunch meeting, fearing a revelation like, "my new man and I recently entered the Guinness Book of World Records for the most orgasms enjoyed in a single sexual encounter," which was rather unlikely, I admit, given the pregnancy. And, luckily for both of our sakes, she didn't get another chance to finish me off. With little time to spare, I rented out my house, dropped off the dogs at her place, and boarded a plane. I was off to Africa.

V

A NOBLE PROFESSION

Teaching is fun, despite the slow pace of progress, low expectations and frequent interruptions (e.g., sickness, funerals, bad weather). There are challenges and daily frustrations, naturally, but planning and delivering a good lesson is exhilarating and rewarding. On the other hand, facing an unmotivated class of dimwits can be infuriating.

— Letter Home, June 2007

And six months later, here I am — living the dream in an African village, teaching at a rural school, the quintessential Peace Corps experience.

But truth be told, it isn't all that dreamy. Outsiders don't want to live in Khwalala because it offers none of the conveniences of modern living, like power lines, sewer systems or public transport. Movement is difficult because dirt roads are treacherous (at least during the rainy season) and the closest paved road is fifteen miles away. The people are kind but unsophisticated, and the chiefs seem threatened by prominent outsiders (like me) with educations and new ideas.

"Teachers are transferred to Khwalala as punishment," Mr. Zimbota says.

"When I received my posting," he continues, "there was one building." Smiling, he adds, "I almost quit our profession."

"Why were you posted here?" I ask, "Was it a punishment?"

Groaning from the dull ache of a bad memory, Mr. Zimbota explains.

"I was Deputy Headmaster at school with many blessings — a paved road and electricity."

"What happened?"

"Our Headmaster was fired for having sex with students," a common occurrence in Malawi, "and I was accused of, how do say, spilling beans?" Malawians love using Western adages.

"So, how did you get here?"

"The Headmaster was shamed by scandal," he explains.

"The Headmaster had the authority to send you here?"

"No, but he was personal friend of Division Education Manager. She transferred me to this swamp as punishment."

"Me, too," I joke, "but I'm being punished by the most powerful government in the world."

"How?" he laughs.

It's safe to say that my Peace Corps experience doesn't quite satisfy the billing. I was recruited to teach mathematics. And I'm teaching mathematics, all right, in addition to Physical Science (combination of chemistry and physics), and English. I also serve as Librarian, Sports Director, Procurement Committee Member, Head of Math and Sciences, and Quiz & Debate Patron. After school I coach the soccer team and oversee the Wildlife Club. Busy from dusk until dawn, I am overwhelmed and making matters worse, I'm not sure whether I'm really helping anyone.

I'm no Mr. Zimbota, that's for sure. During his lengthy tenure (or exile), he has seen Khwalala C.D.S.S. undergo a total makeover. From 1995 to 1998, it had a single school block and only two grade levels — Forms 1 and 2 (high school freshman and sophomores in U.S. parlance). In 1999, the European Union funded the construction of a small building for staff offices. In 2001 and 2002, as the school grew to accommodate students in Forms 3 and 4 (high school juniors and seniors), an outdoor grass shelter served as a makeshift classroom. In 2003, the Malawi government constructed a library and a second school block. Good things have happened under his watch. Slowly. Slowly.

"I oversaw most of those projects," Mr. Zimbota boasts.

"You've gotten a lot done," I say.

"Yes, but I've been here for eight long years."

"I cannot imagine it taking that long to build a school in the U.S.," I admit.

"Well," he replies, "things move much slower here."

"How much slower?" I ask quizzically.

"Very much slower."

"So, what can I accomplish in two years?"

The question lingers in the air, defying an answer. A few days later, Mr. Zimbota calls me into his office. It's a dusty closet reeking of fumes from a parked, cobweb-strewn motorcycle, compliments of the Ministry of Education for "job-related transport."

"You've been teaching for few months," he says, "what are your impressions?"

"My first impression is that you have a tough job and that we have a lot of hard work to do."

"Like what?" he asks.

"More students need to pass the college entrance examination. Teachers need more training. We need a better learning environment, complete with books and supplies. It's pretty overwhelming, actually."

"Tell me about it," Mr. Zimbota smiles.

"What is your expectation?" he continues.

"My expectation is that together, with parents and other teachers, we can re-make this school into something inspiring."

He looks pleased, if not dubious.

"So if that doesn't happen, will you be happy?"

"I don't know," I respond, "Maybe. It doesn't hurt to dream."

"Well, what's the worst thing that could happen?" he foreshadows.

"The worst thing is probably the death of a student," I reply, "but that's not going to happen."

"We lost two last year," he interjects, as I nearly fall out of my chair.

"Well, in terms of education," I continue, trying to change the topic, "the worst thing is that nothing improves, I suppose, or worse yet, things get worse and the student passage rate drops."

"Last year, none of our graduating students passed college entrance examination," he reveals.

"Well," I smile, "I guess we can only improve on that one!"

"Anything else?" he asks.

"One more thing," I say, "another worry of mine is teachers getting transferred without being replaced. We only have six, including me, and we need at least ten."

"Yes, Ministry of Education likes to transfer teachers."

"But even with all these challenges, I believe that things can and will improve," I shout like a cheerleader, not sure whether I still believe what I'm saying.

Mr. Zimbota scratches his head and nods dispassionately, like he has heard it all before, like an honest response from him will send me running home.

Reality informs his skepticism. The students at Khwalala C.D.S.S. come from local primary schools (elementary & middle in America), which have been over-run with students since primary education became free for every Malawian child in 1994. Consequently, most consist of a few dilapidated buildings, skeleton staffs, inadequate latrines, and seas of youngsters. With a paucity of chairs and desks, students jockey for space on cement floors inside empty rooms, or outside underneath trees, amidst hundreds of other chattering classmates, fighting to hear and learn on empty stomachs.

The World Food Programme (WFP) recently acted to address the hunger issue. It swept across the country, equipping primary schools with efficient, wood-burning stoves and soybean flour. The arrangement is that students haul firewood to school so that community women can cook large, bubbling vats of soybean porridge. In theory, each kid gets fed, and the food attracts new pupils, but other aspects of the learning environment continue to suffer, making one wonder whether the Food Programme has bolstered education, created a mega chain of glorified village cafeterias, or possibly done both.

At the end of primary school, students take a national examination, hoping to qualify for secondary school. High scorers and children of the elite go to national boarding schools, some of which rival private schools in America in terms of wealth and prestige. Good (but not great) scorers go to regional government boarding schools, which receive modest funding and resources. The rest (the dregs, so to speak) either stay in the village and become day students at rural community schools or terminate their formal educations. Peace Corps Volunteers teach in the community schools, where the need is greatest.

Under these conditions, the chances that a villager will attain a post-secondary school degree are slim to none. The impediments are many, such as passing the college entrance examination (known as the Malawi School Certificate Examination (MSCE)), securing one of a minuscule number of university slots, and financing prohibitively expensive tuition payments. Still, they try, inching forward headfirst, like soldiers advancing into enemy fire on a bombed-out beach. Their struggle is inspiring.

And they do have some control over the initial barrier — passing the MSCE. To this end, many Malawians, some years removed from secondary school, study in their spare time and sit for the annual test (administered every October). Mrs. Zimbota is among them. Supported by her husband, she wants to pass and join the ranks of the "educated." And there are many others like her, including a village man I will never forget who beamed with pride when he told me that he had passed four subjects. "I need to pass only three more to quality for university," he explained. His last year of formal schooling was 1972.

The Boys have similarly lofty dreams and face equally daunting challenges. Alfred wants to attend college and become a teacher, but his family can hardly pay his meager secondary school fees. Myson wants to obtain a business degree and start a company that provides transportation services to aid workers. Gift has the best shot of attaining his goal of becoming a nurse, but he will need a scholarship. In any event, for each of the Boys, the battle is won or lost in the classroom, with fortunes made or shattered on the MSCE.

* * * *

Still, in the face of overwhelming odds, I rise with them to fight another day. Stepping into the soft, morning light, I walk to the staff room and effusively greet each of my teaching colleagues in succession. As usual, Mr. Zimbota inspects my outfit (slacks and a collared shirt) like a drill sergeant, picking off microscopic lint pieces, and slapping away residual chalk dust from yesterday's lesson. It's safe to say that I wash clothing less frequently than he (or, better yet, his wife) does.

"We are teaching this morning, right?" I ask, knowing that there are always excuses to cancel classes, whether special events, sporting matches, or public holidays.

"I think so," he answers.

"There isn't an assembly, right?"

"No, today is Tuesday," he replies.

On Mondays and Fridays, a school assembly starts the school day, often consuming first period. Led by the Head Boy or Head Girl (gender-specific hemispheres of student body president), the students start by singing the Malawian national anthem, "Oh, God bless our land of Malawi. Keep it a land of peace. Put down each and every enemy…." After the anthem, assemblies feature songs, news reports, dramas and, at the very end, teacher announcements. Assemblies are nice, but they shouldn't displace precious time in the classroom, where the real teaching and learning happens.

Perhaps I'm just sour on assemblies because one was the scene of my most embarrassing cultural gaff. The school always encourages me to speak at the end of assemblies during teacher announcements, and I often do. But, one morning, another teacher shouldered the duty and forgot to make one of my announcements. When he finished, I quickly stood before the students dispersed and addressed them with a joke (delivered in *Chichewa*), the gist of which was something like, "Sorry, sometimes teachers forget to tell you things. I just wanted to remind you that the Wildlife Club will be planting trees today at 2 o'clock."

Unfortunately, my message was lost in translation. Instead of using the *Chichewa* verb *kuiwala* (meaning "to forget") to characterize the teacher's oversight, I foolishly used *alindi chitseru* (meaning "they have stupidity"). The children laughed and seemed to appreciate my wit and language skills. Yet, unbeknownst to me, the teachers were fuming, and immediately after the assembly Mr. Zimbota scolded me, "You have insulted us with disrespect." Frantic, I ran to the staff room and made nice in a flurry of apologies and regrets. In Malawi, apologies are rare, true signs of contrition, and before long, I was forgiven. Thankfully, there are no assemblies to attend or apologies to make, today.

As the school bell rings, I grab my lesson plan and chalk and walk to the school blocks. They are long rectangular brick structures bisected by an interior, dividing wall. Each school block holds two classrooms, dark and dusty bunkers without lighting or sound-dampening carpet (just cement walls and floors, and a metal roof). Inside (if the school is lucky), a classroom has an eclectic mix of wooden desks, in various states of disrepair, neatly arranged into rows and facing a faded, chipped blackboard. On bench seats, two or three students squeeze together to share a cramped, roughshod writing surface.

I walk into a classroom, bracing for the charming drudgery that plays out every time I enter. The students look tired as usual, exhausted from a morning commute (measured in miles) on foot or bicycle, with little or no breakfast in their stomachs. Right on cue, the class stands at attention and collectively moans:

"Hello, sir."

I pause, staring at a meddlesome group of contrarians, waiting for them to rise and show proper respect for an entering teacher, which they do reluctantly.

"Hello," I reply, "How are you today?"

"We are fine, sir, and how are you?" the class responds.

"I am also fine, thank you," I say, eager to soil the clean board with chalk graffiti, trying to reach and inspire as many of them as possible, "Now, take your seats."

I say this as if taking a seat will instantly solve my students' educational woes, reversing years of intellectual neglect. Though remarkably respectful of each other and me, their ability levels are all over the map, causing weak students to drag down the class and strong students to wallow in boredom. I use group work to foster cooperation and overcome any misunderstandings caused by my strange American accent, but using the smart kids to teach challenged ones isn't an educational elixir. The gifted ones eventually get frustrated and find excuses to skip class. Today is no different.

I write simple equations on the board, all from review material that my students were supposed to practice last night. Two or three kids get it, nodding their heads at the mathematical hieroglyphics on the board; they are the students who always understand and teach the others during group work. Negative numbers don't faze them. They will benefit from the trigonometry and Euclidean geometry. They inspire me to teach and to believe in teaching. Gift, my housemate, is one of those students.

The rest are hopelessly confused, casting looks of consternation, maybe constipation. The members of this unfortunate cohort, the overwhelming majority in every class, try their best, but it's never good enough.

"George, would you please come to the board and solve the problem?" I ask, writing a basic fractions expression on the board.

"I can try, sir," he replies.

He starts to write something. He stops. He tries again. He sighs in resignation. The other children mock him.

"Good try, George," I intervene, "Take your seat and keep working hard."

"I'm sorry, sir," he sighs, "I have failed."

Poor George — he's a likeable fellow. He comes to class and studies hard, but his fate was probably sealed in primary school, and he's definitely doomed now, too far behind to catch up. I try not to internalize his performance as a sign of my failure as a teacher. There are just too many challenges for him to overcome.

A major one is lack of suitable teaching aids. There are very few textbooks and other teaching resources, so each day I write the essentials of each lesson on the chalkboard and scavenge for props (made from cardboard or bicycle parts) to convey key concepts. It's more than I can say for other teachers, who often skip class all together and, in lieu of teaching, give students notes to copy. Making matters worse, the official government syllabi are laughably ambitious, requiring indigent village kids lacking books and test tubes to recite Shakespeare and conduct lab experiments.

Another major problem is the language barrier. I try to use English as much as possible, per instructions from the Malawian Ministry of Education, but most students don't understand me, especially the young ones. Determined to prepare my students for the MSCE, I often teach in *Chichewa* and communicate through visuals like freehand pictures, especially with scientific concepts. The results are mixed, with many students appreciating my passion for science and many more growing angry at me for denying them an opportunity to improve their English at the expense of other subjects.

Yet, the thing that Western teachers repeatedly identify as their greatest frustration is the lack of creativity displayed by students. Most pupils "learn" by copying notes from multiple classes into a single exercise book, without any subject delineation. When one fills up, they start another. And nodding to their former colonial masters — the British, rote memorization and recall are the only skills rewarded on tests. Tragically, it's nearly impossible for my students to complete any task requiring analysis or imagination.

But, that's not to say that my teaching experiences are always bleak. Things improve following the George debacle when Zione approaches me for extra help after class.

"Sir, I have question about math," she says.

"Wonderful. I'll try my best to answer it," I reply.

I sit down at a student desk beside Zione and begin to scribble on a small piece of paper. She follows along with tenacious attention, clearly in command of most of the material. A few minutes pass before I look up to find twenty fresh faces huddled around us, each straining for a view of the lesson. Together, we are twenty-two smelly bodies (mostly boys) pressed around a math problem in the heat of an African afternoon, watching Zione figure out the correct solution. Surprises like this are fulfilling and temporarily renew my hope in the teaching profession, the hope that Mr. Zimbota lost a long time ago.

Still, working with Zione is a grave reminder that prospects are dim for village girls. Only academically gifted ones can attend school because families don't pay for average or subpar girls to further their educations. After all, most of them, even the bright ones, will remain in the villages to become wives and mothers, and many already are, confined at home and relegated to familial duties (washing, cooking, cleaning, fetching water), a perpetual cycle of backbreaking work. Scores of remedial boys, on the other hand, flood classrooms and make my life unnecessarily difficult. Sometimes I just want to ignore the dumb students and uplift the smart ones, regardless of gender. Students like Zione.

Yet, Zione is clearly different from the other students, even the gifted ones. Though she is unflinchingly polite, her speech is loud and a bit garbled. She also exhibits mysterious qualities that are off-putting — a deep emptiness in her eyes and a distance in her demeanor. Unlike the other students, she seems to occupy her own world — there but not really there. Why does she inexplicably tilt her head sideways in class and sometimes stare blankly into space when asked a direct question? I want to know.

Asking around, I discover a precious clue — the previous year, she had an "incident" while attending a nationwide Peace Corps camp for the empowerment of women.

"She was teased so badly by other girls," a teacher shares.

"Why?" I ask.

"Because of hearing problem," he answers.

"What happened to her?" I inquire.

"How do you say…she went crazy," he explains.

Dora, my Peace Corps boss, who is responsible for all Volunteer teachers in Malawi, verifies the story.

"I was called in to help her," Dora explains.

"Why?"

"She was very distressed," Dora says.

"What did you do?"

"I made a few phone calls and found a room for her at Zomba Mental Hospital."

It is starting to make sense. Zione has a serious hearing problem. She had suffered a nervous breakdown from the teasing. That explains the emptiness, the aloofness.

Zione is an outcast of sorts. She is the smartest student at school, by far, setting her apart from peers. She lives far from home, by Malawian standards, on the floor of a small, drafty room in the back of a local grocery. Her parents, farmers by necessity, live about eight miles away, and see her only on the weekends. Her existence is lonely and introspective, isolated from the world by bad ears. I can relate to her. I want to reach out and help her. But I cannot do it alone. Maybe the other teachers can assist me: after all, they know her better than I do. On second thought, maybe not.

As a school, we are critically understaffed. Most days, only four teachers report for duty, although six (including me) are on the roster. Mr. Zimbota travels frequently, supposedly tending to administrative tasks, and one teacher is routinely drunk or laid up at home from drinking. All the teachers are male. I am the only non-Malawian and, until the middle of my second year, the only holder of a college degree. Balance that against the needs of between one-hundred-and-sixty and two-hundred pupils, depending on the time of year, and you get an average student-to-teacher ratio of forty-two to one.

Within this environment, teachers have the audacity to call a faculty meeting to discuss a money-making scheme that targets students. Each school year is divided into three terms, and during term breaks (two to four weeks of vacation), teachers often continue educating students for an additional fee. The problem with this practice, in my view, is that none of the teachers has fulfilled his regular teaching obligations, already paid for by government salaries and student tuition payments, because there are always excuses for missing classes, like funerals. Yet, despite what I might think or what I might do in America, it's the system in Malawi, and in order to be an effective Volunteer, I need to work within it.

Still, I pick spots to voice my discontent, usually with a little dose of sarcasm. Smirking during the faculty meeting, I raise my hand and suggest, "It sounds like a good idea to charge students for teaching during term break, but you should first refund money to students for classes you missed during the last school term." The teachers glare at me in disbelief, wondering whether I'm serious. After an extended silence, not the first time my humor was lost on them, one teacher interjects, "Michael, you are somehow CONTROVERSIAL," as the rest erupt in laughter. I'm not going to win on this issue, so having made my point, I laugh along with them. And the situation, I realize, could be worse — at least two of them attend night school without receiving additional pay.

Ah, night school. In the smooth calm of night, a classroom light flickers. Its puny but steady radiance blankets one corner of campus in a soft, gentle glow, casting shadows and chasing spirits. As the only source of electricity for kilometers, it beckons students to come and read by its side, singing the siren song of educational betterment, like the Star of Bethlehem harkening the shepherds to Baby Jesus. Night after night, underneath the rising moon, my students flock to this place to escape the darkness of their village hovels. They start trickling in at seven or half-seven, and leave promptly at nine.

The chaps and lasses (sorry, couldn't resist the British vestige) come for many reasons. For some, especially the hopeless ones, it's an opportunity to socialize during bathroom breaks and stay out of trouble. Ninety minutes spent staring blankly at seemingly indecipherable curricula beats sitting in dark squalor or, for girls, fending off unsavory suitors. A few others, the promising ones, seize the opportunity to supplement their meager classroom diets of instruction by copying missed notes or approaching others (students and teachers) for assistance. In any event, attendance rates are high.

I go almost every night. Night school is a golden opportunity for me to write lesson plans and help students. But with a clean body and a belly full of heavy dinner food, I usually just fight exhaustion. And when sleep overtakes me, I rest my weary head on a wooden desk for a quick nap, waking in a pool of drool when Mr. Zimbota taps me on the shoulder. Somewhat refreshed, I implore myself to carry on until quitting time…just a few more minutes. As the clock approaches nine, I rise abruptly and retreat to my house.

Most nights I enter an empty house. But tonight is different — I can smell the sickness. Alfred moans from the Boys' room, slipping in and out of consciousness.

"Are you feeling better?" I ask.

"Yes, sir. I should be better soon," he replies in a light whisper.

"What is the problem?" I inquire.

"Well, sir, I eat meat that makes me feel funny. My heart beat very fast, and I get weak. I don't know how to explain in English."

"You don't eat meat very often, no one does," I observe, wondering where he found some and whether it was sanitary.

"Myson's father fed us pig," he explains, "Chicken and goat don't hurt me, but pig is different."

I rack my brain for an explanation, wishing I knew more about medicine. Then, after a few minutes of cognitive wrestling, it hits me:

"Oh, Alfred, you probably have a food allergy."

"Yes, yes, that's correct English word," he grimaces, "Do you spell it A-R-R-E-R-G-Y?"

"No, you're mixing Ls and Rs again," I correct him, a common mistake for native speakers of languages lacking the L sound.

"So you spell it A-L-L-E-R-G-Y, right?"

"Yes, very good. Now feel better," I implore.

"I will," he assures me, "I want to be well enough to attend the education celebration tomorrow."

"I'm sure you do. It seems like a pretty big deal."

"Yes. Many people are coming."

"Well, get some sleep, and wake me if you feel worse."

"Yes, sir, good night."

"Good night, Alfred."

With Alfred in recovery, I focus on the precious task at hand. At nine o'clock sharp, I'm seated on my bed, a six-inch slab of fabric-covered foam, giddily fixated on my small, hand-cranked radio. "This is Focus on Africa," it sounds, "But first, the latest world news from the BBC." My ears perk up and for the next five minutes, I have an out-of-body experience, leaving Malawi and flying around the world on a magic carpet of news stories. Best of all, I don't hear bad news from the United States and can confidently assume that my family and friends back home are safe. As my electronic friend signs off, sleep overcomes me. Another day passes.

* * * *

Preparations for the National Day of Education have disrupted the better part of a school week. Mr. Zimbota has traveled for planning meetings with other event organizers, abandoning teaching and administrative responsibilities, and students have missed classes to practice songs, dances and educational demonstrations. In the courtyard of my home, girls use my pots and pans to prepare a traditional dish made from pea flour and oil that reminds me of worm larvae, and boys assemble materials to teach fruit drying, tree growing, and mountain hiking. In the frenzy of preparation, they are too excited to learn.

The stakes are high. Ministry of Education officials from Lilongwe will attend. Motorized transport to and from the event site, a primary school located ten miles from Khwalala, will be provided for all participants. Organizers have even promised each student in attendance not only food (two large bread scones), but also one carton of *mahewu*, a coveted non-alcoholic drink made from corn flour and millet that tastes sickly sweet, like Southern tea, and flows with the consistency of vomit. Food and drink always draw a crowd, just like in America.

And now the event is upon us. Craving some exercise, Eric Cornish (a nearby Peace Corps Volunteer) and I ride to the venue, shortly before the festivities begin. Per local culture, our bicycles are abruptly taken and stowed for safe keeping in a guarded classroom, and we are escorted to the sunny celebration theater, a dusty, open field teeming with school children from all over the region. After turning down an offer of seats in the shade, we sit on the bare ground near our students, a deliberate showing of solidarity with the presumptive guests of honor.

The pastoral primary school ground hosting the event has been transformed into the Malawian version of a country fair. Around us are a ring of temporary structures — large, staked party tents with chairs for VIPs and haphazard makeshift grass shelters without chairs for students. Organizers have plopped a lone microphone in the center of the action, as though we are at a Major League Baseball game and a celebrity is about to take the field and sing the national anthem. Off to one side is a ramshackle line of display tables for student demonstrations, from radio repair to artwork. Outside the ring are rows of shiny SUVs, the preferred means of transport.

Speaking of celebrities, two white faces in the VIP tent immediately catch my eye. They always do, but I'm not alone. My Malawian brethren always find white faces before I do.

"Your friends are here," they say pointing.

"Our friends?" I question, hoping to see a Malawian face but invariably seeing a white one.

"The *azungu* over there," they elaborate.

"I don't know them," I respond defensively, "They are NOT my friends...yet."

The cultural *faux pas* is telling but harmless. There are bigger injustices afoot.

Case in point: the "event." It's a spectacle that gets underway just as two large dust devils rise from the center of the field, as if on cue. There are student dances, speeches and presentations, and during a break in the action, VIPs leave their shaded chairs to interact with student demonstrators, rewarding them with token monetary gifts. Throughout the festivities, a persistent feeding train of student groups quietly circulates through nearby classrooms for food and drink, returning with smiles and milky mustaches.

Still, if it weren't for the school buildings and school uniforms, you wouldn't know that you were attending an educational event. The children and their educations, quite frankly, are secondary, lost amid political regalia and hoopla. The National Day of Education is an event designed and orchestrated for adults, especially politicians seeking glorification and reelection. Fittingly, no one mentions the number of school hours and lesson plans scratched to prepare. No one wants to. Unspoken truth be told, it is a partisan rally held with public funds under the auspices of an educational celebration.

Just ask our cantankerous Member of Parliament — MP Kaliati. She is here in full force, as no political function in these parts is complete without her. Halfway through the program, she confidently bursts onto the scene like a general marching to war, tailed closely by an army of female supporters donning Democratic Progressive Party (DPP) regalia, beating drums, and waving verdant fronds. She takes a prominent seat in the VIP tent, while her infantry sits nearby in a block of seats sacrificed by school children, forming a solid blue cheering section.

Yet, Kaliati doesn't stay put for long. After a few minutes, she leaps forth to join a skit in which school children are posing questions to a Ministry of Education official. Sitting in the dirt, raising her hand high in the air, she peppers the official with questions, and the crowd loves it! It is grand political theater and a powerful reminder of the convoluted nature of democracy — beholden to the people yet often more entertainment than substance. I'm happy when it's over, and so is Eric.

"Can you believe that?" I ask him.

"No way," he chuckles, "that woman is shameless. She'll do anything for a vote."

"Yeah, but she's good at it," I admire, "It's like watching a master at work."

After the Kaliati show, the event ends and the crowd disperses, giving Eric and me the opportunity to meet the *azungu* on our way out. They are attractive, young aid workers based in Lilongwe, recent arrivals slated to work in Malawi for a few months. Having just landed, they're a bit shell shocked, and their *Chichewa* is nonexistent. Yet, they have already traveled to Blantyre and Mulanje (major southern cities) for meetings and attended our modest village event, staying at the finest hotels along the way. This infuses the encounter with a classist tension, like chimney sweepers holding court with two princesses, not wanting to dirty their silk dresses with the soot of proletariat reality. Before long, a driver ends the clumsy encounter by calling them away to an awaiting car.

Yet, once again, the village kids aren't so lucky. Poor planning leads to food and drink shortages, causing some children to leave hungry and confused. Adding insult to injury, although organizers promised every child a ride home, that arrangement is abruptly nixed when they discover a "budgeting error" and decide to ration gasoline. As politicians and aid workers leave in automobiles, Eric and I depart on our bikes, and the bulk of stranded students (including the Boys) set out on foot. Three hours later, after nightfall, the Boys reach our front door. Thankfully, after that long, chilly walk, none of them gets sick.

* * * *

Sickness and death, morose and tragic as usual, occur with unsettling frequency here, at least by Western standards. The sinister combination of overpopulation, hard living and virulent diseases conspire to wreak havoc on a host of societal pillars, like education and business development. How can a country thrive when the average person is frequently under the weather and ultimately expires at the age of forty, barely reaching the zenith of his potential as a parent, village elder or worker?

Within this Darwinian nightmare, I yearn for the caricature of death operating in the States — aloof and fastidious — not his ever-present, indiscriminate cousin in Africa. Funerals in America are infrequent occasions for people under the age of seventy, often arriving predictably after the deceased has suffered a long illness or enjoyed a complete rotation of life's seasons. Young people die occasionally, but not frequently, and often under the guise of immaturity or recklessness.

The opposite is true of Malawi. At least once, and often multiple times, per week, teachers and students miss school to attend the funeral of a friend or family member, honoring the gravest of cultural duties and explaining why coffin making is such a thriving business. And death is a regular visitor at school, too. During a particularly insidious week in 2007, Khwalala C.D.S.S. loses a top student and a revered member of the school committee, plunging the campus into a state of shock. Why so much death?

Malaria is public enemy number one. A parasite transmitted by mosquitoes, it multiplies within the liver of its host, causing periodic bouts of flu-like symptoms, including fever, headache, and chills. During an episode, infected sufferers look and act like zombies, too sick to learn, work or tend to familial duties. Annually, in Africa at large, malaria kills between one and two million people (mostly pregnant women or children under age five), costs twelve billion dollars to combat (roughly forty percent of public health expenditures), and has retarded sub-Saharan African GDP by thirty-three percent.

Yet, it doesn't have to be this way because malaria is largely manageable, if not preventable, when saving lives is made a priority. Sleeping under a mosquito net (a frequently cited deterrent) minimizes exposure at dawn and dusk, the most dangerous times of the day, but nets are relatively expensive for villagers (even subsidized ones). Other options are impractical — preventative medication costs a king's ransom and the removal of standing water (mosquito breeding grounds) is counterintuitive to farmers living in water-starved places. So, in lieu of accessible safeguards, villagers get infected and flock to regional health centers upon the first sign of a malarial episode.

"Can I have some of your malaria medicine?" Mr. Zimbota asks, displaying uncharacteristic forwardness.

"Umm, hmm," I stutter, trying to manufacture an excuse to say no.

Everyone knew that I kept a first-aid kit, and its contents were the fodder of wild speculation. Yet, sharing with villagers, even a friend and confidant like Mr. Zimbota, is tricky business. One pill will turn into two or three, and so on. In an instant, I will become a private dispensary and exhaust my meager supplies, leaving nothing for myself.

"I'm sorry," I answer with great regret, "you need to get medicine from the health clinic in Milepa. Have you already tried doing that?"

"No," Mr. Zimbota admits, "I will send boy to Milepa."

I feel badly denying him, but I need to look out for myself. Without a pharmaceutical fix, foreigners like me would die with even greater frequency than native peoples. Yet, taking a prophylaxis for two years is neither healthy nor pleasant, as each of the three medicinal options has drawbacks like freaky dreams, anxiety, and sunburn. So, many Volunteers just don't take them or do so only during the rainy season. I take them begrudgingly and brave the drug side-effects, reasoning that Peace Corps gives them to us for a reason.

I'm reminded of that reason one afternoon during a bike ride. As I round a bend in the road, savoring the beautiful scenery of rural Malawi, I suddenly come across the frail, lifeless body of Precious, one of my female students, bouncing in the open bed of a wooden ox cart, a makeshift gurney. Being pulled to the local clinic by classmates (including Gift and Myson), she is in immense pain and unable to speak.

"Mr. Buckler, other teachers have gone. We need your assistance at clinic," the students beg.

"No problem," I reply, "What can I do?"

"You need to write note to doctor," they explain.

"What should I write?"

"Say that Precious is student and needs treatment to heal and return to school."

Sending them ahead, I quickly jot a note containing that exact language. I hope it works. Students need a note written by a teacher to prove that they are not skipping school. It's a good policy in theory, but it doesn't work well in situations like this one. Mounting my bike and furiously pumping my legs to catch the group, I wonder what would have happened if I hadn't been around.

At a local clinic, we find an attendant on duty. He isn't a doctor (scarce in Malawi), but he seems to have some medical credentials. He accepts the note, examines Precious and administers an injection, a muscle relaxant of some sort. With used syringe in hand, he cavalierly motions me down a hallway, and as I move forward, the syringe nearly pricks my leg. In a state of shock, I scour it for punctures and blood, dreading the prospect of HIV transmission. Finding none, I take a few deep breaths and utter a prayer of thanks.

We enter a dark room and sit down. In *Chichewa* and broken English, the attendant speculates that the girl is suffering from severe emotional distress.

"These girls," he explains, "get very upset when boy rejects them or they find out they pregnant."

"Oh!" I exclaim, genuinely surprised by the diagnosis, but relieved to have one.

"We often see this problem around examination time," he continues, "I'll monitor her condition. You should return in morning."

"Very well," I say, "I'll be here in the morning."

I step outside of the clinic to the setting sun, just as a large colony of bats bursts from a cranny in the roofline, causing me to duck. I hope it's not an omen.

After worrying about Precious all night long, sleeping on pins and needles, I rise at dawn to leave for the clinic. As soon as I enter the ward, Gift (who stayed with her throughout the night) tells me that Precious is better — her eyes are open and the convulsions have passed. A few minutes later, the attendant from the previous night approaches me with an update: "After you left, her condition not improving, so I give her pills for malaria. Before long I see improvement. She sleep good and is resting with friends and family."

It's a shocking admission — Precious' condition wasn't a run-of-the-mill case of female hysteria after all. "When a patient presents symptoms consistent with malaria in a country ravaged by malaria, your first impulse is to attribute the condition to frailty of the female psyche? Good work, doc, or whatever you are," I yearn to say. Instead, I bite my tongue and thank him for his services. He looks tired, and I know that it isn't easy for him to practice rudimentary medicine in a village without consistent electricity, a staff of trained personnel, or adequate supplies. Now is not the time for judgment.

On my way out, I decide to meet Precious' family. Gathered around her bedside for a prayer session, they offer me food and thank me effusively for assisting their daughter, grateful yet surprised that a white man would show such concern for an ordinary Malawian. As I exit, shouts and cries bellow from the room as spirits are summoned, Bible verses are recited, and promises are made. At the end, Precious utters her first words in thirty-six hours. She has been healed — it's a miracle, and I'm a thankful teacher.

* * * *

The outcome is far worse the second time a student becomes gravely ill. Mr. Zimbota and I are traveling together in Blantyre when his phone rings. Ending the call, he looks ashen and anxious to move.

"We need to hurry back to school," he announces. "A student has died."

"It's not Gift, is it?" I ask.

"No, it's not," he replies.

"And it's not Myson or Alfred, either?"

"No, they are fine," he assures me.

"Who is it, then?" I ask.

"We will know soon," he explains. "We should hurry. There isn't much time."

"Where are we going?"

"A village funeral."

Funerals are serious business — community gatherings where, in the words of a Malawian friend, "You pay respects to person who is gone forever." Another friend adds, "If you attend funerals of others, people come to your funeral."

Alfred waits for us at Khwalala C.D.S.S. Upon our arrival, he escorts us on bicycles to the deceased's homestead, a small compound of mud huts, off the beaten path, that I never would have found on my own. The other mourners, hundreds of them, including most of the students and teachers at my school, are already there, sitting together in the fields among manicured rows of mounded earth and tall corn stalks. There they wait and wait, exchanging greetings and sharing food under an expansive, ominous sky, while a carpenter finishes a coffin (cremation is exceedingly rare here).

I tread lightly. Unsure how to act, the last thing I want to do is offend someone and ruin the community goodwill that I have painstakingly built. Luckily, my teaching colleagues see me and motion me over to their makeshift circle. After obligatory greetings with them and my students, I take a seat in the dirt. Fascinated by the Malawian mourning process, I notice that none of the people around me is visibly upset. Instead, they are surprisingly chatty and casual about the affair.

"The carpenter is taking long time for such small coffin," a teacher comments.

"Yes, he was small boy," responds Mr. Namanya, the Deputy Headmaster, "but he was obedient and very intelligent. Last year he ranked second or third in his class."

"Do you remember him?" he asks me.

"What was his name?"

"David Banda," Mr. Namanya answers.

My mind goes blank with shame. The dead student's name summons no face, and the brief description — short, quiet, kind, smart — invokes no definitive memory. I slump in guilt, knowing that every Malawian I have ever met, even once, knows not only my name, but also a cadre of other personal information about me. I, on the other hand, am failing to identify a person to whom I taught Physical Science for an entire school year.

"Is he the one who won the drama contest?" I ask, trying to hide my ignorance.

"No," says Mr. Namanya, "that was another boy."

"Well," I admit, "I guess that I don't remember him. I'm sorry."

"Don't worry," Mr. Namanya comforts me with a pat on the back, "We have many, many students."

Our conversation ends momentarily when the male students stand and gather together. Starting a solemn procession to the graveyard, they carry the coffin occupied by their fallen comrade, supported lengthwise by two young, felled trees. It's obvious where they're headed — a cluster of tall trees about one-hundred yards away. This is because from a bird's-eye view, all graveyards in Malawi look alike — small patches of lush greenery and mature trees doting the endless hectares of deforested farmland, small sanctuaries of remembrance where foraging for firewood is verboten and sacrilege.

At the graveyard, the hot, humid air is infused with an eerie silence. That is, until women and girls begin screeching, as if on cue, like hundreds of car alarms sounding at once. On the periphery, circumscribing the freshly dug grave, they drop to their knees in agony, convulsing as tears stream down their faces. Men, on the other hand, assemble at the graveside, staring stoically downwards, directing the boys performing the burial. I feel a bit nauseous, like a paparazzo of grief.

The coffin is carefully lowered into a deep rectangular hole, marked at each end by a vertical stick. One man climbs into the unfilled grave and carefully sprinkles a thin layer of dirt over the coffin, one bowlful at a time. Clothing of the deceased, and the trees used to transport the coffin, are added in turn.

"Why did they put trees in his grave?" I ask.

"They were used to carry his body and cannot be used for anything else," Mr. Namanya responds.

Classmates of the deceased approach the grave. Using farming hoes, they forcefully heave dirt downward, filling the hole quickly and replacing it with a steep mound of dirt, carefully sculpted to form a perfect ridgeline extending the entire length of the grave, from stick to stick. Their actions are meticulous and artful, like those of a sandcastle artist at the beach. The wailing stops as Christian ministers deliver closing prayers for the boy and his family. After saying final goodbyes, we leave the graveyard in silence under a cloak of light drizzle.

Back at the boy's homestead, Mr. Zimbota and I fetch our bicycles and set off for home. Pedaling slowly, emotionally exhausted from the ordeal, neither of us wants to talk. And, in the absence of conversation, the strain of death hits me right between my eyes like a lightning bolt, as I brood over mortality's unnerving, ever-present mysteries and the extent to which, as interconnected, sentient beings, we shoulder responsibility for the tragedies of others.

"Mr. Zimbota," I ask timidly after a few minutes, "when you asked me for malaria medication, was it for the student who died?"

"Why do you want to know?" he replies.

"Because I need to know whether I caused his death," I say.

"The answer," he says, "is no."

"Then who was it for?"

"The medication was for me," he answers, "The boy's death is not your fault. None of this is your fault."

"Yes," I nod, desperately wanting to believe his words.

"These are old problems," he explains, pointing to our surroundings, "They existed before you came, and most of them will remain after you leave."

"Whew," I sigh, wondering why I am enduring this emotionally wrenching Peace Corps experience when conditions in Malawi are so hard to improve.

"Don't worry," he consoles me, "We appreciate your help."

"Thank you," I exhale.

"Please continue assisting us for sake of dead boy and others like him."

"I will try."

VI

DIGNIFIED DEVELOPMENT

I have been trying to distance myself from dangerous words like "success" and "failure." Over the course of a day, I make positive gains, sometimes a lot of them, and effectuate progress. I might not satisfy my expectations, but as long as I learn something new and work hard, I sleep well.

— Letter Home, September 2007

Peace Corps Volunteers wear many hats. A primary assignment like teaching is one of them, but Volunteers are also trained to be community organizers, promoting secondary projects (e.g., wells, buildings, trainings, small businesses) that address local needs. Like an injection of grassroots adrenaline, they scrape together funding from various sources to bring about incremental change and hopefully betterment. It is a very nuanced and open-ended role.

Yet, Malawi would be a utopia if good intentions, alone, yielded results. In a country the size of Pennsylvania that lacks a reliable communication system, where computers are as scarce as jobs, and nothing happens quickly or easily (save sweating and tanning), development work of any kind sometimes feels like kamikaze piloting. Many aid workers become overwhelmed and go home early. For those who stay, struggling to find their rhythm and purpose, there is nary a dull moment.

And everyone has an opinion as to why that is.

"Africans are lazy and stupid," he growls. He is drunk, but I'm not amused. It isn't the first time the white owner of a tourist lodge has disparaged my African friends.

"What did you say?" I reply flabbergasted.

"You have to treat Malawians as African animals," he slurs, "They need to be told what to do, kept in their places, you know?"

"If it's so bad here, why don't you pick up and leave?" I ask.

"Because this is my country, too," he roars, "and if we left, the whole damn place would fall apart."

"I respectfully disagree," I say sternly, leaving the table before I punch him.

He sees only one side of the picture — the dark side. In the absence of jobs and educational opportunities, and facing rampant corruption, hope is fleeting, as people operate day and night in survival mode, not for the common good.

The other side of the story, the bright side in my view, is that like most folks, Malawians want to improve their living conditions. Having persevered (albeit precariously) in Africa for millennia, they are resourceful and possess drive and intellect aplenty. What they lack are resources and the luxury of failure. For example, a Malawian who plants a cash crop like coffee in his fields (instead of corn), and hardly has money to survive as it is, risks the daunting prospect of seeing his family starve if the crop fails. That's the dilemma Malawians face every day, and what they need is not pity, but respect and targeted assistance, especially human capital. That's where I come in.

"How can I help the school or community?" I ask Mr. Zimbota on a bright, sunny day.

"Hmm," he ponders, looking up from the bench where he sits, chewing on a fresh piece of sugarcane.

"I teach a full load," I add, "but I have some free time in the afternoons and evenings."

"You came only six months ago," he answers, "and you have planted many trees."

"Yes," I acknowledge, "but so much more needs to be done. I have many ideas."

"You are full of blessings," he says, standing up and taking my hand, a Malawian gesture of affection in male friendships.

"Thank you, sir."

"We need to find more projects for you," he continues, "I will discuss this with community, especially chiefs."

The chiefs, of course — why didn't I think of that? Each village has one to resolve disputes among residents, oversee land distribution, and organize community projects, sort of a small-town mayor, city council and judge rolled into one. Overseeing multiple villages, and their respective chiefs, is a Group Village Headman (a.k.a. head chief). Group Village Headmen report to a Traditional Authority (TA), a regional body of chiefs, and so on. In theory, this hierarchy of chiefs (often hereditary appointments) works in parallel with the democratically-elected Malawian government to bring safety, security, and rule of law to every corner of Malawi.

Mr. Zimbota schedules a meeting with the chiefs, and knowing the stakes, I'm nervous. Whether drunk or sober, corrupt or angelic, chiefs wield tremendous power over their charges and control the most precious resource of all: land. If I want to help Khwalala, I need to please and respect them. Without their support, my development projects will flop, and if I offend them, I run the risk of becoming a village pariah, *persona non grata* in these parts. I also need to listen to them. As sounding boards for the community, they know exactly what improvements local people need and want.

At the meeting, six men sit in a straight line, facing Mr. Zimbota and me. The Group Village Headman, seated in the center, is clearly in charge. I've heard that he's a smooth operator by village standards, sporting a slick grin, multiple wives and several homesteads. Another chief, lower on the totem pole, stares blankly into space, enjoying a drunken stupor. A motley crew, they look and smell like walking exhibits from a periodontal textbook, their pungent breathes nauseating me from across the room. Each looks tired, hungry and skeptical, and none speaks English. Stomachs growl in anticipation of the soda pop and cookie snack to come…at the end.

Mr. Zimbota suddenly stands straight as an arrow, ending the stare down. He smiles and commences the meeting, introducing each chief in order of importance from top to bottom, a litany of too many names and jurisdictions to remember, in one ear and out the other. Then, he turns to me.

"This is Michael Buckler. He is a teacher at Khwalala C.D.S.S.," he says, as the chiefs begin clapping in unison, to the steady beat of a metronome, "clap…clap…clap," a sign of respect.

"Thank you," I nod.

"He is our blessing and opportunity for things to improve," Mr. Zimbota says as the clapping dies down, "I called this meeting for him."

Mr. Zimbota turns toward me, gesturing that I should rise. I stand and try to remember my remarks, carefully prepared in *Chichewa* the night before.

"I will live here in Khwalala for many months," I say, "and I have come to help your villages."

More clapping ensues. It's probably the first time they've heard a white man speak their native tongue. I seem to be a hit, at least so far. It's the Mike show — I can do this all day.

"But to help the villages, I need your guidance and advice," I continue, "What are your greatest community needs?"

The chiefs look dazed and confused.

"Please tell Michael how he can help your villages," Mr. Zimbota adds, using virtually the same words, but with an accent they can understand.

Light bulbs in their brains flicker on. They turn to one another, murmuring and searching for ideas — a promising sign. The room goes silent and starting with the head chief, each takes a turn describing what I can do. I'm hoping for a tidy, manageable list of modest community service projects buoyed by commitments of village resources. What I get is a litany of all things that need fixing, a laundry list of problems and personal requests.

"We need electricity, new schools and health centers," one says in pidgin *Chichewa*, instantly translated by Mr. Zimbota.

"Well, those are pretty big projects," I respond, "Do you have anything smaller in mind?"

"Can you provide car? Wait, wait. Can you take us to America?" another chimes in.

"I need cement for family grave marker, and my house need new roof," the head chief adds, as all the chiefs erupt in laughter.

"Now, this is getting ridiculous," I lament silently, begging for an intervention.

"Let's be serious," an older chief finally interjects, "our community needs simple things, too, like boreholes for water, toilets at market for sanitation, more trees for food and firewood, more books for schools, school fees for children, and school feeding programs. Michael, can you help us?"

"I can help you with some of them," I reply, "but I need your support. I cannot do it alone."

"You have it!" he commits, "now let's enjoy cookies and soda!"

After the meeting, I feel dizzy, overwhelmed and confused. The project options are many — some worthy and some unconscionable, some feasible and some farfetched, some ambitious and some trivial. Picking and choosing is the problem. For starters, I cannot tackle any project with a massive budget or long timeline because as a Peace Corps Volunteer, I have two years and maybe ten-thousand dollars of funding. I also adhere to the philosophy of DO NO HARM. Leaving without a legacy is better than leaving a mess.

Many potential projects, it turns out, satisfy these criteria. So I agonize, "What does the community really want? What does it really need? Which wins out if the two are at odds? Given that ordinary Malawians are deferential by nature, tending to accede to suggestion and suppress personal expression to avoid conflict, how and where can I get reliable information — the truth behind the truth? Who can I trust? Are the chiefs honorable men or opportunists seeking to better themselves? Am I in way over my head, a novice playing a game designed for pros?"

Yet, if I wait for clear answers to these questions, I'll never get anything done. Feeling fidgety, I start doing small things, hoping that something might catch on. Fruit drying, solar cooking, energy efficient mud stoves, mechanical peanut shelling, tree nurseries, ... You name it, I try it. Most of it falls flat and rightly so: having persevered for thousands of years, Malawians have seen or tried it all before. Still, through sweaty, exhausting days, I not only entertain my Malawian friends with dogged determination and toil, but earn valuable credibility and goodwill. Down the road, when I figure things out, these hard-fought intangibles (development capital, if you will) will come in handy.

* * * *

Before starting large projects, I decide to hold tight. I need to learn more about my community, a process that occurs naturally when I hunker down in the village for long stretches of time, bonding with my neighbors and exploring their culture. And the results are immediate: "It is just so good, sir, that you have not left us for several weeks," the Boys comment, knowing my tendency to travel. Likewise, out of the blue, Mr. Zimbota's daughters begin calling me "uncle," and though Malawians abound with uncles, the gesture is genuine and very much appreciated. Slowly but surely, I begin to think like them, act like them, understand them.

Malawian culture becomes my culture, my identity. I love how little traditions of civility, such as greetings, are practiced with military precision. I love the way diplomacy and compromise are prized above all else. I love how food (even the smallest morsel) is shared with friends and strangers alike. I love the way elders are respected. I love how there is always room for one more passenger in a minibus (except when I'm riding in the vehicle). I love the joyful indifference that people exhibit toward life's difficulties. I try to combine American and Malawian cultures, keeping the wheat from both, tossing out the chaff.

Ah, yes, the chaff — the stuff I don't want. Thanks to my American upbringing, there are always things about Malawi that will annoy me like hangnails. For instance, nothing is certain, except for dawn, dusk and diarrhea. Promises are frequently made and broken, reflecting a Malawian tendency to avoid confrontation or disappointment by providing untrue but pleasing news ("lies" in Western parlance). Malawians can be very boisterous — totally oblivious to the Western sensibility of silence. Nothing happens in a timely fashion, and clocks are mostly decorative (even if they happen to work).

Likewise, by Western standards, Malawians are very indirect. I often joke that you can tell the difference between a Malawian and an American by their markedly different responses to a simple math question.

"What is 2 plus 4?" I ask the American.

"It's 6, stupid. Why did you ask me such an easy question? My two-year-old brother could have answered that," the American says.

I hold my tongue and turn to the Malawian.

"What is 2 plus 4?"

"What would you like it to be?" the Malawian replies.

"I want you to tell me," I say.

"Well," he might explain, "it's not 1 or 2 or 3 or 4 or 5 or 7 or 8 or 9 or 10," leaving you to intuit the answer.

You get my drift. Needless to say, the Malawian approach doesn't make for short conversations or timely development projects.

Still, Peace Corps Volunteers learn how to work the system (with some success). You always bring a book to a scheduled meeting because you might be waiting for awhile before it starts. To obtain credible information, you ask three different people the exact same question and triangulate the responses. If your project targets school children, you implement it after the growing seasons, when attendance rates are relatively high. If you want the community to contribute money, you approach residents during the tobacco harvest, when families have some spare cash. Finally, you never undertake a significant project without involving community leaders, especially the chiefs.

You also appreciate that having a good idea is just half the battle. Even development pros steeped in cultural nuance, with well-designed projects, stumble and sometimes fail without thoughtful implementation. As the saying goes, "the best laid plans go awry," and I would add, "especially in Malawi." Case in point is the project at MIT to design a one-hundred dollar "XO" laptop for poor children. MIT might have the world's best engineers, and computers designed by them routinely defeat our greatest chess masters in head-to-head competition, but no one has engineered a computer that wins the aid game.

Stephen Rawls and I know about the MIT gaff firsthand because we join forces again in late 2007 (after the MP Kaliati sleepover) to introduce XO computers to rural Malawian schools. Together, we write and send a proposal to One Laptop Per Child (a non-profit created by faculty at MIT's Media Lab), hoping for the best. But we don't receive a response, and overtures to meet with project staff are rebuffed. It seems that MIT is interested in selling computers in large numbers (e.g., ten thousand or more) to governments, not piecemeal orders from grassroots activists like Peace Corps Volunteers.

On the ground in Malawi, we believe that this "top-down" approach is misguided. What assurance does MIT have that governments will pay their bills or distribute computers equitably? African politicians are notorious for reneging on their commitments (especially promises of payment or repayment), wooing foreign donors with half-truths and failing to deliver, and using aid resources to enrich the lives of a precious, well-connected few. Consequently, it's been our experience that most successful aid projects employ a bottom-up approach, starting small and local, and slowly building momentum.

To this end, we want MIT to sell its XO computers to private individuals — the guys on the street. We know that a teacher in Stephen's community, for example, bought a used, conventional laptop computer. Though he paid too much (about six-hundred bucks), there are many Malawians like him willing to pony up two to five-hundred dollars for a XO laptop. And these purchases would stimulate markets for XO training and repair, and spark a groundswell of political pressure to achieve MIT's ultimate goal — mass purchasing and distribution of XO computers by governments to their underprivileged.

Rebuffed but undeterred, Stephen and I lobby MIT via email to reconsider its distribution policy. Around the same time, MIT modifies its approach, permitting donors to buy one-hundred or more computers and send them anywhere in the world for three-hundred dollars per computer. After experiencing disappointing sales, frustrating negotiations with third-world bureaucrats and competition in the third-world computer market from the likes of Intel, MIT has decided to stop kicking a free-market gift horse in the mouth.

Sadly, the policy change is too little too late for us. Selling small batches of computers to donors is a significant improvement, but it doesn't directly help an average Malawian buy a single computer for his family. Additionally, Stephen and I don't have enough months left in Malawi to obtain funding, perform the logistical contortions necessary to import the machines, and implement a sustainable computing program from scratch. So, we table our proposal, hoping that future Peace Corps Volunteers will implement it. More lessons learned, for all of us.

And such lessons are invaluable on the fairways of Malawi, where development work is a lot like playing amateur golf. During a round, you might hit ninety-nine bad shots, throw your clubs and swear off the game, but one of your shots is bound to be crisp and pure. The memory of that single shot always draws you back to the course. In Malawi, I hit a lot of shanks and ground balls and score my fair share of bogeys. Yet, gradually over time, armed with new-found knowledge of my community and its needs, I dramatically improve my game, and my score card shows several birdies and at least one hole-in-one.

* * * *

Back in Khwalala Village, I try to help Zione (my best student) with her hearing problem. It's painful watching her strain for cognition in class. She doesn't complain or interrupt, but I know she cannot understand half of my words, the subtle tilt of the head saying so much more than a prime time speech. Each day megabytes of information swirl around her, failing to enter a top-notch brain not because the inn is full or the inn keeper is out, but because the door is jammed with cotton. The hearing problem is excruciatingly simple and, yet, seemingly insurmountable. In the States, the solution is a phone call away, but not here.

Then serendipity strikes. During a conversation with another aid worker, I learn about a nearby college (funded by the Montfort Order of the Catholic

Church) that operates a school and testing facility for the deaf. On Wednesday mornings, secondary school students are tested and equipped with hearing aids, free of charge. It's an opportunity I cannot ignore.

"Would you like to get your hearing tested?" I immediately ask Zione.

"Yes," she nods excitedly, "I will go, but I don't have money."

"Let's not worry about that," I reassure her, "Students don't have to pay!"

Unfortunately, several precious months pass before we organize the trip. By this time, Zione has graduated from secondary school and written the MSCE. No longer a student, she is living and farming with her parents in a village ten miles away, making coordination difficult. Our makeshift communication system — passing letters to student commuters living near her — leaves me wondering whether Zione will arrive at my house at the correct date and time.

On the designated morning, I stagger out of bed, hoping for the best. Sure enough, Zione is waiting patiently in the yard, twenty minutes early (rare for a Malawian). She is dressed to the hilt in a blouse and long skirt made from colorful, silky material, determined to make a good impression. By her side rests a rusted demolition-derby jalopy of a bicycle. She has already ridden it for one-and-a-half hours today. Reaching our destination requires two more hours of riding, mostly uphill. Then, there is the return trip.

After a long, slow ride, we arrive early at the facility for the deaf, the first people in line. Around 10 a.m., a young man invites us into a room and, after discussing the particulars of our visit, places oversized headphones over Zione's ears to start a hearing test. Operating a large computer that resembles the cockpit of a 747 airliner, he turns knobs and presses buttons, all the while recording obscure numerical results. After forty-five minutes, a supervisor arrives to break the news.

"She has moderate hearing loss," he explains, "She needs hearing aid to function normally."

"Wonderful news!" I exclaim, "Do you have any hearing aids?"

"Well, we do, but cost is forty-thousand Malawian Kwacha," the supervisor says.

"But, but…," I stutter.

"Students receive free hearing aids," he continues, "but she has already graduated from secondary school. She needs to pay."

The truth stings my ears. I don't have two-hundred-and-seventy-five dollars to spare. In fact, I have only three dollars and a pack of gum. I do have a checkbook for my Malawian bank account, but checks mean nothing here in the village. I wonder whether Zione is following the conversation. I cannot let her down. There must be a solution.

"But she had this problem as a student," I offer, "I know because I was her teacher."

"I'm sorry," he smiles, "That doesn't matter. She's not student any longer."

Having failed at advocacy, I resort to mediation, desperately grasping for creative solutions to remedy the impasse.

"Very well," I acknowledge, "but what if I reenroll her in school?" an annual expense of thirty dollars.

"Why?" he asks.

"She needs to improve her English scores to attend teachers' college."

"I guess that would be fine," he responds after pondering my proposition for an eternity, "But you need to report to us on how she's doing."

"Don't worry — I'll report," I promise, "Thank you very much."

VICTORY. SWEET VICTORY.

Two women appear and lead Zione to a separate room. From a mountain of small, cardboard containers, they select one, open it and pull out a handsome box-shaped electronic device, roughly the size of a pack of cards. They affix the device to her side, fit a curved, plastic piece into her ear, and teach her how to adjust the volume control. It takes only a few minutes of tinkering and, *voila*, Zione can hear clearly for the first time. With routine battery changes, her world will never be the same again. I stand clear across the room, watching in awe.

"Can you hear better?" I inquire in a muted tone.

Zione finds my voice like a laser beam, looks straight at me, and gushes: "Yes, sir. Thank you."

* * * *

I love helping students like Zione, which is the goal of another one of my projects: Camp SKY (Successful and Knowledgeable Youth). Organized by Peace Corps teachers, this annual nationwide camp brings together the best and brightest village students from all over Malawi to supplement their educations with two weeks of intensive learning. It fosters an environment where Volunteers are motivated to teach, students are eager to learn, and everyone has fun. At the end, exhausted but energized teachers and campers return to their communities with new skills and a renewed sense of hope. In theory, it's a win-win for everyone, especially the kids.

Camp SKY 2007 is my baby. With a skeleton team of devoted Volunteers, on a shoestring budget, I lead its planning and implementation, a monumental and maddening undertaking that tests every ounce of my patience and commitment. Within a limited third-world environment, we achieve the impossible from start to finish: organizing committees, holding meetings, visiting venues, drafting contracts, soliciting funding, transporting participants, writing curricula, teaching subjects, feeding hungry stomachs, fixing toilets, nursing illnesses, massaging egos, graduating proud youngsters — you name it, we do it. It is shitty and beautiful and worth every minute.

It all starts with a carefully chosen venue. Ours is Zomba Catholic, one of Malawi's best boarding schools, which sits on a quiet campus a few miles south of Zomba, the former colonial capital. Campers who usually make do in crumbling, rural schools without electricity and running water, receiving a barebones education (whatever teachers have the time and training to cover), luxuriate at Zomba Catholic in the opulence of landscaping, electricity, running water, science laboratories and a computer room. They gorge themselves at a buffet line of course offerings taught by Peace Corps Volunteers and, for the first time in their lives, experience what a good education feels like.

At camp, days are long. Energetic campers rise before dawn to sing and dance in the courtyard, meters away from the beds of exhausted counselors, who continue sleeping like corpses until breakfast. Starting immediately after breakfast, campers scurry to assemblies, classes (traditional, vocational, and arts), laboratories (computers and science), and events like movies and scavenger hunts. After putting them to bed, beleaguered organizers meet to commiserate, plan, and reload. It is an arduous, undeniably successful grind. But the truth is that most people don't know the half of it.

A BIG secret hangs over Camp SKY 2007, threatening to shut it down. Friends and family from the States have donated money to finance the undertaking, but days before the start of Camp, our local Malawian bank won't credit their American checks. Unbeknownst to our campers, suppliers or venue hosts, we are effectively broke, living day-to-day and tracking every expense. After countless meetings and pleas for help, the bank not only refuses to budge, but patronizes us with pithy overdraft protection (at a predatory interest rate) should we sink into the red.

"I have a question," I say to Stephen, our trusty Camp SKY treasurer.

"What is it?" he asks.

"How are our finances?"

"Hmm...I think we won't go bankrupt for another day or so," he replies, "But if we end the camp early, we don't have enough money to get everyone home."

"Wow, better than I expected," I shrug, "Keep up the good work."

For several edgy days, every penny is precious. We have planned to run the entire camp (hosting eighty students, ten Malawian teachers, and thirty Peace Corps Volunteers) for under ten-thousand U.S. dollars. Yet, given the circumstances, we have to make do with a fraction of that amount. Then, at the eleventh hour, after flying for days on fumes (financially speaking), the money miraculously appears in our account. With a collective sigh of relief, we pay outstanding bills and resurrect expensive camp activities. A cloud has been lifted.

Throughout the ordeal, we maintain our composure with adept crisis management skills, which were honed by a major misfire that occurred prior to Camp. The occasion was an upscale fundraising dinner for Camp SKY in Lilongwe (the capital city), which drew well-to-do members of the American community, such as diplomats and NGO workers, to socialize and support the efforts of their lowly Peace Corps counterparts. The cause of the crisis was our cook — Norman, a lovable, but ornery and unapologetic, Peace Corps teacher from Puerto Rico. I should have seen it coming.

Norman is a Latin firecracker with long, straight hair and distinguished service stints in the United States Marines and Peace Corps. Looking for something original, he decided to cook drunken meatballs, a dish he learned to make as a Peace Corps Volunteer in Moldova. There was little resistance to the idea — when Norman decides to do something, you pretty much have to go along with it. And, honestly, it seemed like a good idea at the time. But, in hindsight, "seemed like a good idea" were famous last words.

"How are the food preparations coming along?" I asked him, entering the kitchen of our hosts, the Peace Corps Country Director and his wife.

"Get outta my farken kitchen," he shouted me, "I like to work alone."

"Norman, I just want to check on your progress, that's all," I said in a soft, compromising tone.

"Yeah, thanks for thinking of me, but I'm a big boy" he replied, kissing me on both cheeks, "Now get out!"

"Ok, you've got it under control," I backed off, "The food smells delicious. I'm sure it will be a big hit with the guests."

Turns out that I was wrong. A fabulous chef with no concept of kitchen sanitation or established food handling practices, Norman left the drunken meatballs sitting out overnight to "ferment." Whatever this method did to enhance flavor, it also created a fertile Petri dish for harmful African bacteria. At the fundraiser, most of the attendees ate the meatballs and loved them. But the following morning, several of the organizers suffered intense stomach cramps interspersed with frequent, diarrheal sprints to the bathroom. After learning that most of our distinguished guests (including the U.S. Ambassador's wife and son) were similarly afflicted, we promptly circulated an apology.

> On the evening of Thursday, October 11, Peace Corps Volunteers held a fundraising dinner at Dale and Jeanne Mosier's house. Approximately 60 people attended, and proceeds went to Camp SKY 2007, a summer camp for under-privileged Malawian secondary school students. The event raised about 1,000 US dollars, which will greatly assist Volunteers to organize and manage this year's camp. We earnestly thank all of those who attended and especially Dale and Jeanne for hosting the event.

> After the event many individuals experienced stomach problems. We sincerely apologize for this mishap and for any discomfort experienced by our guests. The cause of the problem has been discussed, and we have taken steps to ensure that it does not happen again. Hopefully this unfortunate incident will not reflect badly on Peace Corps, Camp SKY or our generous hosts.

Little did our guests know, the "steps" taken were to graduate Norman from Peace Corps Malawi (his two years were up) and remove him from the country. As of 2010, he was living in the Pacific-island nation of Vanuatu, in the middle of a third Peace Corps tour. To the good people of Vanuatu, I say, "Beware of the drunken meatballs."

A month later, during the Camp, another major mishap occurs. It involves the counterpart program for Malawian teachers, a small but important component of our overall strategy to improve Malawian schools. Two innovative, one-week sessions are planned: during the first week, participants will design a biology lab manual for use in village schools with limited resources; and in week two, a second group of counterparts will be trained to facilitate miniature versions of Camp SKY in their home villages, so our model can be replicated and reach far more people. The first week is a slam dunk; the second week is a disaster. Why were the results so different?

Money poisons week two. The Camp pays for the transport, food and lodging of participants, including counterparts, but unlike students, Malawian teachers expect "allowances" for their participation, an entitlement common in government and aid work. Motivated by equal parts greed and culture, they feel slighted and disrespected when none materialize. One teacher, in particular, is so upset about it that he openly disparages Ani, the Peace Corps facilitator of the counterpart program, and toward the end of Camp, threatens to run her over with a car, prompting a stiff written rebuke from Camp SKY staff and his immediate expulsion. He was later fired by his school.

After that debacle, the Camp ends on a mixed note. At a graduation ceremony, most of the kids proudly walk across the stage to receive a diploma, marking their successful completions of Camp SKY 2007 (Malawians love certificates). Some of the girls even drop to their knees before taking the diploma from my hand, a showing of respect that never ceases to embarrass me. Two boys, however, sulk in the background, awaiting their punishment for coming to graduation stoned and drunk. Following an impromptu meeting of camp staff, a decision is made — they will not receive diplomas or dance the night away at the celebration disco. After hearing the news, they cry.

So, was the camp worth it? Honestly, it's hard to tell and probably impossible for us to know for sure. Yet, the camp was cheap (about eight-thousand dollars), and removed from our bank problems and ruinous week two of the counterpart program, most of the participants had a great time and got a taste of possibilities that lie ahead if they score well on the MSCE. Speaking for myself and my school, I notice important changes in the kids who attended. They are more self-assured and determined to succeed. They also seem to be taking what they learned from Camp and applying it to their village lives.

Gift is a perfect example. He has a proclivity for risky sex, and before attending Camp SKY, he was getting lots of it with young ladies deep in village fields. But at the Camp, he befriended a Volunteer from Minnesota named Bryce, who works at a health center in Southern Malawi. Bryce, a congenial guy and dedicated health teacher, took a liking to Gift and taught him about HIV transmission. After Camp, armed with this new knowledge, Gift decides to adopt a chaste lifestyle that just might save his life.

Back in Khwalala, I ask him how he's faring.

"Are you still following Bryce's advice?" I inquire one day after school.

"Yes, sir," he replies, "I am very good since Camp SKY."

"What is your secret? How do you avoid risky sex?" I wonder.

"Well," he responds, "When I get excited, I exercise like you and bathe with cold water."

I guess cold showers are universal.

＊ ＊ ＊ ＊

A few weeks later, Gift celebrates by joining his classmates on an epic field trip. The journey takes us to Mulanje Mountain, a massive hunk of Great Rift Valley granite that looms large over our village, dominating its skyline with twenty-seven breathtaking summits. Mulanje's charms are legion, and I frequently explore her wilds with friends, spellbound by the rugged beauty and remoteness, never encountering the supernatural spirits rumored to live there. I love getting lost on her high-altitude meadows and craggy peaks, far from help and close to heaven, in a place few dare to tread.

Naturally, I want to share this wild treasure (hopefully a future UNESCO World Heritage Site) with members of the school's Wildlife Club. Since my arrival, they have dutifully protected and improved the natural environment of Khwalala Village by planting over seventy trees around campus and cultivating vegetable gardens, a perpetual cycle of watering, weeding and fertilizing. On empty stomachs and blind faith, without much support from teachers or other students, they have painstakingly transformed the campus from a deforested dust bowl into a verdant beacon of food and beauty. Outside school groups and organizations visit our campus to marvel at their work.

Coordinating our excursion to the Mountain is the MMCT (Mulanje Mountain Conservation Trust). It's a wealthy non-profit organization charged with the protection of Mulanje, but reviews of its activism are mixed. It seems to spend much of its time locked in power struggles with the Forestry Department over who possesses a governmental mandate to implement an effective conservation strategy. Having spoken frankly with both sides on several occasions, my impression is that Mulanje Mountain is in trouble — the Forestry Department is understaffed, underfunded and marginally competent, and the MMCT is self-important, unprofessional and uncooperative.

Yet, the MMCT has a school program for kids, so I bite the bullet and meet with MMCT personnel to hammer out the details of our trip. Everything is fine, fine, fine, they tell me. Don't worry about a thing, they add, just write a confirmatory letter containing the trip dates, and we will approve it.

"You will hike to Chambe Forestry Center," MMCT staffers elaborate after I submit the letter.

"Very good," I smile.

"We arrange for you to stay in dormitory for school groups."

"That sounds wonderful," I reply, "but do we need a guide?"

"Of course," they continue, "We will pay for guide and provide some food. You pay nothing for trip."

"Sounds great," I say, "but are there daily activities for the kids, to keep them busy?"

"Yes," they explain, "In between meals, they will take hikes and help Forestry Department remove invasive pine species."

I take them at their word, circulating the details around school. Unable to remember their last field trip, the students tremble with excitement, and the morning of the trip, fifteen of them and three teachers meet on campus and begin a three-hour bicycle ride to the base of the Mountain. Arriving in good time, we leave our bikes with a friend, find a guide and start hiking up. I take it slow, knowing that the next four hours will be hot, sweaty and physically demanding. The kids, on the other hand, spring up the steep trails like Billy goats, chattering like magpies and teasing anyone who cannot keep up.

Around dusk, we reach our destination, Chambe Forestry Center, to the eerie desolation of a ghost town. No one emerges from the rows of government buildings to greet us or offer us a place to sleep. And the only soul there, a watchman staying across the river, tells us that the keeper of our living quarters has abandoned his post to tend to his three wives at the bottom of the Mountain. Making matters worse, the derelict keeper holds the only key to a closet containing bedding and cooking supplies. Faced with this news, our hopes fade with the setting sun, as underdressed students shiver in plummeting temperatures.

Stranded and desperate, we decide to take action. Spurred by the sage advice of Mr. Zimbota that "necessity has no law," I break out multipurpose tools and go to work on the closet. On the first attempt, we fail, our tools no match for the stout metal padlocks guarding the plywood doors like Rottweilers. But, on the second attempt, we target the hinges, the closet's Achilles' heel, painstakingly unscrewing each one. After a few minutes of tinkering, the doors fall off with a loud thud, and laughter replaces worry. Each member of the expedition is issued a mattress and warm blanket, courtesy of American resourcefulness and vigilantism, and using the cooking supplies, we prepare a large meal, replacing hunger pangs with the narcotic sublimity of full bellies.

The following day we hike to the heavens. In the absence of Forestry Department officials to lead community service projects, there's nothing else to do, and with mild weather and a partly cloudy sky, the day is perfect for it. Feeling ambitious, we chart a course for the ultimate prize, the granddaddy of Mulanje peaks — Sapitwa (meaning "don't go there"), about ten-thousand feet above sea level. After spending six hours navigating a steep, rocky ascent, bounding over boulders and negotiating treacherous ravines, we giddily climb the final few steps and clutch the metal and cement marker that crowns one of the highest peaks in Eastern Africa.

"This is very memorable day," exclaims Alfred, standing upright and proud, like explorer Vasco Da Gama rounding the Horn of Africa and discovering a trade route to India.

"It certainly is, Alfred," I reply, "You deserve this achievement."

"I never thought that I could come here," Mr. Zimbota chimes in, "Now I can die happy man. Thank you."

"Please, please take picture of students," Myson interrupts, shivering.

"My pleasure," I smile, arranging everyone into neat rows in front of the summit marker as their teeth chatter from exposure.

"Are you done, Mr. Buckler?" they ask, "We are so, so cold. Can we please go?"

We rush off the summit and return to Chambe without incident. As the girls dutifully prepare a large celebratory meal of *nsima* and vegetables, the boys relax and talk. I try to encourage them to assist their female colleagues, suggesting that they clean pots and plates after dinner, but they laugh and shrug me off, convinced that I am a silly American with a farfetched understanding of gender roles. Having learned to pick my battles, I don't press it — tonight is to be enjoyed! Buoyed by the aroma of cooking food and the sweetness of shared achievement, everyone is in a jolly mood.

Unfortunately, the celebration is short-lived. The news of our "antics" has cascaded down Mulanje Mountain, through the ravines and past the cedar groves, faster than a mountain stream. Who delivered it is anyone's guess, but nothing that happens in Malawi surprises me anymore. The lowdown is this: a *wazungu* (white person) pillaged the equipment closet at Chambe using a new-fangled metal device and probably witchcraft. He divided the bounty, pots and silverware, blankets and mattresses with *ophunzira okuda* (black students) and *aphunsitzi okuda* (black teachers). Afterwards, *wazungu* and his black friends embarked on a hike, leaving the place in disarray. It's a good story, but come on!

Not privy to these fabrications, we spend the next morning casually strolling down the Mountain. Returning all of the "borrowed" items and sealing the closet as we found it, our last duty before setting off is bidding farewell to the benevolent watchman across the river who supplied us firewood and provided a comforting presence after our inauspicious arrival. It's a perfect day, but on the long, peaceful descent through virgin forests and alongside waterfalls, our identities morph from intrepid adventurers to dangerous fugitives. We emerge from the bush looking rougher and guiltier.

At the bottom, Forestry officials pepper us with accusatory questions. It's uncomfortable, but after a few tense moments, we dispel the spurious rumors of our plunder by telling the truth and then writing it in a short report that staunchly defends our desperation-fueled actions. The report, signed by a white man no less, seems to satisfy them, at least for the time being. Unbeknownst to us, however, the report is circulated far and wide, and everyone — politicians, education officials, Forestry officers, and MMCT leaders — reads it. In a few short days, we have become local outlaw celebrities.

A brief crisis follows, featuring a uniquely Malawian version of the blame game. Who was responsible for teachers and students nearly starving and freezing to death on the Mountain? Predictably, the MMCT points a finger at the Forestry Department, and vice versa. "This sort of thing cannot be allowed to happen again," both sides posture and patronize. Yet, thankfully, the drama is short lived, and after a bit of cajoling and fence mending, we are forgiven for our sins and encouraged to organize another trip. A journey that started and ended as a fiasco had the sweetest of centers, and in the end, students learn that with proper planning, and a bit of improvisation, dreams really can come true.

* * * *

Speaking of dreams and mountains to climb, another project ("The Project," actually) reveals itself to me one afternoon after school, when I decide to visit a sick student living near Khwalala Market. On the way, I pass scores of female students embarking on their daily marches home, and having ascertained my intentions, several of them escort me to their sick sister, a frail and quiet girl living in a rented closet-sized hovel. When we arrive, she lies delirious on a bare floor, feverish and shivering under a thin sheet, comforted by her three equally destitute roommates. I am disgusted and inspired. Even a blind squirrel, they say, finds a nut every now and then, and I have found mine.

"Can I help in any way?" I ask.

The girls look confused and a bit ashamed that I am standing in their living room, which also doubles as a dining room and bedroom, depending on the time of day.

"Yes, sir," they respond, "You can tell Mr. Zimbota that Mary is sick and needs to visit hospital."

"No problem," I assure them, "I will do it right away."

Delivering the message to Mr. Zimbota is easy, way too easy. There must be something else I can do. I want to understand why children live like this. I wonder whether I can improve the situation. Seizing the moment, I ask some more questions.

"Why do you live here?" I inquire.

"Sir," one responds, "My parents live so, so far. I cannot make journey from school to their home every day."

"How much do you pay to stay here?" I ask.

"Sir, we pay five-hundred kwacha per month," about four dollars.

"If you could live at school for the same price, would you move?"

"Oh, yes, we would love to live at school," they exclaim in unison, "It is very dark and cold here."

"Thanks for the information," I say, walking out the door, "I'll try to help you."

The problem faced by these girls is a common one. Rural secondary schools attract students from near and far. Forced to travel long distances to school (up to ten miles) by foot or bike, most arrive late, muddy and tired. Even during dry spells, rough terrain and empty stomachs make it difficult for many students to show up punctual and alert. And, girls have it particularly bad. In village communities, where boys are placed on pedestals and primped for greatness, they face unrelenting pressure to drop out of school or get married, and spend much of their time performing domestic chores instead of studying. As my dad used to say, "The world isn't fair."

And the current alternative for female students — renting rooms near school from families or businesspeople — is fraught with problems. For starters, there are a limited number of rooms available for rent, too few to accommodate all of the interested students. Moreover, student renters face congested and unsanitary living conditions, with multiple students living in one or two rooms and sleeping on mud floors without the protection of mosquito nets. Other necessities are also lacking, like a source of light for nighttime studying or a nearby bore hole for healthy, clean water. For rural education in Malawi to improve, something needs to change. And I want to be a part of it.

I immediately track down Mr. Zimbota.

"How do you feel about building a boarding facility for girls?" I ask.

"Hmm," he considers, "What are you thinking?"

"We can seek donor funding to help the girls," I elaborate, "because they are more vulnerable, and possibly expand to boys in the future."

"Sound interesting," he replies, "but we need to ask community."

A few days later, at a meeting of parents, chiefs, and students, the response is nearly unanimous: a girls' boarding facility would greatly improve the village. And to support the project, the village is willing to contribute hours of unskilled labor and basic materials (like bricks and river sand). Still, there is a lone dissenting voice, and an important one at that — the Group Village Headman. His reticence is a big deal and a bad sign, but I'm the only one who seems to be concerned. "Don't worry about him," advocates of boarding explain, "He just doesn't appreciate education."

So, the stage is set. With Mr. Zimbota's help, I draft crude architectural diagrams, meet with prospective village contractors and carpenters, and make a long list of required building materials. For our modest undertaking, we need to acquire lots of stuff, including river sand for foundations, wire for various sizes of roofing beams, something called "brick force" to buttress the walls, insecticides for ants and other pests, and hundreds of bags of cement. The only way to get these supplies to Khwalala is to buy them at a hardware store in Blantyre and ferry them back on a heavy-duty transport truck.

My head throbs from information overload and frustration. Too many painfully long, hot meetings hampered by cultural differences and communication breakdowns. Too many unknowns and educated guesses. Thankfully, Mr. Zimbota is with me every step of the way, trying to ameliorate my discontent with smiles and carefully timed interventions.

"How many metal roofing sheets do we want?" I ask.

"The contractor says that we need fifty," Mr. Zimbota replies.

"How did he get that number?" I wonder, "My calculation is different."

"He didn't perform a calculation," Mr. Zimbota reports after asking the contractor about his methodology, "He just knows."

"Ok," I sigh, "but I reckon we need sixty."

The contractor nods and utters something indiscernible.

"You're right," Mr. Zimbota reports, "he forgot about some."

The blessed agony continues. I travel to Blantyre, scouring hardware stores for price quotations, accounting for every last nut and bolt. I also visit transport providers, both in Blantyre and in nearby trading centers, to price the cost of a driver and twenty-ton truck. I run the numbers, not once or twice, but three times, and sigh in frustration. We've fallen short of the "community contribution" requirement (around 25% of total project cost, depending on the donor) by several hundred dollars. The bottom line is that if the community really wants girls' boarding, it needs to step forward and commit more of its own resources.

An emergency meeting is called. Mr. Zimbota begins by explaining the money shortfall, and one by one, the usual suspects — chiefs, parents, teachers and students — rise and deliver impassioned pleas of support for our fledgling project. No one speaks in dissent, not even the Group Village Headman, who sees the writing on the wall. Before long, a decision is reached: to rejuvenate the project, the community will contribute another five-thousand bricks and the money needed to transport the bricks to the school. The offering is substantial and genuine, but at the end of the day, will it be enough?

At this stage, it's just a math problem. I quickly rerun the numbers and signal that I would like to speak. As attendees wait with bated breath, I take the stage, clearing my throat and staring down at my notepad.

"Thank you all for coming," I say, "and thank you for contributing the bricks."

"You help us build boarding school?" a woman asks, jumping the gun.

"Well, I think that if we are frugal, we can find the money."

The room erupts into applause that feels like pressure waves. They really want this boarding facility. Whatever happens, I cannot let them down.

"When do we get money?" a teacher asks.

"Good question," I reply, "We first need to write a grant proposal and get it approved by a donor. That might take several months. I will keep you posted."

Immediately after the meeting, I begin drafting a detailed proposal. "Some of the requested funds," it states, "will be used to convert an existing library into a hostel. Additional funds will be used to construct a bath house, an outdoor kitchen, and a clothes washing station. The remaining funds will be spent on accoutrements of daily living, such as beds and mattresses. Student boarders, and all the boarding facilities used by them, will be located within a secure, fenced campus." It sounds good, a little too good to be true, actually. Yet, all the flowery language and meticulous budgeting in the world cannot hide the truth — the project is an ambitious undertaking, fraught with uncertainties.

And using an existing building (the library) is the biggest one. The ADB is still plugging away at its multi-million dollar, campus-wide renovation project and until it's done, the old library cannot be renovated into a hostel for girls. In other words, our fate is tied to the ADB, our small, local project held hostage pending the completion of a large, centrally administered one. The predicament makes me uneasy, but I seem to be alone in feeling this way. "Don't worry about it," says the ADB foreman, sensing my concern, "We'll be done in few months." Though the ADB is already two years behind schedule, I am cautiously optimistic... cautiously.

I finish the proposal and proudly submit it to a potential donor. The lucky recipient is the Small Projects Assistance (SPA) Fund provided by USAID (agency of the U.S. Government tasked with overseas development) and doled out by Peace Corps staff. It is a modest source of U.S. taxpayer money that caters to discrete projects like ours and has a reputation for making quick funding decisions. Also receiving copies of the proposal are MP Patricia Kaliati and the Division Education Manager, both of whom are women and strong supporters of the project. Now, all we can do is wait.

"Do you think we can pull this off?" I ask Mr. Zimbota.

"Yes," he answers without hesitation, "it is welcome change."

"Do you think it's worth all of our time and trouble?" I wonder.

"In America, you like to say 'the proof is in pudding,'" he replies.

"Yes, I suppose we do."

"Living in your house, near school," he explains, "Gift, Myson and Alfred are top students. Gift is Deputy Head Boy, Myson is Entertainment Chairman, and Alfred is President of the Wildlife Club."

"Yes, but they are boys," I observe, "The boarding facility is for girls."

"You have blessed those boys," Mr. Zimbota continues, "With boarding, we can provide same opportunity for ten times as many girls."

VII

FREEDOM FOIBLES

A presidential election is coming to America next year. You are being inundated with political propaganda and might be questioning the health of our democratic system. Perhaps you want to flee to another country, like I did, and be happily removed and oblivious. Yet, before you burn your passport, and sacrifice your vote, please consider the governance alternatives.

— Letter Home, October 2007

S tarstruck and eighteen, I was speechless. One of the most powerful men in the world stood before me, wearing a charcoal suit, a fat cigar tucked softly into his breast pocket. He looked at me, a complete stranger, straight in the eyes, extended an aging hand, and in a soothing baritone voice said, "Pleasure to see you, Michael." After meeting Speaker of the House Tip O'Neill at the 1992 Democratic National Convention, I believed in government and politicians. Thanks to Tip, and others, I still do.

I become a politician in Malawi. Thanks to the Boys, I literally acquire a title and responsibilities. Together, we constitute the smallest sovereign state on Earth.

"Sir, we need to have Buckler family meeting," Gift says.

"What's the occasion?" I ask, "Is there a problem?"

"The problem is that Alfred is loafing," Gift explains with surprising forthrightness.

"How so?" I inquire.

"In the evenings, he comes late and doesn't help us with cooking and cleaning," he elaborates, "He also doesn't fill water buckets."

"What is Alfred doing while you and Myson are working?" I wonder.

"He likes to chat with his friends and chase girls," Gift responds.

"I see. Let's meet tonight during dinner to find a way forward."

That evening, minutes before night school, Alfred springs through the door, late as usual.

"Alfred, punctuality has become a problem for you," I chide, "Why have you missed dinner?"

"Sir, I was chatting with friends," he says, "I will do better."

"That's what you always say," Myson interjects.

"I mean it this time," Alfred cries.

"That's not good enough," Gift adds, "We need rules and order. Otherwise, nothing changes, and Myson and I suffer."

Gift is right but what rules and what order? The school is a bona fide dictatorship. The country is presumptively democratic. The Bucker household is neither, yet.

"What should I do?" I ask.

"We need to choose system of government for Buckler family," Gift proposes.

"I can write sign with our laws and duties," Myson exclaims, "so everyone can remember and follow them."

"What?" Alfred shouts agitatedly, "Why do we need a bunch of rules? Everything is fine. Malawi is democracy, which means I can do whatever I want. You are breaking my rights."

Gift rolls his eyes, "What rights?" he asks smugly, "What you are describing is anarchy, not democracy. You are why we Africans need strict leaders."

"Very well," I intervene as things start to get heated, "I have an idea."

"Yes, Mr. Buckler has idea," Alfred parrots, "He is very clever man from America. He understand democracy and rights. He know what is best for us."

"Ahem," I interject, ending Alfred's soliloquy, as the Boys fall silent.

"We will research different types of governments. You can ask anyone for advice — friends, teachers, parents, politicians."

Three bald, African heads nod in unison.

"A week from today," I add, "we will meet to discuss what we have learned. By the end of that meeting, we will either adopt a system of government or, if Alfred gets his way, do nothing."

A week later, with all three assembled before me on the front porch, we begin.

"What have you learned about government?" I inquire.

"About what?" Alfred asks.

"About government, you dunce," I joke, "Remember our conversation over dinner?"

"Oh, yes. We have learned so much, sir," Myson answers.

"Me, too, boys...me, too. Let's talk about it."

Myson goes first.

"To do research on government, I asked our social studies teacher, Mr. Nyambalo," he explains.

"What did he say?" Gift inquires.

"He told me that Malawi has been democracy since 1994 and elections are coming again in 2009."

Mr. Nyambalo is right: in advance of next year's general elections, politicians are crisscrossing the country making promises, doing favors, and drawing crowds.

"He also said," Myson continues, "that politicians are visiting us, and promising to help, because of elections. They want to win our votes."

"Do you agree?" I ask.

"I'm not sure," he replies.

"Well, you remember when the President visited last month, don't you?"

* * * *

He smiles, definitely recalling the spectacle. The dearth of air traffic in Malawi is striking. Noise pollution usually comes from roosters and guinea fowl. That made the helicopters flying in tandem over Mulanje District, where I reside, as odd an occurrence as Model T Fords puttering down Interstate 95 in America. Yet, it was a familiar incongruity in these parts, and could mean only one thing — the coming of Dr. Bingu wa Mutharika, Malawi's second democratically-elected President.

Bingu was travelling to a political rally about ten miles from Khwalala. As he was flying in Presidential style, overloaded lorries (large transport trucks) ferried local constituents from the surrounding villages, including my students. Like roving juke boxes, the lorries navigated the dusty, sun-baked roads as their occupants sang and danced, ecstatic about seeing the President and enjoying a hiatus from their daily routines. From the seat of my bicycle, I watched them rumble by, one after another, in wakes of lung-choking dust. We were all moving toward the same place, some faster than others.

Upon my arrival, commotion enveloped the primary school hosting the event. Throngs of people scurried about like ants, wearing light blue clothing with corn-cob-prints, the trademark of the ruling Democratic Progressive Party (DPP). A pack of middle-aged men slowly circled the grounds on eye-catching light blue bicycles tattooed with DPP insignia. Local vendors lined the road selling fruit (bananas and avocados), roasted peanuts, and baked goods (little cakes made from corn flour). It felt less like a political event than a circus or county fair. I could have gone for a funnel cake.

But, of all the interesting sights, what immediately caught my eye was the sea of students. Standing together in cliques, like Medieval clans at a jousting match, each school wore a unique color combination of pants (boys), long skirts (girls), and shirts, setting itself apart from the rest. The primary schools, free to the public and thus plentiful in both number and enrollment, resorted to further gradations to distinguish themselves — hued shirt cuffs and collars. All together, the young-sters resembled an alpine meadow of wildflowers.

Sweating in their suits and shiny shoes, VIPs gathered at one end of the field. Beside them were two curious, cylindrical containers and informational placards, a demonstration of sorts. Walking over to investigate, I learned that the contain-ers were metal corn silos and that the President was coming to commission them as the government's latest initiative to bolster grassroots food security. According to the placards written in *Chichewa*, they were a dramatic improvement over the alternative — storage bins fashioned out of sticks and mud — because the metal silos reduced corn losses (from pests or disease) from forty percent to fifteen per-cent. That's a lot more *nsima* meals.

Back in the center of the field, the stage was set. A raised platform erected by rally organizers was covered to protect VIPs from the sun; political banners festooned like drapes from its crossbeams. In the center of the platform was a sole microphone for the procession of speakers, and just off-stage, video cameras sat poised to capture every moment of the spectacle and beam live footage of it over Malawian television to cities, towns and villages. The air was charged with frenetic anticipation as people braced for the President's imminent arrival.

Needing some water, I marched to the school's borehole. I wanted to quench my thirst and cleanse my soil-stained body before donning pants for the President. Much to my dismay, however, the borehole was mobbed with people, and a ruckus ensued. Hoards of women pushed and shoved their way to the tap, desperately trying to break the logjam. Not even my jocular urgings in *Chichewa* persuaded them to abandon their bickering and work together. Panic set in.

They must have been painfully parched. In this hot, tropical country, people drink shockingly little water — most of it is fetched for cooking and cleaning. Moreover, borehole regulars (mostly women and girls) usually follow an unwrit-ten etiquette, taking turns based on arrival time and ushering exalted community members, like me, to the front of the cue. Yet, this didn't happen, not on that day. With the President coming soon, veritable strangers from all over the region abandoned their congeniality and reverted to their instincts. I was caught in the middle of their desperation.

Still, I tried to pacify the situation. "*Osadandaula, osadandaula*," I repeated, telling them not to worry. A few looked up at me, shocked to hear *Chichewa* words flowing from my lips, but didn't budge an inch. "*Ali okuba* (they are thieves)," a mother screamed, pointing to some women carrying large, full buckets on their heads. She pushed her way to the front with a limp, dehydrated baby strapped to her back. "*Ndinadikira nthawi yaitali* (I was waiting for a long time)," she explained. I moved aside, letting her pass.

Since Plan A had failed, it was time for Plan B. They aren't hard to find in Malawi, where the best laid plans go awry and keeping a stocked and ready inventory of substitutions is wise. On familiar turf at a school, I knew that a fellow educator would assist me, a time-honored professional courtesy. And, sure enough, just as I left the stressful borehole malady, I found the gracious wife of a teacher, who stowed my bike, gave me a pail of water to wash, and led me to a quiet corner of her backyard to change clothes.

As I changed in the dark corner of a bathhouse, my cellular phone rang.

"Hello," I answered.

"Hi, Michael, just wanted to call and check on you," Mom explained from America, barely audible over the ensemble of welcome drums beating in the distance.

"You'll never believe where I am," I said.

"Where?" Mom asked.

"Oh, half naked in a stranger's bath house, awaiting the President's arrival. I'll call you later, ok?"

"What? Michael, that's not funny. Hold on for a moment...."

Click.

As I emerged from the bathhouse, President Bingu arrived. Accompanying him were an armada of automobiles and platoons of advisors, supporters, groupies, well wishers and army soldiers; I quietly wondered how many attendees were receiving something (food, money, political favors) for their attendance. Despite the hoopla, the mood was relaxed, and even the machine-gun wielding soldiers appeared harmless, a humorous line of skinny, little men wearing bubble-like helmets and carrying weapons half their size.

The program began. The national anthem was first on tap, followed by prayers and greetings from local officials. Then, one by one, political lackeys rose to extol the wisdom of the Bingu Administration and castigate the purportedly malevolent meddling of the opposition UDF party and its insufferable leader, Bakili Muluzi. "Vote for Bingu in next year's election," they yelled, "He wants to develop Malawi. Muluzi is wasting our time with lies." They were political preachers of the ruling party government, and this was their evangelical Sermon on the Mount.

Ah, the sweet smell of political bullshit.

You could really smell it when MP Kaliati grabbed the microphone. Making another appearance in my Malawian epic, she spoke with signature gusto and dramatic flair. An ardent feminist, she railed against the status of women in Malawi, screaming her message into the microphone at a blinding tempo, and belittling men bold enough to disagree. Her supporters, a large squadron of village women kneeing beside the platform, filled her brief pauses with enthusiastic cheers. "I don't like her or her friends," a teaching colleague commented, "They hate men." I didn't dare argue with him.

I felt badly for the speaker slated to follow the Kaliati show — none other than our distinguished President Bingu. Perhaps he didn't mind, or even liked, the contrast of his calm and sensible masculinity to her feminine fire, politicians never above playing on stereotypes, but he was far less entertaining than his controversial colleague. Donning a modest straw hat (incidentally, the only one of its kind on the stage), he spoke with temperance in measured tones, his words rubbing your ears like lamb's wool. If I hadn't been standing, I would have fallen asleep.

So, I decided to leave. It was before Bingu finished speaking, but I had scratched my political itch and needed time to win a race home with the setting sun. Seeing my students perform might have delayed my departure, but it wasn't in the cards. Though they had diligently prepared traditional dances and songs to honor the President, long-winded politicos had devoured their performance time. It wasn't the first time their faint voices, resting near the bottom of many interconnected food chains, were sacrificed to the whims of the powerful. It wouldn't be the last. So much for democracy.

* * * *

Back in Khwalala, still trying to choose a government for the Buckler family, the Boys and I reflect on the memory of that day. Gift is the first to editorialize.

"It shows that democracy is wasteful," he interjects, "like my grandfather says."

"Why is that?" I ask.

Alfred and Myson perk up — this could be good.

"Because Bingu spend too much money fighting Muluzi," Gift elaborates, "and trying to get our votes."

"How should he spend the money?" I inquire.

"On the people!" he fires back.

Gift and his grandfather aren't alone. Some of President Bingu's priorities (e.g., cars, speeches, political wrangling) make people resentful and disparage the image of democracy. Poor villagers, like the Boys, have the most to be upset about, especially orphans like Alfred.

"What about you?" I ask him, "Did you speak with anyone about government?"

"Yes, sir," he answers, "I speak with Village Headman."

"And what did the Headman say?" I inquire, always eager to learn new things about our distinguished village leader.

"He doesn't like democracy because it comes from white man," he explains, "White man forces it on us."

"Forced it on you?"

"Yes," Alfred continues, "Headman say that for hundreds of years Africans have used chiefdoms to run society and help people."

"That's true."

"America," he continues, "should not push democracy on us."

I understand where he's coming from, but I'm not sure that he's right. Democracy in Malawi (much like Christianity) is distinctly Malawian: fused with traditional practices and beliefs, it doesn't always look or feel like our esteemed democracy. And it doesn't have to because Malawians are independent people who live in a sovereign country, right? Surely, the Headman is wrong about Westerners forcing the grand institution of democracy on others. Hasn't democracy spread around Africa on its own merits?

As it turns out, the Village Headman is right — America strong-arms its African friends through the practice of "tied aid" (i.e., offering money with strings attached). One form is requiring that a percentage of aid money be spent on goods and services within the donor country, which is akin to American companies like Halliburton monopolizing lucrative rebuilding contracts in Iraq to the exclusion of capable (and cheaper) local contractors. Yet, America conditions aid not only on "buying American," but also "being American," and mimicking our economic and governmental systems like — you guessed it — democracy. Sometimes it's unclear whether needy countries are customers, imperial subjects or friends.

After listening intently to my explanation of aid tying, Gift dances out of his chair and waves his hands in the air, boiling with irritation.

"Why are they forcing us to be democracy?" he yells, "That's not what America is about."

"That's a good question," I admit, "I don't have an answer for you. I don't know why we force people to be free."

What I do know, however, is that our current approach seems risky. Democracy, in all of its flavors, is beautiful to us, but is our fondness for it universal? And assuming it is, or should be, why do we bribe countries to adopt it? By requiring other governments to practice democracy now, on our terms and timelines, aren't we risking a backlash that could spawn a resurgence of dictatorship in Africa and elsewhere? Before continuing down the current path, we need answers to these questions.

"The Headman also says that America doesn't follow its own rules," Alfred says.

"We're all rule breakers," I say, "Is that what he is trying to say?"

"No," Alfred replies, "It is something else."

What the Headman is alluding to is the American practice of criticizing "developing" countries for shortcomings and weaknesses that are commonplace at home, in our own families and communities. Simply put, he is saying that from the amber waves of American grain to the African savannah, people are people, actions speak much louder than words, and nobody likes a hypocrite. As my mother might say, "Don't throw stones when you live in a glass house." We all live in glass houses.

One glaring inconsistency is agricultural policy. The same politicians that trumpet free markets and international development also protect American farmers with subsidies (totaling about $40 billion between 2003 and 2005) that undermine international trade. These handouts allow American farmers (often large corporations) to sell agricultural items at artificially low prices in order to compete with foreign counterparts who can provide the same item at roughly the same price without any government assistance. To witness the fallout of this approach, politicians should come to an African village and watch perfectly good produce — potential trade income — rot away in the fields.

Mr. Zimbota walks by and stops, intrigued by our conversation.

"What are you talking about?" he asks.

"Well," I reply, "We are trying to choose a government for the Buckler family. Right now, we are talking about the shortcomings of the United States, the world's most prominent democracy."

"Ah," he says, "I wish for time to join you, but I must go."

"Where are you going?" I wonder.

"Oh," he whispers, "I need to pay loan."

"What loan?" I pry, "Who is the lender?"

"I get money from grocery owner," he answers, "I use money to help my family pay school fees and buy clothes. Everyone wants to be wealthy, yes?"

"What is the annual interest rate?" I probe.

"Fifty percent," he responds, "We Africans charge high interest and have many, many debts. Do people have debts in America?"

"Americans borrow money just like Africans," I say, "The only differences are that Americans have larger debts and lower interest rates."

Indeed, poor fiscal responsibility is also a universal problem. Spendthrifts come in every shape, size, color and religion. Africa shoulders much of the Western criticism for reckless borrowing, and the total external debt owed by African countries is quite large — about three-hundred billion dollars as of 2006. But, putting things in perspective, the U.S. government operated with a 2009 budget deficit of about one-and-a-half trillion dollars (five times larger than the African debt), and irresponsible lending, borrowing and trading in America sparked a global recession, the worst financial crisis since the Great Depression.

"People have debts in America, just like Malawians!" Alfred exclaims, "Do you have corruption?"

"We do," I respond, "but we don't call it corruption."

"What word do you use?"

"We have several — creative accounting, campaign financing, tax sheltering, political lobbying, and, sometimes, Wall Street banking."

"I'm surprised," Alfred says, "People always say Africans corrupt, not Americans, and corruption is problem of poor peoples like us, not rich peoples."

Turns out, they're wrong on both counts. Yes, corruption is alive and well in Africa, from sewer-infested streets to hallowed halls of government, but in the grand scheme of things, the situation isn't much different in America. Mom and Pop corruption is part of everyday life — kickbacks to Chicago politicos, Medicare fraud, and tax evasion, to name a few. Even at white-shoe cocktail parties we find it — government bailout money being used for corporate junkets and executive bonuses, and in recent years, huge scandals from the likes of WorldCom, Enron, and Bernard Madoff. Corruption, it turns out, isn't just an African problem — its effects are just more sinister in a low-income country.

"I guess that Americans and Africans aren't so different," I sigh, "Yet, Americans think they are unique. They are very pleased with themselves."

"Yes," Myson says, "but everyone love Americans. I want to be American."

"Fine," I continue, "but Americans must realize that what works for them — ideals of democracy, capitalism, and consumerism — doesn't necessarily work for everyone."

"I want to be American, too!" Alfred interjects, ignoring my commentary, "If Myson gets to be American, I join him."

They are smitten with America, and they're not alone. In my travels around the globe, I've found that people generally love and respect Americans, and want to be like them (to varying degrees). Whatever our deficiencies and failures at trying to implement our vaunted governmental and economic systems, we overcome them with superb marketing and branding of the American Dream. The sales pitch — freedom, prosperity, happiness — has become a rallying cry for billions of people around the world. We are dream weavers, and the planet is watching us.

"We do have a lot to be proud of," I acknowledge, harkening back to all the economic growth, and personal and political freedoms, that I have enjoyed by virtue of my happenstance birth during this gilded era of America.

"Exactly," Myson announces, "We want to be like you. Can you make us American citizens? We already switch to American last name of Buckler."

"No, I cannot, but if you like America so much, we can choose democracy as our system of family government. Are you ready to be a democracy?"

Myson starts to nod and suddenly stops, turning his head toward Gift. He has been quiet for awhile, silently brooding over the earth-shattering revelations he has heard about the United States, the land of opportunity that sent me here to help. The frustration on his face grows as he tries to reconcile theoretical democracy with American democracy and Malawian democracy. It's a bewildering juxtaposition.

"I'm not ready to choose democracy," he reveals.

"What do you mean?" I ask.

"People are hurting from democracy. It not going to last."

"What's going to happen?" I inquire, wanting a deeper explanation.

"My aunt says that enemies of President Bingu are busy preparing to overthrow Malawi government," he replies, "Soon, we will return to dictatorship."

He sounds like a conspiracy nut, but he has a point.

"Are you referring to what happened a few months ago?" I ask, "You almost lost President Bingu."

"Yes," Gift says, "Bingu was in hot soup."

"Sir, we almost lost you, too," Alfred adds.

"You're right," I reply, "and I wasn't ready to leave."

* * * *

Sadly, the incident in question was not unique. On the heels of tragic election unrest and violence in Kenya, several regional flare-ups were making worldwide news. Their appeal, once again, was morose, feeding insatiable Western media appetites for the worst Africa has to offer — corruption, HIV/AIDS, wars, droughts, hunger, misery, destitution. I yearn for a day when journalists report the good alongside the bad, with equal amounts of fervor.

In Malawi, the trouble was caused by a bitter rivalry between the two major political parties. Every day their leaders exchanged nasty accusations, spouted over the airwaves and splashed across the front pages of newspapers. The opposition United Democratic Front (UDF) routinely filed legal challenges in Malawian courts to derail the ruling Democratic Progressive Party (DPP) and its anti-corruption, pro-development platform. The DPP returned fire with fanciful allegations of UDF-masterminded assassination attempts. Needless to say, the lawyers were busy, but it was mostly a war of words.

Yet, things escalated when, in a surprise move, the government arrested several high-ranking officials, and prominent supporters, of the UDF. Blantyre, a commercial city keen on avoiding the political drama of Lilongwe, and home to many of the accused, was eerily restless. Government soldiers, beholden to the DPP, surrounded homes and conducted invasive searches. The current leader of the UDF, and Malawi's first democratically-elected President, Bakili Muluzi, was placed under house arrest.

And the legal charge couldn't have been more serious — treason. A powerful cabal within the UDF allegedly planned to stage a *coup d'etat* and seize control of the government when President Bingu departed Malawi on a diplomatic trip to the Middle East. Ironically, or perhaps conveniently, his arch nemesis, Muluzi, also would have been abroad on business. After conducting the *coup*, the conspirators (including former generals with strong ties to the military) purportedly would have exiled Bingu and welcomed Muluzi home with open arms.

Not surprisingly, Peace Corps isn't too keen on *coups* of any kind. As I reviewed our Emergency Action Plans (strategies for bolting when all hell breaks loose), I empathized with the multitudes of Peace Corps Volunteers who, over the years, have been yanked from their villages and projects and suddenly evacuated, sometimes without an opportunity to gather their personal belongings or say goodbye (recently, Kenya). In Malawi, we could have been like them, but we were lucky — Peace Corps never placed us on alert or initiated an evacuation. Still, after things settled down, I wondered how close we had come to scoring a one-way ticket home. The inquiry sent shivers down my spine.

We averted disaster, I suspect, because we were serving in a land of few guns and fewer bullets. Other African countries have resources to fight over, and when machetes prove unwieldy, wealthy outside interests often provide sophisticated weaponry to the warring factions, inciting bloodbaths. But Malawi, one of the materially poorest countries in the world, lacks gold, oil and diamonds, the usual suspects that you can seize, mine and sell. Its revenue streams (agriculture, tourism and international aid) are commodities that lend themselves to peaceful regimes and bloodless (attempted) coups.

* * * *

Back in Khwalala, the Boys and I adjourn our meeting for a few minutes. Putting the time to good use, I walk to campus (about fifty yards) and enter the Form 4 (senior level) classroom to retrieve a book. As I turn to leave and rejoin the Boys, I see something disturbing out the corner of my eye: Esther nursing a reddened, swollen face.

"Esther, are you alright?" I ask, "What happened?"

"David," she cries, "hit me with fist," pointing to the alleged perpetrator.

"Did you do this, David?" I ask.

"Yes," he silently nods, looking down at the floor.

David is the biggest kid at school. Twenty-one years strong and bullheaded, he struts around campus with a chip on this shoulder, showcasing the power of his Adonis-like physique. He is a true personification of "cocky," an aberration in a land of modesty. And not particularly bright, he plays to his strengths — girls, bullying and (most recently) assault. Yet, today is David's reckoning. There is no justification for his barbarism, and I insist that he be expelled, which happens two weeks later. Turns out, his violent temper wasn't a new problem. Khwalala C.D.S.S. was his fifth school in two years.

"Did you hear what David did?" I ask, returning to the meeting with the Boys.

"Yes," Myson answers, "He like to beat people."

"This wasn't the first time," I sigh, "How does he get away with it?"

"Because many Africans want leaders like David," Myson says, "He reminds them of Dr. Banda," a dictator who ruled Malawi for thirty years.

"Most people believe that our country was better off under Banda," Mr. Zimbota interjects, back from the appointment with his predatory lender.

Mr. Zimbota ascribes to a popular, local viewpoint that Africans need to be told what to do and ruled with an iron fist. Many Malawians view democracy as contentious, inefficient and misunderstood by the masses, and fondly reminisce about Banda building roads, shedding the shackles of colonialism, and dispensing food to people. To them, sacrificing personal freedoms for a semblance of order and unity is a fair tradeoff. Democracy, by contrast, is a dependable scapegoat for all the ills that currently pain Malawian society.

Indeed, democracy hasn't saved countries like Malawi (at least not yet). Though African democracies were scarce from 1960 until 1989 (only one African leader was voted out of office), between 1990 and 2004, twenty-three African heads of state were ousted at the polls. Yet, over the same span, economic growth per capita and CPI (Corruption Perception Index) ratings in Africa dovetailed downward together. For example, in 2000, the average African CPI was 3.24, and by 2004, it had fallen to 2.87. Unfortunately, higher scores are better.

And, it's clear that Malawi isn't what it used to be during Banda's autocratic heyday. Since achieving independence from the British in 1964, the country (and sub-Saharan Africa as a region) has experienced negative economic growth. In *Dark Star Safari*, author Paul Theroux lamented how education and infrastructure have worsened in Malawi since his Peace Corps teaching stint in the 1960s. The country's general trajectory has been downhill, and everyone knows it, but whether democracy (introduced until 1994) is the culprit is far less certain.

Myson looks upset. I can tell he wants to say something.

"Myson, what's on your mind?" I ask.

"Sir," he replies shyly, "I want to speak to my side."

"You mean in favor of democracy," I inquire, "and against what Mr. Zimbota and others have said?"

"Yes, sir."

He takes a deep breath and, with the drama of a seasoned advocate, describes the Banda years in horrifying detail. There was no free press, he explains, no freedom of personal expression, no deviating from Dr. Banda's rules. Government workers dressed like clones, their outfits adhering to Banda's standards. Prices were capped for certain goods, like cooking oil, forcing some businesspeople to sell at a loss and suppressing the spirit of entrepreneurship. No free elections, one-size-fits-all governance, no room for debate. In 1971, Banda declared himself Malawi's President for Life.

Further, every citizen was required to carry an identification card at all times, even children. And police forced citizens to produce their cards at random. Myson recounts with trepidation an incident that occurred when he was a young boy traveling with his mother and a police officer at a bus depot sternly refused to let them board a bus because one ID card had been forgotten at home. Another time, an officer made Myson's mother, pregnant at the time, pay a fee for her unborn child — a uterus tax of sorts.

Sound like 1984? Orwell described authoritarianism with shocking foresight decades before Africa experienced the likes of Idi Amin (Uganda), Banda (Malawi), Mugabe (Zimbabwe), and Mobutu (Congo). Mugabe is the only one left, lingering on his throne and infecting the brave Zimbabwean people like a forty-year flu bug. His policies, including extreme price controls and deficit spending, have sparked rampant inflation, ravaging a once promising economy and causing an exodus of educated Zimbabweans. Top that off with widespread intimidation, election fraud, and searing rants against Western "interference," and you have one of the most dysfunctional countries on Earth. "The people will persevere until he dies," I am told, "They are too tired to fight him."

So are the regional leaders. Many are afraid to cross Mugabe, the folk hero, for fear of losing support from their constituents, an ironically populist side effect of democracy's infiltration into Southern Africa. The dangers of criticizing Mugabe are especially pronounced in young sub-Saharan African democracies lacking an educated citizenry, freedom of expression (especially journalism and voting), and widespread dissemination of information. In other words, pretty much all of them.

* * * *

After Myson's history refresher, I know where I stand. Finding a perfect system of government is elusive, but as an American, I vote for democracy (no pun intended), in any of its many instantiations, and against any form of autocracy. I concede that democracy is complicated, messy and inefficient, but it possesses an undeniable siren song — the distribution of power to the plurality; little slices of influence scattered like atoms across many people, each emboldened by a simple sacrament of personal expression — voting. Dependent, as a child, on protections such as constitutional liberties, independent courts, and a free press, voting is the nemesis of tyranny.

Autocracy works well, too, but rarely outside a political science laboratory. Finding a benevolent leader to control everything, with omniscience for the betterment of others, is exceedingly difficult. For every Gandhi or Mandela (George Washington declining an American throne comes to mind), there are hundreds of smart, manipulative egotists whose insecurities and ambitions, when mixed with absolute authority, create Petri dishes for abuse, suffering, and spoliation. Democracy, with its charming flaws and eccentricities, blocks these deities-in-waiting from realizing their ascendancies.

But I am one of four decision makers in the Buckler family. And, in true African fashion, we are trying to reach a consensus. Myson's position is clear — he agrees with me and favors democracy. Gift and Alfred, however, are holding their cards close to their chests.

"Gentleman," I say, "We have heard arguments for and against democracy and dictatorship."

"Yes," they nod together.

"Which type of government should we choose?" I ask.

"Well, sir," Alfred replies, "Gift and me didn't want democracy until Myson reminds us of Banda."

"Have you changed your minds?" I inquire, as Mr. Zimbota shakes his head in disbelief.

"Yes," Gift says, "We don't want to be afraid anymore."

Democracy is the unanimous choice! In the spirit of representative government, the Boys establish a Buckler Family Parliament, seat officers and assign responsibilities. I am President, Gift is Speaker, Alfred is Assistant Speaker and Myson is Secretary. When the Boys have an important issue to discuss, they make an impromptu motion over dinner or from across the hall.

"Mr. President, Mr. President," Gift yelled the other night from his bedroom, as I was drifting asleep.

"Gift, what do you want?" I yawned.

"I would like to make motion in Buckler Family Parliament that we have special dinners to celebrate our birthdays."

"Is that all?"

"Ah, no," he replied, "I also move for more dances at school."

"Dr. Banda denies your motions," I rule unilaterally.

"But, sir," Gift retorts, "The vote is three to one in favor of motions."

"Oh, you're right. I guess they pass."

"Yeah!" they celebrate, "dinners and dances for the Buckler family!"

VIII

WHIFFS OF HOME

Every year around this time in Malawi, Peace Corps teachers graduate from training and move to their village schools. That's where I was a year ago — in a state of shock, longing for familiar holiday traditions, and facing the daunting task of building a new life in a strange place. Stewing in holiday blues, I vowed to spend future Christmases the right way — with my family.

— Letter Home, December 2007

In December 2007, I hop a flight and head stateside. Sporting untamed locks of strawberry blond hair (uncut for over a year), I run around like a coke addict on a drug binge, trying to get my fix of Americana. Travelling from sea to shining sea, basking in a spin cycle of hugs and kisses, delivering presentations about Peace Corps to benefactors of Camp SKY, consuming copious amounts of rich, delicious food, developing a new appreciation for the upright toilet, and trying to figure out why political commentators think that the color of Hillary Clinton's blouse has any bearing on her ability to govern as President — it's carpe diem on steroids.

Seeing my brother makes me realize how delighted I am to be home, if only for a blink. During my fifteen-month absence, so much about him has changed. Now that he's finishing his MBA and becoming a father, he looks older and wiser. It's like he's maturing at a rapid rate, and I'm staying the same, a Rip Van Winkle asleep in Africa. Back in Malawi, relaxing at the end of a long day, I often wondered about friends and family members — what they were doing, how they looked and acted, and whether they were happy. I fantasized about holiday moments like this.

Speaking of family, my parents throw a holiday-themed homecoming party. As the guest of honor, I'm revered like a spiritual guru by armchair travelers eager to experience Africa by proxy. Yet, the barrage of questions and attention is worth it, allowing me personally to thank countless well-wishers and supporters *en masse*. It is the personal connections to them (and Dead Guy Ale) that inspired me to come home in the first place. And going forward, when I'm back in the village watching a gecko dance across the wall and sweating through my shirt, those connections will continue to sustain and inspire me.

As the party dies down, I find a quiet corner and sip a large glass of red wine. After all, I deserve it. Relaxing to the crackle of roasting chestnuts and savoring the buttery smells of holiday cookies, Malawi feels a million miles away, as its charms and problems fade into a sea of joyful conversation and mistletoe kisses. But the distance is an illusion, a temporary ruse. Malawi lives inside me now, a permanent resident coursing through my veins, never far from my thoughts and dreams. And, unbeknownst to me, Malawi is just around the corner, too, lurking in my parents' house. This time it's masquerading as serendipity, and it's about to find me, in the form of a long lost friend.

* * * *

I wasn't far from my American roots in Africa. Half a world away, my hometown of LaPlata, Maryland (or a precious reminder of it) was visible from Khwalala Village. It wasn't literal like Little League diamonds or crab shacks, but something symbolic — the Hills of Namitambo. I stared at those geological oddities a thousand times, at their distinctive conical shapes rising abruptly from the valley floor, dotting the horizon like signposts. They were otherworldly, almost Martian, conjuring images of flying saucers and little green men. "Why am I so drawn to them?" I often thought. Now I know.

At first blush, Namitambo wasn't particularly remarkable or memorable. A typical Malawian trading center, it resembled a town from the Old West — a single promenade flanked by aging buildings and bustling with activity. The usual stuff was there: a health center and electricity attracting surrounding villagers for business, socializing or medical treatment — a shot of urbane espresso before returning to the serenity of rural homesteads. Yet, I cherished Namitambo dearly, above all other trading centers in Malawi, because of a personal connection — a Christmas surprise.

Harkening back to second grade, I'll never forget the look of hurt on her face. Cindy Pfitzenmaier was the new girl in school, and earlier that week, I had wrecked her world on a jungle gym during recess by inadvertently grabbing and snapping her golden necklace. Just my luck, it was her prized possession, a gift from the best friend she left behind in California. As the other girls played hop-scotch or tag, Cindy screamed in horror. As the culprit of her grief, trapped red-handed with the delicate golden evidence dangling from my guilty fingers, I just wanted to disappear. It was wishful thinking.

Hearing about the incident, my parents insisted that I make amends. Together, we purchased a replacement chain at a cheesy strip-mall store, as if Cindy's gold-fish had died and we were conspiring to replace it without her noticing. Driving to Cindy's house, I trembled with shame, nervously stroking the chain like a rosary, wishing that I could just drop the damn thing in the mail. At her house, Cindy answered the door, and gingerly accepted the peace offering and an apology, just as choreographed by our parents. Though awkward, the gesture sparked a friend-ship that lasted for seven years, until we parted company to attend different high schools.

Fast forwarding twenty-five years, I'm at my parents' homecoming party, nurs-ing the glass of red wine. A family friend finds me and sits down.

"How are things in Malawi?" she asks.

"Oh, not bad," I reply, "It's strange being away from it. It's a different world over there."

"I'm sure it is," she says, "I heard the same thing from Cindy Pfitzenmaier. Did you know that she was a Peace Corps Volunteer in Malawi?"

I look at her skeptically, knowing that to many Americans and most Ma-lawians, Peace Corps isn't just a discrete, grassroots development organization established by President Kennedy, but a genre of philanthropic masochism, en-compassing do-gooders of all types and agendas.

"Are you sure that she was a Peace Corps Volunteer?" I ask.

"Yes, I'm pretty sure," she replies.

"Do you know where she lived in Malawi?"

"Hmm, that's tough," she says, "I need to check with her parents to be sure, but I want to say something like Namatombo."

"Do you mean Namitambo?" I gasp, "That's close to where I live."

"Yeah, that sounds right."

Turns out, Cindy was a Peace Corps Volunteer, and she lived in Namitambo from 2000 to 2002, working at a health clinic. I pester my mother for her current phone number, and after tapping into the estrogen network of interconnected mothers, grandmothers, aunts, Oxygen channel devotees and Oprah zealots, she returns with good news.

"Cindy," she proudly reports, reading from her stack of meticulous notes, "is living in New York pursuing a graduate degree. You can call her anytime. She would love to chat."

"Wow," I say, "thanks for tracking down that information."

"When are you going to call?" she pries, as all good mothers do.

"Not sure," I reply, "probably sometime soon."

The truth is that I have mixed feelings about the call. Calling someone out of the blue is unnerving and exhilarating. What do you say to someone you haven't seen in twenty years?

Answer: whatever the hell you want because it doesn't matter. Taking this approach, my conversation with Cindy a few days later is much better than it had been on that fateful day in second grade. Instead of the shy girl I remember, Cindy is talkative and assertive. Bolstered by fate, we reunite effortlessly, reminiscing about elementary school and Malawi, intermixing the languages of English and *Chichewa*. It's amazing how a transformative experience like Peace Corps can bridge the valleys of time and space between two veritable strangers. Before saying goodbye, I promise to visit Namitambo upon my return to Malawi and take pictures of Cindy's old stomping grounds.

A few months later, I make good on that promise by enlisting Alfred to lead a Namitambo expedition. After scrounging around for a bicycle, he digs up a dilapidated junker with wobbly rims, two bald tires and a broken rear sprocket.

"I'm ready for our journey, sir," he happily reports.

"Are you sure about that?"

"Oh yes, sir," he replies, "My bicycle is fine for our journey."

"And you know the way to Namitambo?"

"No problem, sir."

As usual, he is being overly optimistic. The ninety-minute ride takes about twice that long as Alfred repeatedly stops to ask for directions and inflate a hole-strewn inner tube. Yet, we eventually reach Namitambo and discover traces of Cindy: residents who remember her service; a resplendent vine of purplish flowers draped across her former front yard; and a worn foot trail that leads from her back door to Mulanje Mountain. I'd love to stay and investigate this time warp, but the hour is late, so Alfred and I limp home just as we came, returning to the Buckler Homestead shortly before dark. After that, whenever I yearn for home, I think of Cindy Pfitzenmaier and look toward the Hills of Namitambo.

* * * *

Back at my parents' house, the homecoming party is still hopping. And after hearing the good news about Cindy, it's time for celebratory libation. Approaching the wine table, I'm stopped by another family friend, Gary, a former State Department diplomat who served in the Middle East and Africa.

"Michael," he welcomes me, "I know that you are busy, but I would love to chat with you about Malawi. Is now a good time?"

"Sure, I've been looking forward to this," I respond, filling my wine glass halfway.

"Wonderful," he says, "I'm particularly interested in hearing your views on international aid."

"Wait," I reply, "I need a full glass of wine for this conversation."

After sharing a chuckle, we choose a quiet spot by the fire. Sinking into the plush pleasures of cushiony couches, and steadying our glasses, we roll up our sleeves and dive into the debate, one sip at a time.

"So, Michael," Gary starts, "tell me about development work in Malawi," as I wince at the sound of a loaded word.

"Something wrong?" he asks.

"No, I just don't like the term 'development'."

Why?" he asks quizzically.

"Because I don't know what it means."

Development is an amorphous word. Is it flooding a country with automobiles, or encouraging people to abandon sustenance farming in villages and seek work in cities, living away from their families? What about television sets and home shopping channels, or an industrial food system that churns out processed food widgets for the dinner table? Development for Malawi might not be development for another country, and so on. It depends on local conditions like government, culture, religion and history.

"Well, if you don't like using 'development,' what is your term of endearment?" he smiles.

"I don't have a good one," I admit, "Do you?"

"Seems like a game of semantics," he answers.

"All I know is that aid work is not about changing or enlightening, it's about exposing people to options, and letting them choose for themselves. It's about dignity."

"Well," he continues, "what do you think about aid work in Africa?"

"Well," I say, "it needs to improve. Even the aid community admits as much."

"Yeah," he nods.

The picture is not good. In 2005 alone, the overall price tag for aid in Africa was approximately eighty-four billion dollars, and over the last forty years, the West has spent four-hundred-and-fifty billion dollars to improve the continent. Yet, in many African countries, income per person is lower now than it was in the 1960s and life expectancy continues to decline, hardly hallmarks of a job well done or harbingers of hope.

"What should be done?" he wonders aloud, shaking his head.

"Not more of the same," I say, stating the obvious, "but there are other options."

"Like what?"

"We can withdraw aid completely, as some profess."

"But that would be a cruel blow for dependents of the African welfare state," he retorts, "worse than doing nothing in the first place."

He's probably right. In Malawi, for example, foreign aid accounts for approximately forty percent of the national budget. A dozen or so African countries depend on aid for a fifth or more of their national incomes. Pulling out would decimate their economies.

"And don't we, as humanitarians, have a moral imperative to help?" he continues.

"We do," I agree, "but maybe helping is doing nothing at all and abstaining from hurting."

"What are the alternatives?"

"Well," I reply, "we can learn from our mistakes and refine our approach."

"That sounds like a nice goal," he observes, "but the devil lurks in the details. Do you have any specifics?"

My wine glass is still full. I take a large swig and a deep breath.

"I have a few ideas," I start, "The first one is better coordination."

"What do you mean by that?"

"I mean that in Malawi, I see hundreds of aid organizations operating not as a team attacking common problems, but as an archipelago of independent actors."

Malawi is full of aid organizations doing similar work. But each, including Peace Corps, has its own vehicles, t-shirts, budgets, offices, staffs, agendas, rules, reports, logos, mission statements, policies and priorities. The redundancy is maddening.

"Fine, but how do you facilitate coordination?" he inquires.

"In each region, there should be regular aid conferences to share failures and successes, combine resources and strategically map priorities."

"Would anything come from that?" he asks.

"Each conference would produce local development plans describing the particulars of proposed and ongoing aid projects," I explain, "The plans would be written under the direction of local and national leaders, inviting everyone into the conversation."

"Is coordination really that big of a problem?" he questions.

"It's a huge one."

The World Bank has found that the misuse of aid money is directly related to the number of donors operating within a country. Naturally, with large numbers of donors, it's considerably easier for host governments to misbehave with impunity, playing donors against one another to achieve redundant funding appropriations or skimming off modest portions of multiple funding steams without any individual donor registering a problem.

"Another idea for beneficial change is local planning and execution," I continue.

"You've heard of Jeffrey Sachs?"

"Of course," he replies, "he's the famous economist from Columbia University who mingles with rock stars and other celebrities."

Sachs wrote the best-selling book *End of Poverty*. He also heads the Millennium Project, a group commissioned by the United Nations to create an action plan for achieving the Millennium Development Goals, a list of poverty-reduction benchmarks. At the present rate, Sub-Saharan Africa will meet none of the Goals, not for one-hundred years.

"It's too bad," I say, "but Sachs and his supporters are running into trouble."

"Why? What's the problem?"

"They're orchestrating the delivery of aid from above, like puppeteers."

"Why is that a problem?"

"The action is occurring in villages, hard to see from New York City. Grand macro solutions often neglect micro nuances, like culture and capacity."

Examples aren't hard to find. Person A might undermine a project because he doesn't like Person B, a member of a rival tribe. A seed that grows well in one region might not in another. The *sine quibus non* of effective aid work are local projects and local presence.

"I see your point," he nods, "but how do you create a local presence?"

"Well, I think it's critical that aid organizations establish a network of dedicated, competent people to live and work at every link of the aid distribution chain."

"Don't they already have that?"

"Nope," I reply, "especially not at the grassroots level where aid workers need local language and cultural skills to be successful."

"It sounds like Peace Corps for grownups," he remarks, "with a real salary, I hope."

"Something like that."

Exhibit A is the Nordin family. After Kristof and Stacia met in Peace Corps Jamaica, they married and completed a Peace Corps tour in Malawi. Falling hard for Malawi (Africa will do that to you), they decided to stay, live in a village and convert their property into a demonstration project for sustainable agriculture. Ten years later, with their daughter, *Khalidwe* ("culture" in *Chichewa*), they travel throughout Malawi and neighboring countries teaching people how to maximize agricultural yields and improve nutrition.

At the grassroots level, people like the Nordins survive by assimilating and investing their time, money and sweat. They can quickly spot and discontinue ill-fated projects before critical resources are squandered, ensuring that funds are not misappropriated. The city-based, revolving-door approach used by most aid groups, on the other hand, is fundamentally flawed. It pilfers institutional knowledge by replacing veterans with rookies and undermines the goal of foreign aid by feeding copious amounts of money to the aid workers themselves, and their human resource needs, instead of the local people.

"Sounds obvious, but that's not how it's currently done. You are proposing a paradigm shift," he remarks.

"True," I concede.

"I wonder whether aid-loving governments will let that shift happen?"

"Good point," I admit, "if the Malawian power structure doesn't like the arrangement, it will undermine, and ultimately compromise, the mission."

"Based on what I've read," he says, "garnering the support of African politicians can be a bit dicey and expensive."

"No doubt. Leadership is one the biggest disparities in Africa."

According to acclaimed novelist Chinua Achebe, Nigerian leaders languish in a "cult of mediocrity" and display an "unwillingness or inability...to rise to the responsibility, to the challenge of personal example which are the hallmarks of true leadership." Former U.N. Secretary General Kofi Annan explains that in Africa, "people who want to make money go into politics. It is very unhealthy. It is very profitable." Former Nigerian President Olusegun Obasanjo estimates that "African leaders have stolen at least one-hundred-and-forty billion dollars from their people since independence."

"So, how do you stop African leaders from cheating their own people?" Gary posits.

"Wow," I exhale, rubbing my temples, "I think you grow new ones."

"What? People aren't plants."

People aren't born good leaders, either. The hallmarks of an effective leader — ability to communicate, intellect, hard work, patience, creativity, accountability, strategic thinking, and pragmatism — are forged over time through life experience and education and cultivated under the tutelage of mentors. Yet, in many parts of the world, the paradigm of serving, without personal agenda, for the betterment of others or society at large, is nonexistent. It's not even a book chapter in the library of ideas.

"The answer," I suggest, "is to promote civic leadership and the rule of law."

"Once again, I want to know how you accomplish that."

"We should build universities that nurture civil servants," I reply, "much like military academies breed soldiers."

"The answer is constructing universities?" he asks.

"Yes, that's part of it. Every African country should build a Nelson Mandela School of Leadership. What better model than a homegrown hero?"

Mandela set a sterling example. Only a great leader like him could survive the dehumanizing hell of Apartheid, spending twenty-seven years in prison for voicing an opinion, and upon liberation, exhibit grace and foresight. Instead of seeking revenge, he not only forgave his captors, but embraced them as partners in reconciliation, forging a new South Africa and diffusing a potential civil war in a country itching for bloody retribution. Our world, especially Africa needs more leaders like Mandela.

"Very well," he interrupts, "You've said some interesting things, and I want to hear more, but nature is calling. Let's take a break and come back in five minutes."

"Sounds good," I reply.

The respite is appreciated. Talking about international development is draining. To rejuvenate myself for the next round, I top off my wine glass and pillage some cold *hor d'oeuvres* scraps from the main table. A few minutes later, my friend returns.

"We need to wrap this up soon because my wife wants to leave," he says.

"Well, before you go, I want to mention business."

"Ah, yes, I'm a businessman," he says proudly, "Business has been my livelihood since leaving the State Department."

"So you appreciate that entrepreneurship is ubiquitous, in a million places and culturally-infused forms to be sure, but it's there?"

"Sure," he says, "everywhere I have lived."

I don't necessarily mean entrepreneurship in the Western sense of risk taking and money making. Rather, my focus is the original spirit of providing goods and services for which there is a public demand, acknowledging that, at its core, entrepreneurship is as much about self-sufficiency and problem solving as privatization and wealth generation.

"Long term progress in Malawi," I say, "is inextricably linked to the development of sustainable businesses. There are lots of promising market opportunities given the English-speaking population, fertile soil, and low wage rates."

"Like what?"

"Well, for example, I don't understand why one of the world's friendliest and most beautiful countries doesn't have a booming tourism industry."

Actually, I do. For starters, the government doesn't foster a healthy business climate. It should make basic infrastructure improvements (e.g., hotels, roads, Internet), sponsor financing programs for small businesspeople, fortify the banking and judicial systems, and become a lot less tax happy. According to a 2005 World Bank report, sub-Saharan Africa was the most difficult place to do business when it came to red tape. The report also found that in 2004, the region ranked last in terms of introducing business reforms.

"Is there any hope for African business?" Gary asks.

"Yes, but it requires a different set of skills than in the West."

"What skills?" he asks.

"Social entrepreneurship," I reply.

Social entrepreneurship is an approach popularized by Muhammad Yunus, a Bangladeshi economist. Applying business principles, social entrepreneurs craft commercial ventures that address societal problems. Dr. Yunus demonstrated the power of this approach at the Grameen Bank in Bangladesh. The Bank has loaned over nine-billion dollars to the poor and enjoyed repayment rates as high as ninety-seven percent.

"The basic principle of business for social wellness is reproducible in Malawi."

"How?" he asks, "It's hard to build a successful business in a culture where people are seething with jealousy and skeptical of outsiders."

"It's hard but doable," I retort, "The key is tailoring the business approach so that it doesn't run afoul of culture, and social entrepreneurship has the flexibility to do just that!"

Recognizing that Malawians have a strong aversion to socioeconomic stratification, a social entrepreneur could tie the success of a business to community betterment by promising improvements (e.g., a health center) when certain financial goals are reached. Another possibility is training Malawian employees to run the business and handing it over to them after a sustained period of profitability. In these ways, social entrepreneurship could synergistically align culture and economic growth.

"Ok, my wife is giving me the evil eye. Just look the other way. What's your next idea?" he asks.

"It's infrastructure."

"Let's jump over this one," he replies, "infrastructure makes sense to everyone."

My brother, Bob, strolls into the room with a wine bottle.

"Looks like you guys need a refresher," he says, filling our glasses for a final flurry of conversation.

"Sounds good!" we toast, "Thank you."

"What are you talking about?" Bob asks.

"Oh, just international aid policy," I explain, "We're solving all of the world's problems right here, right now."

"Wish I could stay," he jokes, "but I'd rather be sitting in a dentist's chair getting a root canal."

Once Bob has left, I return to my friend, the nervous husband.

"The next point," I say, "is that Malawi needs some tough love."

"What do you mean?"

"The Malawian people need to take responsibility for improving their country. Malawians can and should solve Malawi's problems — period."

"Why haven't they?" he asks.

"Well, one reason is that Bakili Muluzi, a former President of Malawi, used to tell them that things couldn't improve without Western aid. It was a dispiriting and defeatist message that inspired apathy, excuses and misunderstanding in the villages."

"How so?" he inquires.

"If I had a dime for every time a Malawian begged me for money, I would be a very, very rich man."

And Muluzi is not alone. Aid organizations often perpetuate the myth of helplessness. They blame colonialism, HIV, environmental austerity, trade policy or whatever for the persistent under-performance of Malawi. In so doing, they often overlook the fact that in other poor regions of the world, like Southeast Asia, people have overcome similar problems with initiative and far less foreign donor money.

"Is there any hope for Malawi?"

"Definitely," I explain, "if you articulate clear and fair expectations of self-empowerment from the beginning and adhere to them, you will mobilize progress, earn respect and minimize unsustainable dependencies."

"You've taken this approach?"

"Yes," I reply, "with a Wildlife Club at my school, a nationwide education camp for underprivileged youth, and a girls' boarding facility."

"Good for you."

"Thanks," I say, "the strategy worked well for the Wildlife Club and education camp."

"What about the boarding facility?"

"That project is in limbo at the moment," I explain, "We've applied for funding but haven't heard whether we'll get it."

"Good luck."

I space out for a moment, thinking about the potential impact of a boarding facility, about my female students living in squalor in Malawi as I sip wine in America.

"My final issue is money," I say, as my head clears, "I guess it always is."

"That's right," he agrees, "at least in my experience."

"Despite a legacy of failed projects and wasted funding, there are compelling arguments for increasing foreign aid to places like Malawi."

"What are they?" he asks sarcastically, shaking his head.

"Come on," I say, "You know which countries are the biggest recipients of aid from the U.S."

Of course he does, having spent a decade working in the Middle East. Until we became mired in Iraq, Israel was number one, and Egypt was number two. Since 1949, the wealthy country of Israel, which has seven-hundredths of a percent of Africa's landmass and seven-tenths of a percent of its population, has received about one-hundred billion dollars in aid from the United States alone. The entire Continent of Africa has received just ten times that amount from the entire world.

"Seems like appropriating taxpayer money to international affairs is a matter of political will and strategic choices," he says, "more so than equity."

"Bingo," I reply.

But that might be changing. In 2005, the Commission on Africa, founded by former British Prime Minister Tony Blair, challenged wealthy countries to contribute just seven-tenths of one percent of their national incomes to aid for poor countries, much of it for Africa. By way of comparison, for four years after World War II, America spent one percent of its national income on the Marshall Plan to rebuild Europe. Still, as of 2010, Blair's challenge hasn't been met.

"More aid isn't as important as thoughtful aid," Gary interjects.

"Very true," I agree, "Foreign aid is not a simple and relatively inexpensive solution to African poverty, as some have argued, but a band aid at best and a curse at worst."

Research shows that aid is susceptible to the law of diminishing returns. That is, a second batch of aid money given to a country is less effective than the first batch in terms of achieving poverty-reduction goals, and so on. And the Center for Global Development has calculated that when aid expenditures reach approximately sixteen percent of a country's GDP, additional aid fails to effect economic growth. Many African countries receive aid packages that exceed that threshold. Where is the excess money going?

"We've created quite a mess with it, haven't we?" he asks.

"Yes, we have."

"Why?"

"Because we are blind to the reality that much of international aid is a self-serving gesture to appease the guilty consciences of Western donors, not help the recipients."

"But, it's not that simple, is it?"

"Not at all," I reply, "It's very complicated."

The aid game is a web of causes and effects. You cannot understand economics without studying culture. You cannot understand culture without studying language. You cannot understand language without studying history. You cannot understand history without studying power. You cannot understand power without studying fear. You cannot understand fear without studying people. You cannot understand people without engaging them. You cannot understand international aid without engaging real people, in real places, with real humanity. That's the beauty of the Peace Corps approach.

Speaking of engaging people, Gary's wife is patrolling the house like a hawk, searching for her ride home.

"Honey, where are you?" she yells.

"Oh, there you are," she says, "Hello, Michael."

He and I exchange guilty looks.

"Sorry for keeping your husband," I apologize, "if it makes you feel better, we had a great time."

"Yes, Gary likes to chat," she smiles, patting me on the shoulder, "especially when I want to leave! Now, Gary, get your butt in the car before I make a scene."

"Good talking to you, Michael," he says, shaking my hand, "You should share your ideas and perspectives with more people."

"If I write a book about this stuff, do you think anyone will listen? Do you think anything will change?" I ask, as his wife tugs on his lapel.

"I wouldn't bet on it," he smiles.

* * * *

Unfortunately, three weeks of talking about Malawi at home does little to prepare me for a return to the real thing. Only days ago, I was basking in the aura of friends and family, saturated with stimulation like a card counter at a packed Las Vegas casino. Yet, the instant the plane touches down in Malawi, life goes blank

— the sun doesn't shine, the birds don't sing, and nothing seems real. I stand alone in a white-wash vacuum calling out for someone, anyone to find me, and hearing only echoes of my desperate voice. Stunned, and seeming powerless, I struggle with sadness for days, wondering why I came back to the Warm Heart of Africa.

Then, in the nick of time, some mail arrives at the post office — a possible sign, a turning point? I'm afraid to open it at first, worried that it will make me feel worse. But after resting in the corner of my bedroom for a few minutes, the parcels serenade me, and I cannot resist the temptation to rip them open like a ravenous wolverine. I never cried during or after my divorce (not once), but hunkered down in bed, in a nest of Fed Ex shipping labels and Styrofoam peanuts, I weep over the heartfelt notes and thoughtfully prepared packages from home, drowning my sorrows in gourmet chocolate.

"We are so proud of you," my mother writes, "Keep up the good work."

"I wish that I could be in your shoes," says Dave, "You are so lucky."

"Cannot wait to visit you in July," Aunt Joan promises, "Stay well and be good."

"Enjoy your second year," Bob writes, "You'll never have this experience again."

He's right. They're all right. Perspective is a powerful thing, especially when it comes from trusted, loving sources. It catapults me forward, allowing me to turn a corner and gradually reenter the flow of everyday life, and mindset of service, that I need to regain the mojo of an effective Peace Corps Volunteer.

The Boys help, too, as an inspiration. They cannot join me in depression, a first-world luxury, so they uplift me.

"Sir, we need you to assist us with Mathematics," they explain over dinner, "We will write MSCE in October this year. Every day we work extra harder to receive passing score."

"It is true," Mr. Zimbota says, entering the house without knocking, and inviting himself to dinner, "They need your help."

"What can I do?" I ask.

"Hmm," Gift ponders, "When you travel to Blantyre, please buy mathematics textbook for Buckler family? We three can share."

"How many books does the school currently have?" I inquire, knowing that most of them have either been stolen or overused beyond recognition.

"There are two books for thirty students," Gift answers.

"Whoa," I sigh, "I'll definitely buy a third one soon."

"Thank you, sir," he says, starting to get up and leave for night school.

"And, Gift," I call out, causing him to halt in his tracks.

"Yes sir?"

"Before you go, I need to know a few things."

"What?" he asks.

"Have you completed your mathematics homework from yesterday?"

"My homework is done, sir."

"Very good," I continue, "Alfred, it's your turn. Has his Wildlife Club been watering the trees regularly?"

"Yes, sir, I check every day."

"Thank you. That leaves Myson. Have you cleaned the dishes from this morning's breakfast?" I ask.

"No, sir, but I will do that after night school."

"Fine," I say.

"Will you release us for night school?" they inquire, "We not want to be late."

"Yes, but remember something, Boys. We have ten months to prepare you for the MSCE."

"Yes, sir" they nod.

"There's no time to waste. Let's get down to work!"

"We will," they cheer.

"Very good. You are released."

Mr. Zimbota and I glance at one another and smile. He knows what just happened. The Boys feel the sea change, too, like a breeze of fresh air at the dawn of a new day. Once again, all things are possible, and my life has meaning and purpose. Everyone is relieved to know that Mr. Buckler is back in the game.

IX

TERRA CORNA

On a lazy afternoon, I pause for a moment, putting aside auxiliary verbs and logarithms, grant proposals and banana wine, to reflect on my experiences in Malawi. I apologize for not writing more, but free time has been scarce, and hastily prepared correspondence is not my style. So much has happened since I joined Peace Corps.

— Letter Home, February 2008

I cannot believe that a year has passed since the journey began.

Back then, twenty-five strangers sat in a circle in a nondescript hotel conference room in Philadelphia — random names and faces stealing nervous glances. Ben from North Carolina was absurdly tall (about 6'7"); Karen from California was petite, almost breakable; Donovan, a thirty-something guy from Colorado, appeared more Wall Street than Peace Corps in a cardigan and loafers. Chris, a beatnik guitarist from Rhode Island, brought corn nuts to share. Excited and terrified, we knew very little about one another.

The occasion was Staging, a short orientation before taking the Peace Corps plunge, stepping onto the plane and embarking into the great beyond. Peace Corps hired a charismatic facilitator to break the ice and animate the sterile hotel conference room by leading us through a series of games, skits and reflection exercises.

"Who is a smoker?" she asked, as the room went dead silent.

"Come on, someone is a smoker, I know it! Who is it?"

Nobody responded (a total lie).

"Ok, who packed the most shoes?" she proceeded.

"I brought twelve pairs," a diminutive Californian said.

"Really?" replied the facilitator.

"Too many, huh?" the Californian asked sheepishly, as the room stirred with disbelief.

"Twelve pairs?" we all thought, "She doesn't know what she signed up for."

And we were right. She would be the first casualty, leaving early the next morning while the rest of us were snoozing, too embarrassed to say goodbye. Hanging like a black cloud over the rest of Staging, her *adios* forced each of us to ask the unsettling question, "What are we getting ourselves into?"

In truth, none of us knew, not even the facilitator.

"Malawi is going to feel totally foreign to you at first," she explained.

"No kidding," we were thinking, "Tell us how foreign it's going to be."

"How do Volunteers live there?" Ben asked, probing for details, "The materials we received from Peace Corps weren't very descriptive."

"I'm sorry, but I really cannot help you with that," the facilitator said with a movie-star smile, "I've never been to Malawi or, for that matter, served as a Peace Corps Volunteer."

Survey says: wrong answer, lady! Her response caused an eruption of nervous chatter. She was smart and entertaining, but she'd never been a Volunteer or even visited Malawi?

"Holy crap," I said, "We won't know the real deal until we step off the plane."

"I'm worried that we won't have anything in common with Malawians," Chris whispered.

"That's a legitimate worry, but maybe we'll be pleasantly surprised."

"How are we going to cope?" he asked.

"Drink beer and eat bacon double cheeseburgers now, while you can," I joked,

"They might be hard to find in the village!"

"We will tonight — Philly style. You're coming out with us, right?"

Of course I was going out: it was our last night on American soil and my thirty-second birthday. Joined by the other recruits, I wandered into the Philadelphia night in search of fun and camaraderie, an alcohol-fueled parting shot before kissing it all goodbye and starting the Africa chapter of my life. Along red brick side streets, and in quaint city pubs, we let the enormity of our quest burst like the bubbles in our pint glasses — out of sight, out of mind.

The following day, getting to Malawi was neither quick nor easy. From a bird's eye view, we bussed to New York and hopped a sixteen-hour flight to Johannesburg, South Africa, where we stayed at a swanky hotel near the airport, gorging ourselves on all-you-can-eat buffets and all-you-can-drink wine bars, fearing they would be our last tastes of civilization.

"Sir, sir," the hotel *mater dei* said to Cory, a trainee with a savant-like mind for random sports trivia and a fondness for the bottle.

"Yes," Cory smirked, trying to play dumb.

"Guests are limited to two complimentary glasses of wine. You've had six."

"Oh, sorry about that," Cory smiled, "I was just compensating for the members of my group who don't drink."

The next morning we awoke early (even Cory) to complete the trip, boarding a two-hour flight to Lilongwe, Malawi's capital. All told, it took two days and eighteen hours of flying to transverse the nine-thousand miles between our old and new homes. But we didn't care — it all seemed worthwhile, a small price to pay for Peace Corps fame.

And instant fame greeted us at the airport. My lifelong wish of feeling like a rock star was granted as we emerged from the plane and walked down a long staircase onto the runway for our first tastes of Malawian flavors — air, sky, soil, and…groupies? In the distance, hordes of screaming people welcomed our arrival with banners and signs. After a few minutes, I realized they were Peace Corps Volunteers eager to sample the latest batch of fresh meat. Enjoying the attention, I wanted to join the party, but after passing through customs, we were whisked away from our adoring fans to a remote facility.

Needless to say, training began immediately.

"*Muli bwanji?*" our language trainer said, "Now you try."

"What the hell does that mean?" I replied, jet lagged and peevish, having garbled the foreign words on my first attempt.

"It means 'How are you?' in our national language, *Chichewa*," she smiled, putting me at ease and encouraging me to try again.

This time I pronounced the words in a mostly intelligible manner. The accent, a bastardization of Southern Maryland meets village African, must have been painful to her ears, but she nodded and tried to push me further.

"*Ndili bwino,*" she said, "*Muli bwanji?*"

"Hmm…ah…sorry," I stuttered.

"You can do it," she prodded, "try again."

I froze and turned sheet white, a blank mind mocking a twisted tongue. I was an idiot, a total language dunce.

Another voice quickly interceded. It was distinctly American.

"This exchange, a simple greeting, is on page two of the language guide, which we were supposed to read last night," it said.

I shot looks at other trainees in the class, as if to say, "Really?"

"Oh, yes," they shot back, "Really."

I turned in the direction of the voice, searching for some sympathy, feeling like the dumb kid at math camp. It was coming from Ani, a fellow trainee who minored in linguistics as an undergrad at McGill.

"Forgive me," I apologized, "I didn't realize that we had homework in Peace Corps."

"We don't," Ani said, "I memorized the basic Malawian greetings this morning over breakfast."

"Well then," I replied, taking a deep breath and imagining myself in a happier place, "When is the next popcorn break? I'm yearning for something Mesoamerican."

"Not for another two hours," said our language trainer, "Can we continue the lesson?"

"Sure," I sighed, "if that's alright with Ani."

Things were looking pretty bad. But, it wasn't Ani's fault — I had done this to myself. I was a thirty-two-year-old burned-out lawyer trying to learn an African tribal language. My only foreign language experience was Latin, eons ago in high school. I was hot and tired and nine-thousand miles from home. I was screwed.

And for better or worse, I had been assigned to the gifted-and-talented group. Stephen Rawls would become one of my closest friends, but at the start of training, I wanted to strangle him for learning half the *Chichewa* language in America, before we stepped on the plane. Ani is similarly gifted and one of the most holistically talented people I know, equally comfortable solving an advanced calculus problem (she majored in math) or transforming a blank canvas into a gorgeous painting. Jesse (also no academic slouch) distinguished herself from Stephen and Ani's nerd alliance by playing the bad girl - smoking, drinking, and castigating others with a Jersey-girl tongue. I just tried to keep up.

Leading our brainy, eclectic language group was Dyna, a vivacious and dynamic Malawian trainer. During the week, she lived with us in the sticks, separated from her husband and children in Lilongwe and utterly devoted to our linguistic edification. To teach body parts, she gyrated around the room, grabbing various appendages and jotting word phonetics on a cracked, portable blackboard. In the evenings, one-on-one language sessions were the norm, when other trainers were resting or socializing.

Dyna's relentless drive came from Cedric, the director of the language program. Like an old Southern woman who refuses to appear in public without all of her ladylike "particulars," he was dapperly dressed at all times from shoe tip to widow's peak, sporting three-piece suits when the rest of us were wearing shorts and t-shirts. A debonair gentleman with the charm of George Clooney, tongue of Barack Obama, and looks of Robert Redford, he could have been a model or politician in America But for better or worse, he was stuck in Malawi with us. And as a natural salesman, he rallied us to stay the course when things got tough, reassuring us that "everything gonna be alright."

Training was a seemingly endless ten weeks of living in a typical Malawian village. By "typical," I mean a dense array of family compounds, each built around a cluster of huts with mud floors and straw-thatched roofs, and connected by dirt roads and a morass of foot paths. Surrounding the village were hundreds of acres of hilly, dark-reddish farmland, plowed by hand around granite boulders and fruit trees. Most of the inhabitants were unemployed yeoman, powerless to the whims of weather and dependent upon government fertilizer and seed subsidies. Life was slow, steady and physically demanding, defined by chores and seasons, not schedules or clocks.

Training in this environment was arduous. Under the kind tutelage of a host family, we struggled in the absence of running water, electricity and contact with real family. Almost every day we assembled for "programmatic exercises" — student teaching in the mornings at a local secondary school and, in the afternoons, intensive language classes and group sessions on various facets of survival in the African bush. During hot days and cool nights, we bathed from buckets under expansive African skies and relived ourselves in claustrophobic outhouses filled with flies and roaches. The schedule was packed from dawn to dusk, our daily activities dictated and directed by others, especially the meals.

Make no mistake about it: in Malawi, the food is bland and heavy. On a steady diet of *nsima*, *nsima* and more *nsima*, constipation and weight gain were rampant. And these were the good times — out in the field, we wouldn't have host families, nor Peace Corps deliveries of meat, eggs and bread. In a few short weeks, we would have to cook for ourselves, and that scared the crap out of me. So, I enlisted my host sister, Cecelia, to teach me the art of village cooking. On Sunday afternoons, in her dark, smoky version of *Le Cordon Bleu*, we cooked food over an open fire until I proved to her that left to my own devices, I wouldn't perish from starvation.

And, of all the things we made together, *nsima* required the most skill and physical endurance. First, we took corn kernels to the grinding mill to make flour. Next, we warmed water over a fire and added a small amount of corn flour (perhaps only twenty percent of the total amount we intended to use). Occasionally stirring the mixture, we let the flour and water cook on high heat for about fifteen minutes, until the solution emitted a corny smell, looked a bit gloppy and rattled with large, stout bubbles. Finally, at precisely the right moment, we dumped in handfuls of flour, stirring furiously until the mixture was stubbornly viscous and our arms were about to fall off. A wet, wooden spoon was used to form *nsima* patties and stack them on a plate. *Voila!*

Twice during training, I became violently ill. Both episodes followed the ingestion of "chips," greasy French fries painstakingly prepared by Cecelia.

"Excuse me," I moaned to Cecelia, rushing to the outhouse.

"You feeling ok?" she asked.

"No," I shook my head, fearing that I would hurl if I opened my mouth.

"Oh, no," she sighed.

"Hold it down, just a few more steps on these wobbly legs," I told myself, "You can do it."

"I grab towel," she shouted from behind me, "Just in case."

"Oh, no, I'm not going to make it," I realized, "Just don't puke on the dog."

"Yip, yip, yip," the dog screeched, frantically licking its body.

"Sorry," I apologized to Cecelia, having showered her dog in greasy, potato vomit and bile — a direct shot.

"Do not worry," she said, "I'm not mad."

"Thank you," I whispered, crawling back to my house with a booming headache.

"I will get help," she announced, as I slipped in and out of consciousness and passed out on my porch.

Bereft with guilt, she rushed to our Malawian trainers and reported, "I think that Michael is allergic to potatoes," which was unlikely given my Scotch-Irish roots. The ultimate cause, I suspect, was the cooking water, which Cecelia often siphoned from a nearby stream when she was short on time. Yet, fingering potatoes as the pathogenic scapegoat was a glorious mistake, a boon for me and my digestive system. For the reminder of training, my snacks were healthier: peanuts, boiled eggs, bread scones and popcorn.

The particulars of this dietary reformulation were negotiated by Malawian trainers like Dyna. With the patience of Job, they were lifelines who not only taught us how to speak local languages and teach in Malawian schools, but elegantly mitigated miscommunications, snafus, minor bouts of illness, and festering personality conflicts. They also explained our presence to the community, which must have been dumbfounded by our gaggle of fair-skinned do-gooders. It was a study in grace and professionalism.

I wonder what the trainers told the village about our parties. Every Wednesday night, under the cover of darkness, we tiptoed away from our modest huts, past sleeping dogs and snoring children, and headed for Mary Cate's — a fully furnished village bungalow that was downright palatial. There, over shared swigs of liquor and beer surreptitiously procured in town with meager trainee allowances, stories were swapped, poems were read, and lifelong bonds were forged in furnaces of laughter and camaraderie — a Malawian Dead Poets' Society. I lived for those cathartic interludes — precious respites from the suffocating blanket of Malawian-American cultural dissonance.

Yet, a complete escape was unattainable, as nothing was truly private or confidential. Gossip being the lifeblood of conversation, our unofficial Wednesday-night gatherings were ripe fodder for the village rumor mill. For example, after I walked Jesse home one night, scuttling past shadows and silhouettes, her village family spread rumors that she was my love interest — "girlfriend" to an American and "wife" to a Malawian. I wasn't interested in a second marriage, and hadn't forgiven myself for the first one, but overnight I became a village stud, and Jesse was spared advances from unwanted suitors.

Nothing was solitary, either. Technically, you did bathe and relieve yourself alone, but just a few feet away, a flurry of activity (e.g., animals, people, voices) surrounded you. And, in the open, you were fair game for unsolicited encounters initiated by curious Malawians. Highly social and collaborative by nature, they assumed that Americans were like them and wanted an escort for every meal, walk, and laundry wash at the river. Many host families, including mine, refused to let their trainees do anything without assistance and supervision. Consequently, sleeping was our only escape.

Speaking of privacy, or lack thereof, the uninvited presence of my host brother, Osman, was jarring at first. Night after night, we sat in my house on rickety wooden chairs, a low card table between us. As a kerosene lantern cast soft glows on our faces, I looked him straight in the eyes (American assertiveness), and he glanced back, frequently averting his gaze (Malawian modesty). At first, he didn't blink or talk, nor did I. And each of us breathed a sigh of relief when a knock on the door broke the stalemate and women entered (on their knees no less) with dinner. He didn't speak much English, I didn't speak much *Chichewa*, but we both knew the international language of food.

Frankly, I preferred to eat alone. Yet, I was too polite and intrigued to object to his presence, so my eating companion and I invented a language of improvised hand movements and sounds, which generated more laughter than legitimate dialogue.

"There, there," I would point at the salt, hoping he would understand.

"What? What?" he shook his head.

"I want a thing that is this color," I said pointing to my white t-shirt, like we were playing charades.

"Uh-huh," he nodded.

"The thing I want is also small like dirt," I continued, lifting some sand grains off the floor and rubbing them between my thumb and index finger.

"Uh-huh," he nodded, seemingly putting two and two together.

"You understand?"

"Yes," he said, using one of the few English words in his vocabulary.

"Ok, please pass me the salt."

He picked up dirt from the floor and sprinkled it on my shirt. *Oy!*

As our communication improved, things got better. I learned that Osman was a farmer about my age, and that every day he would rise early to hoe the fields or ride his bike into town to lay bricks, earning precious money for his wife, children and extended family, all of whom lived in our compound. With a big gap-toothed smile, Osman tolerated my language gaffs and probing (sometimes inappropriate) questions about Malawian culture. Over time, I grew to appreciate Osman's company and long for it when he was absent. He was my first Malawian friend.

Graduating from training after ten weeks aroused mixed feelings. I missed Osman and my host family. They mourned my departure like a death in the family and gave me parting gifts — a stirring stick and pot for cooking, beans from the garden, and *chigumu* (traditional Malawian bread made from corn flour). On the other hand, back at the Peace Corps training center, it didn't take me long to embrace warm showers and coffee breaks. They mollified endless hours of "processing," a nebulous term used to describe the grueling exercise of assessing our experiences and giving feedback to the staff.

Before graduation, the last significant training exercise was the LPI (Language Proficiency Interview), a one-on-one conversation with a native speaker in a local tongue. Used to assess a trainee's readiness to communicate in the field, the interviews are taped and evaluated on a ten-grade scale ranging from Novice Low (weak handling of rote phrases) to Superior (capable of abstract conversations). A score of Intermediate-Mid (command of simple situations) is required, but after ten weeks of study, merely passing is disappointing. So, I prepared diligently, and the stars aligned, blessing me with a score of Advanced High (conversant on topics of personal and public interest). Good local language skills would give me a head start, a crumb of respectability in my village of service, where every morsel counted.

But which village would get me and my language skills? That was the million-dollar question, and its answer was a closely guarded secret. After all, stakes were high: sites in the central region were close to the Peace Corps office and its free Internet; lakeshore placements were perfect for beach bums but very hot and sunny; many of the northern sites were beautiful, in a mountainous way, but remote and chilly; and the poor bastards assigned to *Chikwawa* in the Southern Malawi would spend two years in an unforgiving oven. Some trainees begged for electricity and plumbing; others wanted nothing more than a mud hut and two years of desolation. Peace Corps staff spent gobs of time on the thankless task of identifying potential sites and trying to match people to them.

Our villages were finally revealed with great fanfare at a ceremony held during the last week of training. Doing the honors was Dora, an elegant, middle-aged Malawian woman (and longtime Peace Corps employee) responsible for managing all of the Volunteer teachers in Malawi. To heighten the drama, a map of Malawi was placed on an easel in front of us, and as each volunteer's site was announced, his or her picture was pasted onto the map at the appropriate location. I anxiously awaited my turn.

"And this Volunteer," she read, "will have a beautiful view of mountains!"

"Who is it? Who is it?" the crowd buzzed.

"It's Michael," she exclaimed, "He is going to Khwalala Village in the Mulanje District of Southern Malawi!"

"Yeah, yeah," the crowd cheered.

I ran to the front, as the trainees before me had done, and accepted a slip of paper bearing the name of a village, the name of a contact person and a phone number. It was anticlimactic to say the least. We wanted maps and detailed descriptions of our future homes, complete with pictures and testimonials (hello, GPS coordinates!). When that didn't happen, we peppered our trainers with questions to fill in the gaps.

"Have you ever been to [village name]? What is the weather like? Is the house decent? Are the people nice? Is there electricity nearby?"

"We really don't know," they patiently answered, "You need to investigate for yourselves."

The mystery left us hungry for answers and eagerly awaiting our fates.

We became official Peace Corps Volunteers in December 2006. It happened at a ceremony held at one of the nicest venues in Lilongwe: the U.S. Ambassador's residence. We were proud Americans that day, happy to be done with training and anxious to disperse to our schools and start two-year service clocks. After the Ambassador spoke of our valuable service and patriotism, we raised our hands and recited the oath of service, swearing to "support and defend the Constitution of the United States against all enemies, foreign and domestic." The Peace Corps Director played a video about President Kennedy and the history of Peace Corps. It was very romantic.

But it didn't take long for reality to set in. Sensing our imminent departure, we scoured Lilongwe for accoutrements of daily living, struggling to navigate the streets under heaps of purchased household goods — kerosene stoves, buckets and pillows.

"Should I buy toothpaste or can I find it in the village?" I asked Stephen.

"I'm not sure," he replied.

"What about shampoo?"

"Don't know," he repeated.

"Well, I guess we have enough stuff," I said, straining to carry two bloated shopping bags.

"Yeah," he agreed, "and it's getting late. We need to return to the Peace Corps house before it gets dark."

That evening our group cooked delicious homemade food and partied like rock stars into the night, trying to celebrate our status as freshly-minted Peace Corps Volunteers. I say "trying" because although the party was a blast, it was tainted by an air of imminent departure, a foreboding reinforced by the disconcerting sight of packed bags.

The next morning we awoke to the distinctive growl of diesel engines, as Peace Corps vehicles assembled to gather our belongings and transport us to our new homes. In groups of twos or threes, amidst hugs and tears, we packed the military-issue personnel movers to the gills (bikes on top) and hit the road.

"To the folks headed south, see you soon. To the central folks, see you every so often. And to the northern folks, have a nice life," I bid farewell.

"Come on. It's time to go," yelled the drivers, honking their horns, "Time is beating us. We don't want to drive at night."

"Alright," I said, "Let's move out!"

My vehicle was driven by Chris, a gentle and articulate Malawian man who would have become a doctor or lawyer if he had been raised with the resources of a typical American child. But he was in Malawi, where driving aid workers around was the best way for him to feed his family. He could have become embittered taking orders from white foreigners with MP3 players and pockets of cash, but he didn't. Instead, he embraced his lot in life with passion, and challenged himself to become the finest Peace Corps driver that ever was. Decked out in a tie, collared shirt and impeccably shined shoes, he drove with the skill of a surgeon and heart of a saint.

The two-hundred mile journey to Khwalala would test both of these qualities. After a late start, good weather and paved roads hastened our journey, and even the jaunt from Zomba to Blantyre, reputed to be the most accident-ridden road in Africa, was a breeze. Yet, a foreboding sky loomed over Blantyre, and as we turned off the tarmac toward Khwalala Village, a torrential downpour morphed dirt-track roads into a soupy mess, sliding sideways like lava. Still, we pushed forward in four-wheel drive, crossing dangerous gullies and rickety bridges. Slowly... slowly...slowly, we eluded the quagmires and pulled onto the grounds of Khwalala C.D.S.S. to the sight of a relieved Mr. Zimbota.

* * * *

Now, those memories seem eons old. Entering year two, I'm a grizzled Peace Corps veteran. Bathing out of a bucket is old hat, and cooking over a fire feels normal. If I miss class or students fail to complete an assignment, no worries. If a friend comes two hours late to a meeting, I say, "Wonderful, you're early today." Everything is possible and, at the same time, nothing is or ever will be. Yet, I haven't given up hope, and my weathered calendar fills with optimistic goals. Chief among them is a girls' boarding facility, although I haven't heard from Peace Corps staff about the status of our grant proposal.

My school commitments vary depending on the day. After last year's punishing schedule, I decide to teach only three subjects, about eighteen hours a week, giving me ample time to lesson plan and organize community service projects. Classes end around 2:30 p.m., followed by after-school activities like sports training (soccer and netball) and spiritual groups, but my modus operandi is to teach in the mornings and blow off the afternoons. They are precious opportunities to pursue personal pleasures, like exploring the area or visiting friends. As an unofficial Peace Corps bike mechanic, I often make house calls.

Yet, each day before I depart for my adventures, I join colleagues in the staff-room for a small lunch, a treasured tradition of ours. Each of us contributes money at the beginning of the month to buy bread, tea and sugar, and we rotate the teacher responsible for managing the logistics of the operation. I started the practice during my first year to alleviate hunger pangs of colleagues (who would teach the entire day without eating) and to promote camaraderie and fellowship. At first, I had my doubts about the latter, but these days, it's fair to say that there's no shortage of conversation — school affairs, politics, culture, sex — you name it, we discuss it.

"Mr. Michael, I have question for you," Mr. Namanya says, sitting down at his desk with a fat hunk of bread and a cup of sugary, piping hot tea.

"Fire away," I say.

"Is it true that black men marry white women in America?" he asks.

"Oh, yes," I reply, "and black women marry men from other races."

"Really?" he whispers in disbelief, imaging the possibilities.

Other colleagues look up from their desks. They are too stunned to eat — their jaws frozen in the open position.

"If you're not eating that piece of bread, I'll take it," I joke, as Mr. Namanya comes to his senses, feeling his hunger.

"So, I could marry a Peace Corps woman?" he garbles, after taking a large bite of bread.

"In theory, you could, but you already have a wife and children."

"Yes," he smiles, "but we Africans have many wives and many children."

Talking temporarily dies down in the staffroom, replaced with sounds of slurping and chewing. It's a window of opportunity, but I need to eat quickly because more inquires are surely coming.

"Mr. Michael, I have another question," Mr. Namanya says, right on cue.

"Sure, go ahead."

"Everyone in America is very rich, right?"

"No, many people are poor," I say, "even poorer than you."

"What?" he shouts, "I am not believing you. More poorer than me?"

"Yes," I explain, "You have food to eat because you grow it yourself, but some poor people in America have no money and no food."

"You are teasing us," he says, as the other teachers laugh in unison.

"No, I'm not," I reply, a bit frustrated, "Let me show you. Wait one minute."

"Look, here," I point, having returned from the library with a volume of Encyclopedia Britannica showing grainy images of Dustbowl desperation, "These are pictures of poor Americans from the Great Depression."

"Hmm," the teachers remark, having gathered around my desk for a better view, "These people are poor?"

"Yes, they are very, very poor."

"But, they have nice clothes," Mr. Namanya observes, "and one is standing next to car."

"Yes, but...," I start to respond.

"Look," they interrupt, "Poor people in America wear suits and fancy hats!"

"Ok," I sigh, "time to put the book away."

People will see what they want to see, I suppose. I swung for the fences and whiffed the ball entirely — another cultural strikeout. Thankfully, I have better luck with the students.

About once a week, one asks, "Will you join my family for lunch?" I usually accept, appreciating the free meal and the importance of honoring them with a visit. Coveting the opportunity to host me, the families are dressed to impress and pull out all the stops, blowing their savings on a village feast of rice, beans and meat, and sometimes springing for bottles of Coca-Cola. Conversations are rudimentary and experimental, at best, but the experience is always genuine and rejuvenating. After the meal is over, I'm thanked profusely for coming and given a live chicken or bag of tomatoes to take home. It is the zenith of Malawian hospitality, and I never tire of it.

On nice afternoons, when I'm not riding my bike or eating with the families of students, Malawians often find me working in the schoolyard, weeding and watering rows of delicate seedlings, and chasing away ravenous goats trying to eat them. For Malawians, watching a white man work in a field and battle livestock is very entertaining.

"There's brown male again," a student shrieks, "He eating that tree."

"Look, Mr. Buckler is coming!" another student yells, pointing in my direction.

Sadly, the problem is all too common — a wandering, male goat, anchored by testicles the size of boulders, blithely denudes a mango seedling on school property, savoring the fresh, chlorophyll-rich shoots. He should be tied to a tree, but villagers sometimes get lazy with their livestock. I sprint to the scene of the crime, rock in hand, itching for some live target practice. The goat rotates one of its ugly, distended eyes in my direction, stops its nonchalant chewing and flees like a bullet. I take aim and violently hurl the rock.

"Wonderful! Another miss," I lament, as the rock sails over the goat's head and shatters against a brick wall.

"Good try, Mr. Buckler," the students laugh, as the escaping goat bellows an all-points warning to his bovid friends waiting in an adjoining field.

"I'll get him next time!" I vow, "I'll get all of them."

"Yes, sir," they say, "We know you not let our trees be hurt. Thank you."

What can I say? The local people know and trust me, even if I attack their goats.

As an "acclimatized" Volunteer and card-carrying goat hater, I fashion a list of Top Ten Rules for Village Living:

Rule 1: Don't do anything a local wouldn't do.

Rule 2: Don't do everything a local would do.

Rule 3: Constipated? Eat a mango or a papaya.

Rule 4: Speak the local language and eat the local food.

Rule 5: Get used to daily exercise, whether you like it or not.

Rule 6: Don't look down the latrine. Just do your business and get out.

Rule 7: Eat cooked food within a day and uncooked, perishable food within three days.

Rule 8: Never leave home without a water bottle, raincoat and good book.

Rule 9: Resist the temptation to kill the rooster that interrupts your sleep or the goat that ravages your garden.

Rule 10: Don't worry. Be happy.

It serves me well, although (as explained above) I have difficulty following Rule 9.

Per Rule 10, alone time and personal reflection are mandates. Tackling demons, exploring facets of my personality, evaluating and refining my value system, and processing my past and present are bittersweet habits. Nature always works to fill a vacuum, and in a theater of silence, the human mind crackles with activity. Yet, when fatigue and burnout threaten to overload the system, yoga takes the edge off by pacifying the psyche, just as writing is a creative and soothing outlet. I just wish the latter didn't stir me awake in the middle of the night with a thought that just couldn't wait until morning to meet paper.

Still, I sleep soundly most nights because in the early evenings, I release frustration and unspent energy in the soft glow of fading sunlight. Having jerry rigged an exercise room in the library, I grind out pull-ups from a suspended tree limb, dips between reading tables, and pushups on chairs. Some days I perspire through the thick, sticky air with a music player. Others, I just turn my ear to the wind and enjoy the live harmonies of a local church choir — Catholic, Presbyterian, Evangelical — it all sounds the same: absolutely beautiful. It's exercise, African style.

For about a week, students (mostly boys) flock to my nightly workouts, trying the latest American fad to hit Khwalala. They test their masculinity by straining to do the most exercise repetitions and demonstrate their elasticity with teeth-clenching back bends. Fuming when a girl outperforms them, pride bubbles to the surface.

"You better be careful," I say.

"Why?" they ask.

"Because if we build a boarding facility here, girls will exercise every day and get stronger than you."

"Women are weak," they say, "This is man's work."

"Actually, women beat men in athletic competition," I counter, "One of the best long distance runners in the world is a woman."

They are temporarily speechless.

"You are joking us, Mr. Buckler," they retort.

"No, I'm serious."

"Maybe the woman you speak of," they continue, "eats magical food from witchdoctor that turns her into man."

"Nope. Wrong again."

"Then, what does she eat?" they ask.

"She eats the same thing you do," I answer.

"She eats *nsima*?" the students ask.

A year ago, I would have told them that American runners eat nothing that vaguely resembles *nsima*, such as pasta or energy bars. I also would have told them that Americans don't have a staple food because they eat food from all over the world. And, it's true to a certain extent: American cuisine is regional and varied, at least the specialty items. Marylanders love their crab cakes; Wisconsin folks love like their cheese and bratwurst; and Oregonians love their salmon. But, that's not the whole story.

This year I know much more about food.

"No," I reply, "she doesn't eat *nsima*, but she does eat corn. We all do."

"What do you mean?" they inquire.

"Americans grow and eat a lot of corn."

"As much as Malawians?" they ask.

"Much more," I explain, "but we eat it differently."

"How do you eat it?"

"Well," I continue, "You eat it as flour, but we eat it in other forms."

Malawians and Americans, in turns out, share a common love affair with corn, the Mesoamerican crop that English writer William Cobbett declared, "the greatest blessing God ever gave to man."

Corn is America's staple food. The usual suspects are obvious: corn on the cob, popcorn, grits and cornbread stuffing, but there are many less obvious examples. As Michael Pollan explains in *Omnivore's Dilemma*, despite their looks, most popular supermarket foods come from the American Corn Belt. On ingredients labels, Americans often find corn syrup, corn starch, and corn oil. And don't forget about corn-fed livestock, the source of our low-cost meat. We, like Malawians, are walking, talking ears of corn.

But is Cobbett right about corn being a blessing for humanity? Politicians certainly think so. The Malawian government has promoted its production since the 1960s, when Dr. Banda, the former dictator, forced every family to grow it. And, since 2005, the government has subsidized corn seeds and fertilizers for farmers, a program praised by Malawian people and criticized by the World Bank. Still, corn subsidies aren't new — they've been flowing in America since 1973, when the Nixon administration used them to rewrite New Deal agricultural policy and abolish corn production limits. From 1995 to 2006, American taxpayers spent fifty-six billion dollars subsidizing cheap corn.

Yet, corn isn't a panacea for the world's food problems. It is a nutrient-intensive crop that quickly depletes the soil and provides very little nutrition to its consumers. Consequently, most Malawians are quite small in stature, and standing at 5'11½" (hey, that ½" matters to me!), I'm a giant in my village. Similarly, in America, dependence on corn has yielded disturbing results. A generation of youngsters reared on high-fructose corn syrup and corn-fed beef has seen an epidemic increase in diet-related diseases like hypertension and high cholesterol. The Centers for Disease Control predicts that American kids born in 2000 stand a one-in-three chance of contracting Type II diabetes. Thanks, corn.

Back in the makeshift gym, all the talk of corn makes my students hungry, and they leave for dinner. I stay for a few minutes of peaceful solitude, finishing my exercise routine and singing aloud like a drunk at a karaoke party. Unfortunately, my dissonant vocals draw the attention of a school "watchman," a shabbily dressed, scruffy man charged with protecting the campus against thieves, but really just looking for a good place to sleep. Passing by, he pauses to listen through the broken windows, staring like I'm a zoo animal.

"Have a good night," I say, trying to shoo him along.

"Oh, thank you, sir," he answers, continuing to stare.

"Don't worry," I try again, "I will lock the library when I finish."

"Very good, sir," he replies, "I stay here until you leave."

"Sounds good," I sigh, "How is your family?"

"Very well, sir. And yours in America?"

"They are also well, thanks."

Ignoring my audience, I finish my sets of push-ups and lock the library. Finding the strength to shut the door and turn the key is challenging with a body and mind spent from a full day of reading, teaching, cycling, mentoring, philosophizing, goat chasing, exercising and, now, in the shadows of night, cross-cultural compassion. But it goes with the territory — center stage is where I sleep and wake and go about my day. I wish the watchman good night and walk toward my house, eager to eat dinner with the Boys. As I take my first step, I'm reminded of something that Eric Cornish (nearby Volunteer) often says: "Peace Corps is a 24-7 job. Lots of downtime, but no time off."

* * * *

Speaking of no time off, the Buckler Homestead is a handful. A daily infusion of goofy energy, the Boys rise at dawn singing and joking and don't stop until their heads hit the pillows. They call me father (their cultural perspective), and I treat them like younger brothers (my cultural perspective), praising and scolding depending on the situation, but always loving. We share laughs, food, and stories. They work hard to make me happy, and I reciprocate by trying to make them feel protected and secure, somehow removed from a litany of everyday challenges.

Still, living with others is never easy. Being boys, with typical masculine bathroom habits, they routinely forget to cover the hole in the outhouse (a must for suppressing the mosquito population), the Malawian equivalent of leaving the toilet seat up. A few of my bananas disappear, no doubt bringing relief to an empty stomach on a hungry afternoon. And particularly irksome is their practice of leaving dirty dishes sitting out on the clean dish rack, inviting an army of food-pillaging ants to coat them like tar. They are not the cleanest of housemates, but then again, neither am I.

Thankfully, the Boys have learned that Westerners like bad news better than bad information. Malawians have a tendency to tell you what you want to hear, even if it means leaving out important (invariably unfavorable) facts. Yet, the Boys make great strides toward adopting a Western approach after I tell them that problems are manageable but lies are erosive, creating mistrust and slowly dissolving relationships. As a judge I worked for used to say, "Protect your reputation. It's the hardest thing to build and easiest thing to lose." After hearing that, when a problem arises (e.g., a broken plate), the Boys come to me immediately, confessions pouring out of the responsible party.

Still, most of our interactions are positive. For example, at the spur of the moment, the Boys decide to throw a bash for Mr. Zimbota's oldest daughter, who is leaving Khwalala C.D.S.S. to attend Mulanje Secondary School, a boarding school for gifted students, and arguably the best government-sponsored school in the district.

"This party will be so, so nice," Alfred says.

"How so?" I ask, knowing Alfred's fondness for hyperbole.

"We should be eating rice and beef, and we can invite all our friends. After food, let's have disco and dance into nighttime. I cannot wait to dance with so, so many girls."

"Whose paying for all of that?" I inquire, "Do you have some money that the rest of us don't know about?"

"No sir," he giggles, "but we will find funds somewhere."

"Mr. Buckler is right," Gift interjects, "Rice and beef are too expensive. We have very little funds, but we can have party if we work together. Instead of rice, let's cook *nsima*."

"Only *nsima*?" I inquire.

"No," he replies, "Mary's parents have greens that we can buy for good price, and my garden has tomatoes and eggplants."

"What about entertainment?" Alfred asks Gift.

"There will be traditional songs and dances, not a disco. I have drums."

"You guys are doing excellent job," Myson weighs in, "but we need to tell people soon."

"Don't invite too many people," I suggest, "Malawians eat a lot of food!"

"No problem, sir," Myson says, "but don't forget Henderson. He invited us to party last month."

"Very good," I say, "It will be a nice event."

"Oh, one more thing," Myson interjects, "Mr. Buckler, can we use your pots and pans for cooking?"

"Of course you can, Myson, but please clean them shortly after you use them!"

"Yes, sir, with soap this time."

The party is a hit. The guest of honor, Chiripiriro (derived from "belief" in *Chichewa*), entertains guests, graciously accepting going-away gifts from village friends — grainy photographs taken by a village photographer with a vintage sixteen millimeter camera. Her traditional *chitenje* lower-body wrap and sleeveless top (emblazoned with a traditional African shield) do little to feminize her gangly, pre-pubescent frame, which plainly lacks the voluptuous curvature and heft coveted by Malawian men. To the relief of Mr. Zimbota, our little party is a platonic, adolescent gathering, not a debutante ball.

Sitting beside me at the party, Mr. Zimbota's youngest daughter, Memory, bounces playfully. She used to erupt into tears around me, but recently has come around, pointing and dancing when I return from bike rides. I try, as I have for months, to engage her in conversation.

"*Muli bwanji*, Memory?" I say, expecting another snub and watching a spectrum of emotions — silence, concern, recognition, anticipation, relief — flash across her face.

"*Ndili bwino*," she whispers.

"Yes, yes!" I shout, pumping my fists, "She said it! She said it!"

"She said what?" Mr. Zimbota asks.

"She said '*Ndili bwino*,'" a typical *Chichewa* response meaning "I am well."

Everyone looks up and cheers — enjoying the breakthrough. Everyone, that is, except Memory. She looks confused and violated, and responds by bawling and running to her mother, who rolls over laughing. Then, as icing on the cake, she pees her pants, causing everyone to laugh more. Good job, Mike — you scared the piss out of a three-year-old.

"Memory is afraid of Mr. Buckler!" Alfred jokes.

"Seems that way," I reply, wishing it weren't true.

"Don't worry, sir," he cajoles, "she will understand when she grows up."

"Yeah," Myson adds, "when she sprouts like corn stalk."

"Speaking of food, what are we having tonight for dinner?" I ask.

"*Nsima*," the Boys say in unison.

"*Nsima*, again?" I moan, "Can we cook something else?"

The resounding answer is "no." *Nsima* is their staple, their lifeblood, and they crave it constantly. They consume heaping plates of it on a nightly basis, displaying an uncanny ability to stretch their stomachs with ever-increasing amounts of the dense, sticky corn mush. When I cook an American meal for them as a special treat, serving homemade tomato sauce and mountains of pasta (purchased at a premium in town), they finish their plates "hungry" for *nsima*, and sometimes sneak away to cook a batch of it on the sly before bedtime. In short, Malawians are shameless *nsima* addicts.

And, truth be told, so am I. Possessing a solid, grainy texture, *nsima* goes down with a subtle corny taste and fills the stomach, lingering there for many hours of uninterrupted fullness. Though my first two meals of the day are *nsima*-free, the Malawian staple is front and center at dinner alongside boiled vegetables (various greens infused with onion and tomato) and, depending on the season, fresh avocados, mangoes, guavas, passion fruit, and pineapples. Around dinnertime, I find myself craving *nsima*, and when I leave the village for a few days, my body goes into *nsima* withdrawal.

And, on this particular night, some of my favorite students (including the

Boys) make me *nsima* accompanied by eggplants sautéed with tomato and onion. I work slowly on a plate of my own, savoring the generous helping of vegetables and modest serving of *nsima*, just the way I like it. Four students sitting in front of me share just two plates — one containing a meager allowance of vegetables and the other bowing under the weight of a mountain of *nsima*. Having waited all day for a meal, they devour it instantaneously.

"How many bites of *nsima* do you eat?" they ask.

"I have no idea. Enough to make me full. It depends on the day. You actually count?"

They actually do, tracking the numbers like American kids follow baseball batting averages, despite the practical difficulties of comparing bite statistics (e.g., differing mouth and hand sizes). Language being a reflection of culture, Malawians even have a special word in *Chichewa* for a single bite of their cherished, finger-licking delicacy.

Over dinner, the Boys report dramatic news of the day from school. The front-page story is that a senior boy has taken a freshman girl as his "girlfriend," an arrangement that can lead to a parent conference, at the very least, and possibly expulsion from school. In Malawi, "girlfriend" or "boyfriend" means there is sexual intercourse, probably in some hard-to-find place in the surrounding fields, behind a privacy wall of corn stalks. I'm not surprised. I've spoken with this particular boy about sex on several occasions and given him a few condoms to encourage him to practice it safely.

The drama reached a climax today because the boy was sulking at school. Turns out that his "girlfriend" received an envelope from another boy, a corn farmer living about forty-five miles away. The contents of the envelope were scandalous and incriminating: a love letter and a picture. Such cold-hearted betrayal! I sit at the dinner table smirking, reminiscing about high school tomfoolery and wondering whether the boy and girl in question will be disciplined. After delivering the news, the Boys rush off to night school. I stay behind for a moment of reflection (and digestion) about corn and sex — the intercultural obsessions that spellbind the world.

A short time passes before Mr. Zimbota stops by, an evening tradition of ours. He likes to check on me and chat, and by asking the right questions, I learn from his lessons on local language and culture. He is also someone I can trust with my true feelings, and having been discouraged for the last few weeks, I choose to tell him the reason — a nagging concern that my overtures of goodwill and hard work are having a miniscule impact on the community, a common complaint of Peace Corps Volunteers. As always, he provides much needed perspective.

"No, don't think that way," he cajoles, "Thanks to you, teachers drink tea and eat bread for lunch."

"That's my legacy?" I joke.

"Maybe you will help us build girls' boarding school."

"Ok, that's better," I say, "but no guarantee on that one."

"You also show us that men can cook and do things that only women do here. We like your food so much, most especially, how do you say, guacamole?"

"But you still eat mountains of corn," I sigh, picturing a Malawian swimming in a silo of the yellow grain, in Iowa.

The humorous image teaches a simple lesson: we're not so different. My conversation with Mr. Zimbota reminds me that people are creatures of habits (food or otherwise) that are loathe to change anywhere, regardless of culture or color. It also makes me appreciate that just as corn has won over the world slowly but surely, our impacts on each other are incremental, elusive and deceptively profound.

"We learn from each other," Mr. Zimbota says, "You are American. I am Malawian. You always tell us that Americans and Malawians are the same — *tili chimodzimodzi.*"

"Absolutely," I say, feeling the cross-cultural love.

"But do you believe it?" he continues.

"Well, friend," I answer, "if you are what you eat, I certainly do."

X

The Gods

I, um, experienced a minor hiccup recently. As a passenger in a car that was "allegedly" traveling about thirty kilometers over the speed limit, I was taken into custody by Malawian Police. During a brief confinement (all charges were eventually dropped), I became dizzy agonizing over the potential punishments, which range from a fine to jail time. When I asked the supervising police officer about my likely fate, he said, "Sir, it is in God's hands."

— Letter Home, April 2008

Living in Malawi, it is easy to wonder about God. Most days I feel like a god because Peace Corps Volunteers (especially white men) enjoy a God-like existence. They dart in and out of situations, seeing many worlds and peoples at once, enjoying rarefied status but also bearing an expectation of assistance. There is impunity when mistakes are made, and societal constraints don't apply. Through it all, I conclude that if there is a God, she must be very lonely, as I am most of the time.

Thankfully, loneliness is not on today's menu. Eric, hungry for American fellowship, is cycling my way. He should arrive around 9ish or 10ish or 11ish, depending on uncertainties like inclement weather and road conditions. He's welcome anytime, announced or unannounced, and he knows as much. Around half past ten, the Boys find him pedaling his mountain bike, just outside the village.

"Mr. Cornish, you come to visit us?" they ask.

"I always come to see you," he replies with a hint of sarcasm, a trademark of his.

"Very good," they reply, "we make you *nsima*."

"I would love that. Thank you," he smiles.

After his bike is safely stowed in my house, and the reception pleasantries (visits from neighbors, greetings and handshakes) have been honored, we sit in the grass, a few steps from my front porch, underneath a canopy of lashed poles and fruit vines, watching the sun cross a baby blue sky. The Boys lounge with us.

It's Sunday.

"Sundays just seem slower than other days of the week," Eric observes.

"Yeah," I say, "there isn't much to do on Sundays, except read and pray."

"Prayer very important," Gift interjects, "Are you going to church today?"

"Don't think so," I admit, lifting my arms and yawning into a slow stretch of apathy, tainted by a slight twinge of guilt, "Eric, do you want to go to church?"

"Hell no, but thanks for the generous offer," he snaps, "I'm just fine right here. You can go without me."

"Mr. Buckler, people get very happy when you come to church," the Boys explain.

"I know, I know," I sigh, "but the services last for three hours, and I don't understand much of what is being said."

"The people love so much to see you," Myson says, twisting the knife of guilt a little deeper.

"Boys, they love receiving you, too," I fire back, "and I don't see you dressed for church. Are you going?"

The unspoken answer is "no." They look at one another, giggle and grab chairs from inside the house, a clear sign that they are staying put. Mr. Zimbota, another church fugitive, strolls over from his house and joins us. He loves hanging out, especially when my Peace Corps friends are visiting.

"Are you going to church today?" I ask Mr. Zimbota.

"No," he replies, "I want to spend time with you and our visitor, Eric."

"Did you go last week?"

"Yes," he says, "My daughter led choir. I wanted to see her."

"You go pretty regularly," I observe.

"Yes, I try. It is good to praise God for blessings."

"True," I agree halfheartedly, trying to hide my real motivations for going to church in Malawi — community relations and language learning.

"When are you returning to church?" Mr. Zimbota asks, calling my bluff.

"I don't know. Sometime soon."

He looks at me, vexed.

"Michael, do you believe in God?" he asks abruptly.

The circle of conversation goes silent. All eyes turn toward me.

"Well, I was raised Christian," I reply, choosing my words carefully, "and my father is an ordained Methodist minister."

"Yes," he nods.

"So, I'm a Methodist in America, but in Malawi, I pray with you as a Presbyterian."

His eyes, and the corners of his mouth, curl in dissatisfaction. If he were American, he might remark, "You're full of it. Your response sounded good, but you didn't answer my question."

"I see," he continues, "but do you believe in God?"

"Well, ahem," I cough, "that's the hard part. It's difficult to know what to believe."

"Not for me," Eric interjects, "I don't believe in God, and I wish that religious people would realize that their beliefs are silly."

Mr. Zimbota smiles, as though Eric has exhibited the honesty he was fishing for.

"Ok, I believe in God," I acknowledge, feeling exposed.

"You do?" Eric remarks in surprise.

"Yes, but I don't have proof of God's existence. I don't know God's ways or thoughts or motivations. My faith is a choice, plain and simple, perhaps a convenient one."

"Fair enough," he replies.

The Malawians look perplexed and uncomfortable, as though I've introduced them to a radical, new concept that smacks of heathenism and sacrilege. Cats got their tongues.

"Then, why do people go to church?" Myson asks.

"I think people like being part of something bigger than themselves," I explain, "and finding meaning in life within a supportive community."

"People are just scared and driven by fear," Eric chides, "on a fool's errand for truth."

"Michael, are you fearful?" Mr. Zimbota wonders.

"No, I'm not motivated by fear," I explain, "My beliefs ring true to my everyday experience. Many have been passed down to me from generations of collective wisdom."

"What wisdom?" Mr. Zimbota inquires.

"It comes from my forefathers, just as your beliefs come from yours."

"Wisdom is wisdom," Eric adds, "It just gets handed down in different ways at different times by different groups of people who chose to associate with one another."

Our circle offers plenty of examples. I'm a Methodist of Scotch-Irish descent from America sitting next to a Malawian Presbyterian and supporter of the Democratic Progressive Party. Eric is a Southerner and registered Democrat, and Gift is a devotee of the Arsenal Football Club. Groups, groups and more groups — a multi-layered patchwork of influences and, often, contradictions. They make us feel interconnected and give us purpose. Religion is one example, but there are many others, like tribe.

Malawi is composed of many tribal peoples. *Timbuka* inhabit much of the north, except along the lake shore, where *Tonga* communities flourish. The first President of Malawi, Dr. Banda, was a *Chewa*. During his reign, he relocated the capital to the *Chewa* stronghold of Lilongwe, in Central Malawi. There are also *Ngoni*, an offshoot of the militant Zulu from South Africa. Along the southern lake shore, where they once facilitated the East African Slave Trade, *Yao* are abundant. In Southern Malawi, close to Mozambique, there are many *Sena* and *Lomwe*.

These groups coexist peacefully, for the most part. Despite strong tribal affiliations, Malawians are beginning to identify themselves as a unified people. Within my house, for example, Alfred is a *Lomwe*, Gift and Myson are *Yao*, but all of them are resolutely Malawian. Everyone celebrates national holidays, uses a national currency to conduct business and follows the lives of national celebrities, like President Bingu (a *Lomwe*) and the Malawian soccer team. When Bingu's popular and philanthropic wife died of cancer, Malawi mourned together, as one.

Still, tribal tensions are a clear and present reality, particularly among the older generations. Politicians accuse one another of practicing tribal favoritism or playing to stereotypes, such as the widespread belief (especially among whites) that people from tribes in Northern Malawi are the most educated, creative and ambitious (i.e., better workers and partners in development). At nationwide gatherings, Malawians from different regions interact with each other skeptically, often self-segregating with those from their home areas. People from different regions or tribes rarely intermarry, and when they do, it's a big deal.

Consequently, living in Malawi provides a fascinating sociological and geopolitical perspective on nationalism. This is especially true for an outsider from America, where, after nearly three-hundred years of patriotic conditioning, people tend to identify themselves with country more than ethnicity. Contrasting styles of national identity — strong for Americans and lukewarm for Malawians — often emerge when I meet American strangers in Malawi.

"Hello! Where are you from?" I say, after stumbling upon a random Iranian-American woman perusing the curio markets of Lilongwe.

"Oh," she answers, "I'm from Detroit."

"What are you doing here?"

"I'm completing a six-week rotation at the hospital, treating medical conditions that have been eradicated from the West."

"Very nice," I remark, "I'm a Peace Corps Volunteer in Malawi. If you need any help getting around or figuring stuff out, just let me know."

"Thanks. I might take you up on that. See you around."

Exchanges like this one, repeated on a monthly basis, dumbfound Malawian friends traveling with me. It would be unusual for a *Tonga* man from the north and a *Sena* man from the south to have an equally carefree conversation, despite the fact that they are probably closer in terms of culture and life experience than I am with a Persian woman from the Midwest.

Back in Khwalala, where the circle of conversation remains lively with frank dialogue about religion and tribe, Mr. Zimbota shakes his head and laughs.

"Americans are so different from us," he observes.

"How?" I ask.

"You come from different tribes, but you love each other!" he explains, meaning to say "like" in place of "love," but making the grammatical mistake because in *Chichewa*, there is no distinction between liking and loving.

"I suppose we do," I say, "Will Malawians love one another someday?"

"I hope so very much," he says, "if God will allow," a common Malawian response to anything uncertain.

Indeed, God might be the common thread that does the trick. Malawians of all stripes believe in greater powers at work around them, above them, and often against them. Most (about seventy-five percent) identify themselves as Christians. Another twenty percent are practicing Muslims. Yet, nearly all of them are Animist, adhering to a traditional belief system that recognizes the active involvement of witches and devils masquerading as humans or animals. For most people, Animism is de facto, a rigid base that newer religions can overlay but not supplant.

Interesting juxtapositions arise in the mixing of belief systems — Western-style orthodoxy, on the one hand, and African voodoo, on the other. Religious centers (churches and mosques) abound, regularly filling with parishioners toting Bibles or Korans. Yet, animist sects and traditional African doctors also thrive, plainly advertising their services at homesteads and open-air markets. The leaders of each camp openly question each other, but instead of choosing one, average people practice both, inconsistencies be damned. Human beings have a knack for amalgamating the mutually exclusive.

Gule Wamkulu is the poster child of Malawian animism. A *Chewa* secret society, whose name literally means "big dance," it boasts members who disguise themselves as animals or trees, and dance wildly at funerals, weddings and other village gatherings, to serve as a medium between the ancestral world of spirits and the mundane affairs of living people. *Gules* are known for being insular, spirited and lewd, often drinking to excess and running around villages with oversized masks covering their faces and drawn machetes waving in the air. In short, they are the Caribbean pirates of Malawi.

Another prominent aspect of Malawian animism is village medicine. Hesitant to abandon their culture, even in the face of Western pharmaceuticals, villagers flock to "African doctors" ("*sing'anga*" in *Chichewa*) for advice or potions to cure their ills or solve their problems. All of these practitioners, however, are not created equal. On one end of the spectrum are purveyors of natural medicine, wielding knowledge passed through the generations to prescribe treatments derived from roots, barks and flowers. Their services of traditional wellness and healing often complement the conventional medicine practiced at local clinics. It's a win-win for health.

Traditional medicine gets its bad name from folks on the other end of the spectrum. Witchdoctors, as they are known, purport to be shamans with psychic powers to divine truth, cast spells, and mingle with spirits. Their remedies are esoteric at best and, at worst, downright dangerous. A frequently cited example is the advice that sleeping with a virgin will cure HIV. Of course, Christian pastors aren't doing much better asserting that a sincere and unwavering belief in Jesus Christ (notwithstanding frequent and polygamous, unprotected sex) will prevent you from becoming infected in the first place. Still, there is a difference: while pastors are advisors, witchdoctors are enablers.

They enable by practicing "witchcraft," an umbrella term covering two categories of mischief: true witchcraft (*mfiti*) and magic (*masenga*). The former is dangerous and sinister, an instrument of pain and suffering. It is practiced only by witchdoctors as a form of mystical mercenariness. The latter is more innocuous, akin to a card trick or a prank (e.g., relocating someone while they are sleeping). It can be practiced by witchdoctors and lay villagers alike. Confused? Perhaps this consumer tip, brought to you by the Malawian Village Chamber of Commerce, will clear things up: use magic to spook an adversary, but invoke witchcraft to put an enemy permanently out of commission.

Nikki, a nearby Peace Corps Volunteer, didn't know which to employ when she sought answers to a robbery at her home. Dissatisfied with the investigatory work of the local police, she decided to venture into the Malawian occult and consult a witchdoctor. Finding one wasn't a problem — he lived right down the road and openly advertised his services on a simple, black-and-white sign in his front yard. Nikki didn't know the cost or scope of his services, or whether there were any supernatural risks associated with her whim, but as a free-spirited Oregonian, she figured that she had nothing to lose by trying.

The witchdoctor must have been surprised to find a tall, blond-haired, blue-eyed American woman knocking on his door. But, in typical Malawian fashion, he graciously invited her inside and offered her a seat. The small, village house was sparse and dark, and had all of the usual accoutrements — wooden chairs and a small table, a reed mat for sleeping, and bags of corn flour. Yet, against one of the walls, obscured by the shadows, was something unusual — a collection of distinctive statuettes made from gourds, and decorated with paint, beaded necklaces and human hair.

"What are those?" Nikki asked, pointing to the idols.

"The big one," the witchdoctor replied casually, "is *Amayi Dua*. She allows me to channel my deceased mother."

"Oh," she gasped, "and the others?"

"The next one, *Mwatida*, protects us from sicknesses and harm caused by others. *Kusala*, there, identifies witches, and *Mwuzajani* promotes fertility."

"What's the last one?"

"It's a snake puppet that can turn into a real snake and bite someone."

Her jaw dropped. Having come for pleasure more than business, she was definitely being entertained.

"Why have you come?" he asked.

"I was robbed last week," she explained, "I just want to find out who stole my things."

"Very good," he replied, "I can help you."

For the price of about sixty American cents, the witchdoctor went to work. After Nikki described the robbery in more detail, he approached *Amayi Dua* and asked her to awake. He blew on her hair and entered a trance-like state, mumbling to himself in an indecipherable language, like an evangelical Christian speaking in tongues. The statute never left its inanimate state, but the witchdoctor put on a show, alternating between meditations and convulsions, seemingly unfazed by his audience. After a few minutes of drama, he returned to reality, eager to provide some answers.

"The criminals are two boys from technical school, known to be thieves in community," he uttered.

"Yes, what else?" she asked.

"They watch your house and tell each other when you are away," he answered.

"Do they have my things?" Nikki inquired.

"No. They sold them at market."

He opened his eyes and shot Nikki a cold, dry stare of sobriety.

"There are three punishments for stealing," he said.

"What are they?" she asked.

"First, I can cast a spell that will trap thieves on your property next time they try to steal. I can also cause painful sores to appear all over their bodies. Lastly, I can bring about their deaths!"

Nikki gulped, speechless. Stealing a water bucket and a few pounds of sugar didn't warrant the death penalty. What started as lighthearted folly on a slow afternoon was getting serious.

"I can also give you magic seeds to plant around your house," the witchdoctor continued, seeing the worry on Nikki's face.

"What will they do?" she replied, "I don't want anyone to die or get hurt."

"They will prevent thieves from entering your house," he laughed, "Nothing more."

"I'll take the seeds," Nikki politely smiled, quickly paying for the psychic services and excusing herself from his company.

It's safe to say that she didn't become a regular customer.

* * * *

Frankly, witchdoctors are a bit intimidating, especially after Nikki's experience. So, for spiritual matters, I gravitate to their antithesis, the Church of Central Africa Presbyterian (CCAP). On any given Sunday around 11 a.m., the Khwalala contingent of this large and influential African Christian congregation has been singing and dancing, and praising and praying, for almost three hours. I, on the other hand, arrive late (on the rare occasion that I arrive at all), determined to adhere to the longstanding pillar of American Methodism that no church service shall exceed one hour. Finding Mr. Zimbota, I try to slide into the back of the men's section like a stealth plane, but white skin instantly blows my cover.

My bobbing head also draws attention. In the stale, hot air, fatigue sets in, sedating me like anesthesia. By sheer will alone, I almost make it through the endless litany of scripture passages read in *Chichewa*. To Malawians, they sound like, "God, we love you. Please bless us with food and good health. You are the one and true God." But to me, they sound like, "God...love...bless...health...God." Then, my inner voice takes over. It says, "getting very sleepy...starting to doze... good night."

"Wake up!" Mr. Zimbota whispers, "Minister is starting to preach."

"What's he saying?" I ask, unable to decipher the brisk *Chichewa*.

"He is reading from Book of Matthew," he replies.

"Which part?"

"Beatitudes," he responds, "Blessed are peacemakers, for they shall be called children of God."

The minister continues his sermon. As he lectures the congregation in dramatic crescendos and decrescendos, I start to nod off again. Mr. Zimbota sees me and frowns. Yet, my fear of disappointing him is no match for my urge to sleep. My eyes are closing.

Just in the nick of time, the minister takes a seat and the choir erupts into dance and raw village melody, filling the room with vigor and perfect harmony. I jolt awake and watch. Emerging from the back of the church, each choir member shuffles in perfect synchronization in a long, thin line. Instrumentalists with traditional drums and makeshift three-string guitars bring up the rear, igniting the beats and rhythms that feed the advancing column. They arrange themselves in rows near the altar and sway in unison to the song.

Parishioners come forward in groups toward a single collection plate perched on a small table in the center of the room. The church leadership starts, followed by men, women and children, and, lastly, distinguished guests. Each contributor dances around the plate, flinging money in the air as two church members hurriedly collect and count the contributions. It's the most joyful form of tithing I've ever seen. But I don't just sit and watch. No, no, that wouldn't be very fun — for me or the others. Instead, the attendees wait with bated breath for my turn to contribute. The giving cannot end until I come forward to toss money and wildly gyrate my body for their amusement, causing the parishioners to hoot and applaud. I am divine entertainment!

Following my performance, the choir saunters back to its benches, and the congregation sings a slow, minor-keyed closing prayer. The church elders depart, using a special door to recognize their elevated status, while the remaining faithful gather their belongings and move toward the public exits, doorless portals to the awaiting overcast day. Outside, beside rows of bicycles, I mingle with Mr. Zimbota and other men, exchanging greetings and receiving countless handshakes of gratitude for honoring them with my presence and imparting my "interesting" dancing moves. Mr. Namanya, an assistant pastor and the Deputy Headmaster at Khwalala C.D.S.S., greets me warmly, joking:

"Mr. Michael, I saw you come late. You don't arrive late to school! You have problem with church?"

"No problem," I reply, "I just don't need as much time with God as you do."

"That's very funny," he chuckles, flashing a boyish smile that belies his true age.

"Well, I must be going," I say, hungry for lunch, "I'll see you tomorrow at school."

"Nice afternoon," he smiles.

In the staff room the following day, I find Mr. Namanya in a familiar position, intently listening to his transistor radio and glancing over a one-week-old newspaper. He's our news junkie, always eager to give me a rundown of the top stories. "The radio man says that Americans are addicted to oil, and another suicide bomber killed herself on the streets of Baghdad," he reports, "Oh, and Western powers condemned the violence in Zimbabwe." Turning to the newspaper, thumbing to the front page, he reads an account of a local witch who purportedly flew to South Africa aboard a winnowing basket. I laugh aloud at the article, but the Deputy shakes his head, utterly convinced.

"Don't be silly," I shout incredulously, "That's ridiculous."

"It happens," he argues, seriousness filling his face.

"What happens?" I inquire.

"Witchcraft! It makes people fly and do other things."

"What other things?"

"People have gone to sleep in their homes," he says with a twinge of hurt, "and woken up in fields with their beds and blankets."

"Sounds like a practical joke or some sort of sleep walking condition."

"Sleep walking?" he asks, "No, no. I've seen it with my own eyes. They were bewitched."

Ah, Mr. Namanya — a human menagerie of complexity and conviction — educator, Christian pastor, news junkie and, last but not least, devout Animist. I don't get it, I don't believe it, but I cannot prove him wrong or completely dismiss his beliefs, no matter how inconsistent they may seem. It's his reality.

* * * *

Back at my house, the church absconders are still enthralled. After hearing about Nikki and Mr. Namanya, people they know and love, they are afraid to leave the circle for even a bathroom break or bite of food, certain that they will miss something riveting and memorable. Playing hooky and listening to stories about the collision of witches and Westerners in the wilds of Africa is ten times better than enduring a marathon liturgy.

Case in point: Mr. Zimbota's wife and children limp back from church looking weary and spent. They say hello before proceeding to the kitchen to make lunch for us, a reminder that lazy days such as these are luxuries enjoyed only by men and boys. For the women and girls of Malawi, there is no such thing as a day off. Eric and I offer to help them cook, but Mrs. Zimbota tells us to rest and continue our conversation.

"That is funny story about Nikki!" Alfred chuckles.

"Yeah," Eric says, "I'm impressed that she had the guts to use a witchdoctor."

"Many Malawians do it," Mr. Zimbota says, "Witchdoctors are busy people."

"Similar to Western religions," I add, "witchcraft and witchdoctors are just another way of explaining reality and enforcing societal rules."

"What rules?" Eric asks, "I know that villagers use witchcraft to punish wrongdoers, but give me some examples of how they do it."

"Well," Mr. Zimbota answers, "Witchcraft is used when people become too wealthy or proud."

"You mean when people are jealous of each other?" Eric inquires.

"Yes, but in Malawi, we call it envy."

Reinforced by animism, envy is a stalwart of Malawian culture. National anthems speak volumes about countries because, in theory, they were written by the people, for the people and about the people. Tellingly, the Malawian anthem, which students sing at every assembly, goes: "keep out each and every enemy — hunger, disease, envy." Labeling envy an enemy is a tacit acknowledgement of its importance. It causes average Malawians to be highly suspicious of each other and, true to their animist beliefs, to attribute their misfortunes, and the successes of others, to the dark art of witchcraft.

Yet, at its core, envy is a well-intentioned safeguard. It is woven into the fabric of Malawian society as an inertia encouraging everyone to succeed or fail as a collective, guided by the invisible, iron hand of "cultural socialism." Any perceived differentiation, whether in terms of wealth or opportunity, is carefully scrutinized in order to guarantee the survival of the greatest number of people for the longest period of time. Consequently, Malawians share almost everything (e.g., money, childcare, farming implements), trying to ensure that everyone operates at the same socioeconomic level — a low but survivable one. This is an expectation, a non-negotiable directive.

To enforce this edict of egalitarianism, individuality is suppressed. Those seeking to get ahead or stand out are ridiculed as selfish miscreants and become targets of thefts and other crimes. Potential victims build walls around their homes and hire guards, but these barriers are no match for passive aggressive spiritual warfare. For example, a local headmaster living high on the hog (probably because he embezzled student tuition payments) nearly drove himself crazy over the course of several sleepless nights worrying that jealous colleagues had bombarded him with harmful spells. It was probably just his conscience getting to him.

Still, crafty villagers employ strategies to amass a bit of wealth without drawing the ire of their neighbors. Instead of leaving cash lying around to share, they buy bricks or other construction materials to build homes, interminable and socially acceptable projects that divert household money away from other uses (Africa is littered with unfinished houses). Likewise, women buy and sell goods at local markets, often at little or no profit, to keep money occupied. Liquidity is dangerous — currency can be drunk by your husband or shared with your sister. But it's socially acceptable to deny another's request for money when your wallet is empty. So, everyone has an empty wallet.

Within this environment, it isn't surprising when Western-style development efforts land with a big thud. Dead on arrival, many of them are based on notions of *laissez faire* capitalism — free markets, self-interested decision making, accumulation of capital, and socioeconomic stratification. Malawian villagers might be given a small business loan and told, "This is enough money for three goats. Use profits from the goat milk to pay back the loan and buy more goats. Before long, you will be a goat magnate." If Adam Smith were alive, he would be proud.

A year later, when the goats are dead, a shocked aid worker investigating the failure might hear the following explanation: "I tried to charge everyone for the milk, but my friends and family members wanted it for free. I also used some profits to buy clothing and pay school fees for my niece. My father took the rest to pay for a burial stone. The goats were healthy for six months, but then they started foaming at the mouth and died. I think that someone cast a spell on them."

The Malawian "all-boats-sink-together" mentality is a far cry from the Western paradigm of individual persistence, accountability, achievement and personal betterment. Americans, for example, desperately cling to the notion, however mythologized, that success is earned, not bestowed. The Star Spangled Banner (America's national anthem) honors perseverance, hope and ambition. We envy others with awe, not just disdain, and strive to emulate those who seem to have more or do better, believing that they are somehow deserving of good fortune. As Abraham Lincoln said, "Things may come to those who wait, but only the things left by those who hustle." Malawians tend to wait; Americans tend to hustle.

Hence, in Africa, Western-style hustlers (often outsiders) reap the lion's share of business spoils. Most of the powerful businesses in Malawi are owned and operated by Indian immigrants, and China recently inked a nine-billion dollar deal with Congo to build infrastructure in exchange for mineral extraction rights. Still, in the wake of colonialism, for-profit firms and foreign governments aren't surprised when their investment plans encounter obstacles. First and foremost, African governments (local, regional and national) want to enrich themselves and their people, not foreign investors. It's a classic showdown of two competing philosophies — African envy versus Western greed, but under these circumstances, Africans have the home field advantage.

Back at my house, on that lazy Sunday, Mr. Zimbota gets bitten by the Western business bug. Before a delicious lunch of *nsima* and beans, artfully prepared by his gracious wife and children, he pulls me aside, volunteering himself as an agent of change.

"I want to be entrepreneur," he reveals.

"How?" I ask.

"By buying and selling clothes. I can buy them in the north, near Tanzania, and sell them around here."

"That's sounds like a promising idea," I say, "Can you make money doing that?"

"Yes, it is very profitable! I did it many years ago and made much money."

"What do you need to start?"

"I need loan of twenty-thousand Malawian Kwacha. Can you help me?"

"Hmm, that's over one-hundred dollars," I reply, "That's a lot of money."

"Yes, but I will pay you back."

"Well, first, I have an important question," I stutter, a bit taken aback by his request, torn between helping a friend and investing the money in more socially beneficial ways.

"Ask me anything," he says.

"What happened to your old business?"

"I ran out of money," he admits, "because I needed to pay for my son's funeral."

"I'm very sorry about that," I say, feeling guilty for asking.

"Do you have more questions?" he inquires.

"Probably, but not now. I'll consider your request and get back to you."

Unfortunately for Mr. Zimbota, I know too much. I know that other teachers would jealously resent my investment in his business. I know that the business would distract Mr. Zimbota from his school responsibilities. I know that another unexpected expense might arise, forcing Mr. Zimbota to plunder his business capital once again. I know that in Malawi, money is often borrowed without a sincere commitment of repayment. I also know about accusations from the Ministry of Education that Mr. Zimbota misappropriates money, especially school funds. I know he would never intentionally "steal" school money, but borrowing a little here and there without repaying has the same effect.

I want to help Mr. Zimbota, but there are better ways to invest the cash if my goal is to reach as many people as possible. For example, I have already spoken with Mr. Kachingwe, an exceptional teaching colleague, about turning our school into a hands-on entrepreneurial laboratory. Business Studies is a required subject, but it is taught theoretically. Telling is knowing, and seeing is believing, but doing is understanding. With the cooperation of the community, students could start or expand businesses, which would provide hands-on training and inject cash into the school.

"I'm currently doing that," Mr. Kachingwe explained when I floated the idea.

"In what way?" I asked.

"It's very small, but Form 2 students buy notebooks and pens in town and sell them in village."

"What does that teach them?"

"They learn many things," he responded, "like how to set good price, keep inventories and calculate profits."

"If you had more money, would you expand the program?"

"Yes!" he shouted with glee, "We can involve more students and sell more things."

"And, if we build a girls' boarding facility, maybe you can help the residents start a business of their own?"

"Excellent idea!"

I stand confused and paralyzed. Why is helping so hard? Do I fund Mr. Zimbota, the school, neither or both? It's a tricky tight-rope walking act. I just want to throw all of the money aside as a poisonous distraction, and continue building personal relationships.

After lunch, I pull Mr. Zimbota aside.

"Have you considered starting a business to help the school?" I ask him.

"What kind?" he asks.

"Well, one that employs students and returns profits to the school, so that everyone benefits."

"No," he says abruptly, "I want my own business."

I was afraid of that answer.

"I'm sorry, sir," I sigh, "I want to invest in projects that help the broader community."

"Yes," he nods, "I understand."

"So, I cannot help you now," I continue, trying not to register the look of disappointment on his face.

"Very well," he says, pretending to understand.

"Thank you very much for lunch. Are you ready for more chatting?" I say with tempered optimism, trying to diffuse tension and soothe any hurt feelings.

"Yes, that would be nice," he replies coldly.

We exchange parting smiles, but something in our relationship has clearly changed, and it doesn't feel right. It's hard to juggle the roles of money man and friend, white man and native African, investor and entrepreneur, teacher and headmaster, mentee and mentor, visitor and host. Both of us are vulnerable, and both of us have been hurt. In a monetary sense, I have the most to give, and I failed to give it. Yet, in an emotional sense, I have the most to lose, and I know it. Mr. Zimbota's friendship means everything to me, and I fear that going forward, it will never recover from this unfortunate episode. Perhaps there is hope for reconciliation, but only if "God will allow."

****

The roundtable discussion reconvenes after lunch. Eric is full and drowsy, slipping in and out of consciousness. Mr. Zimbota seems apathetic, perhaps stung by my betrayal. The Boys, however, are raring to continue our metaphysical conversation, eager to discover what adults from different cultures and places have to say about religion. As usual, they inject pure adolescent energy into everything around them, recharging the three older participants for a final round of dialogue. Myson, in particular, has something on his mind.

"Mr. Buckler," he says.

"Yes, Myson?"

"We talk about Animism and Christianity," he explains, "but there is something else."

"What?" I wonder.

"Sir," he continues, "I am Christian, like my father. But most of my family is Muslim. They pray many times each day and wear white hats. My uncle has travelled to Mecca."

"Yeah, he's right," Eric interjects, "how did we forget Islam?"

"We should discuss more about Islam, sir," Myson suggests.

"Very good idea," I say, "I've learned a lot about Islam in Africa."

In Malawi, I come face-to-face with Islam for the first time. Although most of my students are Christian like me, mirroring the country at large, several are Muslim, leaving early every Friday to attend religious services. Mosques are plentiful, especially in the cities, where Muslim-owned businesses dominate the economies. In rural areas, geographic pockets are decidedly Muslim, especially along Lake Malawi, and the first elected President of Malawi (serving from 1994-2004) is a Muslim from the *Yao* tribe. Islam might not be an overwhelming presence, but it is a distinctly powerful one.

Although foreign at first to a white Christian from Southern Maryland, Muslim areas are orderly and calm in a reassuring way. Drinking holes are hard to find, but restaurants serving delicious *Halal* food are omnipresent, and streets are clean and safe. Most men wear one-piece, body-length white robes and embroidered cylindrical hats (*kufi*). Women cover their bodies in dark fabric, donning headscarves and, sometimes, cloaking themselves in *burkas*. Everyone participates in the faith, from beggars giving passersby the opportunity to fulfill their Muslim obligations of charity to olive-skinned businessmen, bargaining hard but with tenacious virtue, as would please Allah.

Five times per day life temporarily halts. Like clockwork, *muezzins* (leaders chosen for their good character and voice skills) face Mecca, arouse the loud-speakers of mosques and broadcast the call to prayer (*adhan*), a melodious com-bination of guttural chanting and moaning. Stores close, conversations are placed on hold and thousands of Malawians drop to their knees and lower their heads to the floor in submission. The experience is moving, a palliative public service reminder of the invisible hands of God at work in Christian, Muslim, and Jew, alike. Indeed, watching the silent surrender of a setting sun to a call to prayer is one of life's greatest joys.

Speaking of *muezzins*, I once stayed with one in Zomba. The uncle of Myson, he summoned me like a family member pursuing a lost relative, eager to thank me in person for helping his nephew. I surprised and delighted him by coming — a white man lowering myself (in his view) to a Malawian's level. As a distinguished guest, I was shown royal treatment — the best food and accommodations (includ-ing the uncle's room and bed). Between meals served by his young, devoutly Mus-lim wives, we sat together in the living room sharing our respective traditions and watching religious programming on satellite television, reveling in commonality. As we exchanged goodbyes the following morning, the uncle surprised me with a beautiful white *kufie*, which I treasure to this day.

Yet, such fellowship is rare. Even though Malawi is celebrated as a place where various religious and racial groups coexist harmoniously, the animosity between Christianity and Islam lurks just beneath the surface, threatening to erupt. During my first year in Khwalala Village, a prominent Muslim cleric in Blantyre accused Peace Corps Volunteers of acting as agents of the CIA, provoking an immedi-ate denial from Peace Corps and placing staff on high alert. Thankfully, nothing came of it. On another occasion, Taliban were reportedly seen coming and going at Malawian airports, spreading anti-Western propaganda and tapping into the vast reserves of Muslim wealth in East Africa.

All told, however, civility prevails, a harbinger of hope for the future. Among Muslims, I am generally shown respect and kindness, and treated fairly in busi-ness dealings. For every bad seed who accuses me of working for the CIA, there are ten strangers who stop to offer me directions or tell me to have a nice day. My overall impression, based on my intimate encounter with Islam and its followers, is that, removed from the vitriol of politics and propaganda, most people want the same basic things in life (e.g., food, shelter, health, family) and make wonderful business partners, friends and neighbors.

* * * *

Back at the roundtable discussion at my house, the conversation starts to wane as afternoon clouds float by. But no one wants to leave without a proper conclu-sion of one sort or another, preferably a take-away lesson. Eric gets the ball rolling.

"Why can't we all just get along?" he asks rhetorically, "I don't understand the animosity."

"I don't either," I agree, "We're all so similar, but some people seem determined to accentuate our minor differences and overlook our wealth of shared human experiences."

"We are all God's children," Mr. Zimbota says, "We are one in eyes of God."

"Agreed," we all nod, satisfied that we have reached our stopping point.

"Well," Eric interjects, "In the eyes of God, I'm one tired puppy. I need to ride home. Thanks for a wonderful and insightful day."

With that parting comment, he bids farewell and rides west, into the setting sun. The rest of us return home to relax before dinner. In the distance, a *muezzin* climbs to the top of a minaret and begins bellowing. Seizing the moment, I drop to the floor with my compass, point my body north (towards Mecca), and utter a quiet prayer. Someday maybe the angry cleric in Blantyre will realize that I'm not a spy. Maybe Mr. Zimbota will accept that I meant well when I didn't lend him the money. Maybe a god, or the God, will send me a sign of her presence and concern, a precious reminder that although life can be mysterious and painful from our perspective, it is the loving handiwork of a higher power.

* * * *

A few weeks later, Mr. Zimbota finds me working in the staffroom at school. We haven't spoken since I denied his request for money, pushing him away and creating an eerie void of adult camaraderie in my life. Since then, I've been doing a lot of thinking about my decision. It wasn't a coldly rational aid-project determination without personal consequences, but a slap in the face for a man who stood beside me as a close friend and mentor, through thick and thin. It was a choice that changed our relationship, and left us both with bitter-tasting mouths. Hopefully, the time has come for us to start anew.

"How are you?" he asks.

"I'm fine," I reply.

"How is my friend, Eric?" he inquires.

"I'm pretty sure that Eric is fine as well. He's away at the moment, off visiting his girlfriend in the north."

A sudden gust of air interrupts our conversation. With a violent punch, it rattles the corrugated steel roofing, slams unlatched windows, and sends papers flying every which way. Once it passes, Mr. Zimbota and I work alone in the dingy, cramped room, picking up the pieces, distracted from the awkwardness by the immediate task at hand. When we're done, Mr. Zimbota slides into a chair behind his desk and crosses his hands across his lap. I organize the retrieved papers and return them to their proper homes, one of five teacher desks lining the white-washed walls. Not sure what to expect, I return to my seat, preparing to grade a mountain of exercise books, but hoping for more.

"Remember what we discussed when Eric was here?" Mr. Zimbota inquires suddenly, after a brief silence.

"Hmm, you mean about religion," I wince, straining for recall.

He nods.

"What's on your mind?" I ask.

"I want to hear more about what you believe," Mr. Zimbota says.

"Well, I believe that our world was created by a just and loving God that has an important plan for each of us, and that serving as an instrument of God's will is the highest of callings."

"What are details of God's plan?"

"Good question," I reply, "I run into trouble when I fret over details. Sometimes I just need to turn off my brain."

"Turn off your brain?" he says, lost in the English euphemism.

"I mean that I cannot possibly grasp all of the information required to understand God or the human experience."

"So, your faith is about not knowing anything?" he asks.

"No, I'm just satisfied with believing the basics and not knowing all the details. I leave them up to God and trust that she puts all the truth I need right in front of me. People with all the so-called answers scare me."

"I'm confused," he admits, "Without details, how do you serve God?"

"You meditate and listen," I reply, "because God often speaks softly."

"Where do you hear God?"

"It's very personal. Some people go to church, but I find God in all places, in all things, especially the natural world and personal relationships like ours."

Mr. Zimbota looks a bit stumped. He needs time to digest my answers. While he's thinking, I turn the tables and ask him some questions.

"So, that's my perspective on God," I say.

"Thanks for telling me how you really feel," he says.

"No problem. But how do you really feel about God?"

The question makes Mr. Zimbota uncomfortable. He looks down and rubs the back of his smooth, razor-shaven head.

"Sometimes I don't understand God," he explains, "It all started when my only boy passed."

"How did it happen?" I ask.

"One day, he was healthy baby. Next day, he was very sick."

"Did you take him to the hospital?"

"Yes, of course," he says, "but the doctor made mistake and didn't give him medicine for malaria. He died next day."

I'm stunned and shaken. Should I hug him? How do I express my support and condolences?

"I'm very sorry for your loss," I say gently, "It must have been difficult."

"Yes, it was. But now my son is with God."

"Were you angry at God when he took your son?" I ask.

"No, no," he replies, "God knows best, and African proverb says 'When you throw stone at God, it lands right on top of your head.'"

"But God confuses you?"

"Yes," he admits, "I am wanting to know how God allows innocent children to die."

"Good question," I reply, "I often wonder whether God exists in places with HIV pandemics, high infant mortality and unspeakable tragedies of human suffering. I think we all do."

"So, you don't have answer," he says dejectedly.

"Well, instead of focusing on God, I think the better question is, how do we as people allow that to happen?"

"Huh?" he squints.

"I believe that humans have free will."

"Yes" he nods, suggesting that he gets the gist of the concept.

"God wants us to be happy, healthy and fulfilled," I continue, "but when we use our free will to do bad things, God stops herself from sending help."

"Why?"

"Because doing so would cheapen her most precious gift. Free will is not free. It doesn't relieve us of responsibility for ourselves."

"Why don't people use free will in good ways?" he asks.

"Many do," I answer, "but some let fear drive their actions, instead of realizing that loving others, and helping them, is the pinnacle of human greatness."

"Like the Golden Rule, as you call it," he adds, as a wave of peace washes over his face.

"Do unto others as you would have others do unto you," I recite.

"That is why you come to Malawi, to help others, to practice Golden Rule?"

"Yes," I say, "I think so."

XI

TRUTH & RECONCILIATION

The guests at the lodge are a microcosm of white Africa. An ornery, middle-aged woman, who migrated from Australia eons ago, berates me between cigarette puffs. My crime, it seems, is not recognizing the name of her elitist neighborhood in Blantyre, Malawi's largest and wealthiest city. "Oh, you've only been here a year," she laments, as if she were an authority on all things Malawian. I respond defensively in Chichewa, confusing her with words she was too proud to learn in her youth and is too old to learn now. She turns away in frustration, as I breathe a sigh of relief.

— Letter Home, June 2008

White people come to Africa for all sorts of reasons. As a British protectorate from 1892 to 1964, Malawi saw its fair share of white government officials on assignment from the Crown. After independence, bureaucrats left, but British tea and tobacco companies, and their white managers, remained behind. During the last half century, enterprising white farmers have settled throughout Southeastern Africa trying to make a go of it on the land, and many of their descendants have stayed, raising African families of their own. In recent years, the aid community has introduced scores of short-term white residents, trying to farm not the land, but the people, into prosperity.

Yet, very few white residents live in a village. Instead, whites keep to themselves in the cities, enjoying martinis at the country club, imported ham at the dinner table, and vacations at cushy lodges. These comforts provide them — as foreigners in a foreign land — with a reassuring reminder of home, but their aloofness comes with a price: fanciful tales about them, fanned by speculation and misinformation, run wild in the villages. The one about white people being vampires bent on eating African children almost got one man killed on Mulanje Mountain.

"I was hiking down the Mountain at dusk, around the time vampires are supposed to feed," he explained when I met him at a traveler's lodge.

"What happened?" I asked.

"Several people rushed toward me with machetes and knives, intending to do me in!"

"How did you survive?"

"Lucky for me," he replied, "my Malawian guide set them straight and let them touch my skin and hair to see for themselves that I wasn't a blood sucker."

Thankfully, nothing like that has happened to me.

Still, people in Khwalala Village make me feel like a freak. Greeting me with whistles, shouts, stares and hisses, they believe that *azungu* ("white people" in *Chichewa*) are healthier, smarter, wealthier, and generally better — the standard bearers of humanity. I wish that I had a dime for every time I heard a teaching colleague say, "You know, we Africans are not as [insert positive attribute] as you *azungu*." And students are no better at overcoming the inferiority complex. Eschewing established mathematical principles, they fabricate new and creative (but ridiculous) solutions to algebra problems, believing that conventional mathematics is above them, a discipline reserved exclusively for whites.

Few seem to appreciate that confidence, practice and perseverance, not race, make perfect. So, I tell them a joke to make math more fun and understandable.

"An infinite number of mathematicians walk into a bar," I begin.

"Are they white or black?" Myson asks.

"It doesn't matter," I reply, "Let's just say they're white and black."

"What do you mean?" a girl asks.

"Good point," I acknowledge, "that was confusing. To clarify, some are white, some are black and some are both because they come from interracial parents. Is everyone satisfied with that?"

"There are black mathematicians?" Alfred asks.

"Black and white people make children together?" another boy inquires.

"Ok, ok," I sigh, "I think we're getting distracted here — back to my joke."

"Yes, sir," they nod.

"So, there are an infinite number of white and black mathematicians," I continue, "and they walk into a bar. The first orders a cup of beer. The second orders half a cup. The third orders a quarter of a cup. What's happening here?"

Gift raises his hand. He is the best student in the class, and a glimmer of hope for desperate teachers like me.

"They are trying to save money," he says, "Beer is expensive."

"Perhaps," I reply, "that's a very creative interpretation, Gift, but at the end of the night, how many total cups of beer will the bartender pour for the mathematicians?"

I wave my arms wildly in the air, like sorcerer trying to conjure the answer from their brains: Abbra Kadabbra, make these children produce the right number! My antics (probably an unnecessary distraction) are met with uniform stares of confusion.

"Well," I sigh, "Does anyone know the answer?"

"No," Gift shakes his head.

"Before the next mathematician can order," I deliver the punch line, "the bartender says, 'You guys are clever,' and pours two beers."

I laugh aloud at my dorky joke. Needless to say, I'm the only one laughing.

"How do infinite number of people drink beer from two cups?" Gift inquires.

"They share cups just like we share plates," Myson adds, "They are African mathematicians. That's why Mr. Buckler is laughing — it's funny because there is no such thing as African mathematician."

"No, no, that's not the joke," I say, desperate to move on and tie the lesson into a neat, little knot of educational clarity, "I have a final question to test your understanding, and the student who provides the correct answer will win a prize."

"Yeah," Alfred shouts, "prize, prize!"

"If the bartender had allowed all of the mathematicians to order, how many total cups of beer would they have purchased?"

"Oh," Gift says, raising his hand high in the air, tugging at my heart strings.

"Good, Gift," I say, "go ahead and answer."

"Wait, wait, sorry," he apologizes, "I am forgetting answer."

"Come on!" I yell, "I already gave you the answer."

Dead silence. One one-thousand, two one-thousand…thirty one-thousand, I continue counting, waiting for an answer or a school bell or anything to break the monotony. Finally, the bell rings, emptying the classroom. I stay behind, defeated and incredulous, acknowledging that students definitely don't understand geometric series and continue to believe (perhaps more than ever) that white people are superior mathematicians. Yet, in a roundabout way, I may have made some progress by demonstrating, in no uncertain terms, that white people aren't very good at teaching or telling jokes.

* * * *

On second thought, I probably haven't altered the status quo much. As anthropologists will tell you, getting upset was exactly what the students expected me to do.

"Yeah, bro, it's really interesting to study the dynamics of white-black relations in Malawi," exclaims Justin, a white South African teaching at a Malawian university.

"How so?" I wonder.

"Well," he explains, "Malawians associate white people not with the color white, but with red."

"Why?" I ask.

"Because white is a symbol of purity and godliness, which white people are not. Red, on the other hand, is the color of anger and aggression, which is how Malawians see white people."

"That kind of makes sense," I say.

"How many times have you seen a white person have a temper tantrum here?"

"Too many to count," I admit, "And the sad reality is that sometimes I've been that angry white person."

"Me, too," he sighs.

Whites aren't alone in this regard. Many business enterprises in Malawi are owned by families originating from the Indian peninsula. And, in recent years, the Chinese have become a noticeable presence, starting businesses in Africa to feed their burgeoning economy and unprecedented development ambitions. They, too, lack patience with the "Malawian way of doing things."

Within this racial stew, stereotyping is prolific. To Malawians, British are arrogant, Indians are cruel, and Chinese are opportunistic. Each of these groups has been perceived (at various times and to varying degrees) as an imperial presence. Americans, surprisingly, are feared as pugilistic, but also revered as approachable conversationalists and generous providers of international aid. Malawians strike most foreigners as not only gentle and friendly, but corrupt, prone to begging and theft, and lacking in ambition.

Of course, none of the dueling racial profiles holds much water. And ironically, upon closer inspection, they share a lot in common, having originated from the same human propensities — a need to define oneself through an immediate community and an unwillingness to mingle with unfamiliar brethren. Yet, when I override my brain circuitry, and make the effort to engage Malawians in their environments, their behaviors start to make plenty of sense. Understanding, in short, is the greatest debunker of racial myths.

For example, by Western standards, Malawians do move slowly. To the casual observer, this behavior, annoying and inconvenient as it seems at times, might be mistaken for laziness or apathy. But a well-informed Westerner would know that Malawians are always moving — cooking, farming, walking, cycling, childrearing, cleaning, carrying water — within a physically draining tropical environment where every drop of energy counts. Hence, Malawians use energy like a candle — gradual and steady, a little bit at a time, hoping that they won't burn out before the end of the day. They might be slow, but the corresponding stereotype is preposterous — there's nothing lazy about them.

There's also nothing particularly esoteric about me. Yet, as the first white friend of many villagers in Khwalala, I spend inordinate amounts of time trying to dispel myths and educate about my cultural perspective. Through daily contact and reinforcement, teachers and students at my school accept me as a unique species of human who values independence and doesn't like starting meetings late or being followed around the market by beggars and children. From first-hand experience, they confirm that I don't eat their babies, suck their blood, or collapse from exhaustion when I perform manual labor.

* * * *

Promoting understanding is an uphill battle, but first and foremost, it's an internal one. So, on particularly hard days, I retreat to Sanjika Rock, an oasis in the trees with a beautiful view of Chiradzulu Mountain. It's isolated in a peaceful way but, in the greatest of ironies, it's also a place that I visit to escape a profound sense of alienation. Though adults below me go about their daily lives, and children play in the surrounding fields, I don't feel their company. I'm just alone, like the last Dodo bird, longing for anyone who looks or acts like me — anything culturally consonant to take away my otherness.

My only friend on the Rock is a Malawian ghost — the spirit of John Chilembwe. It doesn't say anything, but I know its story: raised in a nearby village, Chilembwe was discovered by an American missionary and sent to a Baptist college in America, where he earned a divinity degree. Upon Malawian repatriation, he founded a self-sufficient, African-owned and operated mission that assisted thousands of local people with food, schools and churches. In the early 1900s, when Chilembwe was one of the most respected people in Malawi, he used to mediate right here on Sanjika Rock.

Unfortunately, Chilembwe's thriving mission threatened the local British governor. A corrupt, white despot with a scathing reputation, his cruel treatment of subjects, and distaste for African sovereignty, created racial tension that sparked a violent uprising. Vastly outmatched, Chilembwe and his supporters were defeated, and Chilembwe was killed, but not before taking the ultimate prize — the governor's head! Malawian currency bears Chilembwe's image, paying homage to his martyrdom, and every year the President of Malawi visits the remnants of Chilembwe's mission to pay respect.

With Chilembwe in mind, I arrived in Malawi expecting to find a country seething in racial tension. After all, white people had killed Malawi's favorite son, and his execution was a hate crime no less, comparable to the assassination of Martin Luther King. Add to that decades of white colonialism, and surely there was residual bitterness, some "screw you white man" mojo. At first, I found just the opposite — pervasive Caucasian hero worship. But, suddenly, during my second year, the mojo reared its ugly head in the form of a racially motivated assault that will stay with me forever.

It begins when I decide to escape Khwalala for a few days. Awaiting me in Blantyre are friends, cold beers and warm showers. All I have to do is get there, a multi-leg journey of uphill cycling and minibus rides. The cycling I like; the bus rides I hate. Minibuses (minivans in American parlance) are dilapidated, crowded, unreliable, dangerous and often operated by hopelessly stoned and drunk miscreants. They leave when they fill, and not a second earlier, and you hold your seat by sitting and waiting. What's not to like?

After an uneventful bike ride, I reach the minibus stage and find a vehicle raring to go. Despite the cramped conditions, female passengers kindly move their luggage, exposing a sliver of floor space for me near the front. There I stand for most of the journey, slouching over the other passengers like an old man, absorbing the jolts and bumps of the rocky, rutted road with slightly bent, and increasingly sore, knees. After several kilometers of discomfort, a woman exits the bus, forfeiting a dilapidated folding seat that looks heavenly but immediately buckles under my weight. I was better off standing.

About two miles from Blantyre, the minibus runs out of fuel, which is a common occurrence. The driver parks the bus along a busy road with no discernable shoulder and leaves to find gasoline, expecting me and the other passengers to await his return. At the half-hour mark of waiting, my patience runs out, and I decide to try hitch hiking the rest of the way into town. But this upsets the stoned minibus money collector, who has stayed behind to guard the vehicle and corral the passengers. As I walk away, he follows me down the road, demanding his money. I turn and tell him that I will pay him if I get a hitch, but not before. He doesn't understand, and repeatedly slaps my hand for cash.

As I weigh my options of paying or staying, there is no shortage of advice. Bored out of their minds, people on the bus yell at me not to pay. They already argued with the money collector over his exorbitant rates earlier in the journey, and due to the delay, they are now doubly irritated with him. A smartly dressed passerby, however, sees things differently. She tries to assist by ordering me in broken English to hand over the money. I tell her politely in *Chichewa* that I don't need her help, but she stomps away, insulted. The money collector slaps my hand again, getting in my face with his stale alcohol breath.

The situation worsens when a passing horde of primary school students gets involved. They know three things about what they are seeing and hearing — I am white, the conductor is Malawian, and he wants me to pay money. Sensing a grave injustice, they surround me and scream at the top of their lungs for me to pay, hurling racial taunts and insults, and shooing away cars trying to come to my rescue with a ride into town. Though threatened and intimidated by their mob tactics, I hold my tongue, feeling disappointment more than anger, resignation more than confrontation.

Hoping to resolve the impasse tactfully, I try to engage them in dialogue. In perfect *Chichewa*, I explain that I mean no harm and intend to pay, certain that my deft diplomacy will carry the day. Yet, my words land flat as bricks, failing to reach their deaf ears or penetrate their stony visages. I am a crooked white person trying to cheat one of their own, an unwelcome pest in their country, plain and simple. Realizing that my options are limited, and fearing a physical confrontation, I pay the conductor the full fare and start walking down the road, swallowing a huge pill of humility and hiding beneath the rim of my baseball cap. It is an embarrassing learning experience.

After surviving the mob and reaching town safely, I pause to reflect on what happened. My sense is that my unfortunate brush with intolerance is a sign that there are fences to mend, both in my relationships with Malawians and in the broader context of race relations in Malawi. So, I seek out opportunities to redeem myself and my *azungu* brethren, hoping that someday, after enough toil and heartache, we will cut away the shackles of racial prejudice and injustice and truly realize Martin Luther King's dream.

"I don't want that to happen again," I tell Mr. Zimbota after returning to Khwalala, "People need to work together and overcome their differences."

"Don't worry," he assures me, "Those children were being very disrespectful. It wasn't your fault."

"You're right," I continue, "but it happened for a reason. There is a lack of trust and understanding between your people and mine. We need to change that."

A few days later an opportunity arrives in the unlikeliest of forms — a wedding invitation.

* * * *

Nothing stirs villages quite like weddings. They are massive, expensive undertakings involving hundreds of guests and tons of food. People arrive from near and far to pay their respects, contributing what few resources they have to assist the host family. As an honored member of my community, I receive countless wedding invitations, and accepting them is a privilege and a valuable opportunity to prove that just as stereotypes are bred by separateness, they are shattered by engagement.

On this particular occasion, the invitation arrives through Mr. Zimbota. His older brother is a well-respected man who became modestly wealthy (by Malawian standards) as the manager of several corn-grinding mills. I met the brother several months back at a funeral, and we took a liking to each another. Ever since, he has been lobbying me to visit his home, and now he has upped the ante by requesting that I attend the upcoming wedding of his youngest child, a son no less. It is the perfect excuse to go.

There is just one catch. Knowing that I enjoy photography and own a nice digital camera, he wants me to take pictures: a guest for hire, a worker for free. Utilizing me in this way is unfathomable to most Malawians, who want to pamper and spoil me like a visiting king, expecting me to remain sedentary — sitting in the finest chair and eating the best cuts of meat — it is their culture. But my Malawian friends know how I operate, that I cannot sit still for long and like staying busy. The smart ones put me to work.

The site of the wedding is a small village in the District of Thyolo, an agricultural Shangri-La. Blessed with rich, dark soil and year-round rain, it was commandeered by the British during Malawi's colonial era. The colonialists kicked established families off the best land and, by planting green, undulating carpets of knee-high plants, remade its rolling hills into some of the best tea plantations in Southern Africa. To this day, these enterprises provide jobs and stability to thousands of Malawians, although many workers (especially tea pickers) are woefully underpaid for their backbreaking labor.

Donning corduroys and my finest collared shirt, I am still underdressed for the wedding. After arriving at a modest compound of homes deep within a tea estate, and being introduced around, I'm fed in a private room, away from unwanted attention. Swollen with food, I excuse myself and start walking to the celebration venue, the auditorium of a local mission school operated by the Seventh-Day Adventist Church. Yet, I don't get far before my gracious hosts insist that I accompany the father of the groom to the wedding in a private automobile. I try to resist, citing my love of walking, but my efforts are futile.

At the auditorium, my status switches in a flash. There, amid organizers frantically putting the final touches on streamers and balloons, I go to work taking pictures. The large hall is full of plastic chairs, arranged in two large sections divided by a wide center aisle. Snap. On the stage at the head of the room sit chairs for the wedding party and a table displaying a modest, three-tier wedding cake. Snap, snap. Just off stage, occupying an entire corner of the room, is a disk jockey manning a large sound system.

When the auditorium is ready, we fetch the guests of honor. A motorcade, led by a second-hand Mercedes Benz, drives down a tree-lined road to a nearby manor house. Out strolls the lucky couple, their wedding party and little ring bearers, all dressed to the hilt in rented suits and dresses. Once they are loaded, the motorcade departs, and I am in the lead, bouncing in the open bed of a pickup truck, struggling to take crisp pictures. We drive around the mission grounds honking, as the bride and groom stand through the Benz's sunroof and wave to spectators, like celebrities in the Macy's Thanksgiving Day Parade.

Rounding the last road bend, we hear crowds of people screaming. Mad for our arrival, they rush the cars, momentarily trapping the wedding party and delaying its grand entrance. Snap. After the bride and groom are delicately extricated, a torrent of guests floods the auditorium, as uninvited onlookers crowd around exterior windows for a good view of the action. From double doors at the rear of the auditorium, the wedding party enters and promenades two-by-two down the center aisle toward the stage, dancing to festive, reggae-inspired Malawian music as onlookers throw money. Snap, snap.

Before long, I realize that by Western standards, I'm not attending a wedding or a reception, but an elaborate fund raiser. There isn't a clergyman or organist, or any alcohol or finger food — just music, dancing and lots of moolah. The couple, it seems, has exchanged vows that morning, probably at a quaint, religious ceremony attended by loved ones. The groom's family must have paid a mint for the entire occasion, and this post-nuptial party is a clever way of defraying the expenses. Ingenious. Snap.

After taking their seats on stage, the bride and groom are stone-faced and somber, like someone has died. It is the traditional way of showing grace and modesty at public events, but it reminds me of soldiers standing guard at Buckingham Palace. Snap. One by one, groups of guests come forward to dance before the stoic couple. As they shake their booties, the master of ceremonies roars into a microphone, goading them to empty their pockets into a large basket. Snap, snap. He is spastic and overbearing, like a Southern Baptist preacher on speed, but no one else seems to mind.

Yet, things get a bit awkward when the only two white people in the room (me and another Peace Corps Volunteer) are called forward to contribute. Initially caught off-guard by the money throwing, we have formulated a strategy.

"Ok," I said, "we have a problem?"

"What?" Keegan asked.

"I don't have much money. Do you?"

"No," he answered, "but I have several small bills."

"Great," I replied, "let's use all of them."

"Brilliant," he agreed, "that way we can dance for a long time, giving people the impression that we are being very generous."

"Exactly!"

When our time comes, we dance and throw the bills. But when the MC sees our meager offerings, he announces to the crowd, "The *azungu* are cheap. They need to give more money." I freeze with nothing more to give, humiliated before two-hundred strangers. Snap. The hall goes silent, waiting for something to happen…waiting…waiting…and in the nick of time, Mr. Zimbota dashes to the loudmouth and whispers, "Don't do this. They are poor Peace Corps Volunteers." It's a dubious argument given my shiny digital camera, but it works. The MC orders the DJ to restart the music and the crowd comes back to life. As more guests are summoned forward to contribute, we make our escape.

Later in the day, I find Mr. Zimbota.

"Thanks for saving us at the wedding reception," I say, "We were pretty embarrassed and didn't know what to do."

"No problem," he laughs, "Those people thought that you had more money. White people always have money."

"Yeah, I understand why they feel that way," I reply, "but I hope that the wedding guests realized their mistake."

"People are always learning from you," he explains, "You are full of surprises."

"Like what?"

"Like coming in first place and taking pictures," he says, "People were asking me how I got my white friend to work at Malawian wedding."

"Really?"

"Yes," he explains, "They've never seen white person working for Malawian."

"Wow," I reply, "I try to expose them to new things, and I guess it's working."

"Keep trying extra hard."

"Well," I sigh, "there is no shortage of opportunities."

A few weeks later, another one rolls around, but it's not a happy occasion.

* * * *

A man died, and a good one at that. Between softly sung hymns, I hear cries and wails coming from his house. I smell the preparation of food — sliced cabbage, tomatoes, onions, beans and chicken to complement the *nsima* staple. Freshly cut tree branches lie in the yard. They will be arranged in two parallel lines across the nearby road, each demarcating a boundary of the deceased's homestead, and together forming a brief zone of respect in which passersby disembark from bicycles and passing cars slow to a crawl.

The air spins gently but steadily with activity. Entire villages, hundreds of people, have come to participate in the carefully choreographed, estrogen-fueled spectacle known as a Malawian funeral. The men rest and talk about current events, business, politics, and weather. The women alternate between mourning and cooking. The children help the women or play in the dirt. Unfortunately, Malawians are quite good at arranging funerals because they have had so much experience parting with the dead.

Speaking of experience, I spot her stoic face, framed by lines of wisdom, as she exits a hut. Her eyes, moist with fresh tears, speak to a sleepless night of remembrance. Oh, what those eyes have seen! Intergenerational births and deaths, dictators and statesmen, witch doctors and aid workers, colonialism and democracy, famines and droughts, pandemics and wars, and now the passing of a husband. Finding my familiar white face, she embraces me and weeps powerfully, her strong, heavy body collapsing around my slender frame. "The *azungu* is here. We are blessed," she's probably thinking.

I have come to pay my respects. My solitary white presence in a sea of Malawians is far more important than I can possibly know, especially for the deceased's son, Mr. Zimbota. It's the least I can do, honoring a man and a family that graciously received a visit from my parents at this very compound last year. It was surreal seeing my mother, wrapped in a *chitenje* (traditional lower-body wrap), sitting in the dirt next to Mr. Zimbota's mother, like two old friends chatting over tea. With that image fresh in my mind, I sit in a chair in the shade, thankful that my parents are still around, as Mr. Zimbota (now one parent poorer) runs around making arrangements, greeting guests, and checking on me.

"Come, let's go," he says after a couple of hours, motioning me toward a mud hut. Following his lead, I step inside and find a small dark room with a reed mat spread across the floor like a picnic throw. Others file in one by one, all men, staring ravenously at an array of food — tea, sweet potatoes, *mandazi* (Malawian donuts), prepared by the women to pacify our grumbling stomachs. The feast begins immediately. And, as we converse in *Chichewa*, dipping our hands in and out of the same bowls, the other men stare at me, appreciative but surprised that we are acting as equals in a land of perverse inequality.

"You sit with us on the floor, eating our food, drinking our tea and speaking our language."

"Yes," I nod.

"You are not like the rest of them."

"Them?" I ask.

"*Azungu*," they reply.

"How?" I ask, flattered by their observation.

"*Azungu* never come here, never chat with us, never eat our food," they explain.

Momentarily, the stories pour out, each man with his favorite testimonial of abhorrent colonialism and its enduring vestiges. Malawians are unbelievably diplomatic and reserved (at least when sober), but after decades of mistreatment, they are highly attuned to disrespect.

Most of their bitterness concerns low wages or poor working conditions on tobacco farms. But one man tells the tale of a white tea estate owner who keeps several Malawian mistresses and forces them to wait on him hand and foot. Among them is the man's daughter.

"That's awful," I say, "I'm so sorry."

"Yes," he nods.

"Can you do anything to stop it?"

"Nothing," he explains, "I hated white men for this...all of them."

"All of them? Not just the owner?"

"I think all white men bad like him," he admits, "until I meet you."

"Thank you," I reply, so touched by the gravity of the moment and the honesty of the man that I cannot say more.

"Yes. You good white man," another interjects.

The rest of the funeral is lost on me. Through the hymns, the Christian service, and the burial, my head and heart are elsewhere — they haven't left the mud hut or the conversation with the Malawian men, and probably never will. I realize that although I've come to Malawi to teach children and build schools and have devoted thousands of hours to achieving those goals, I haven't been very successful, at least not in my estimation. Yet, the simple gesture of attending a funeral, and showing some respect to the disaffected, leaves me feeling like a runaway success.

A few days later, Mr. Zimbota returns to Khwalala in a strange mood, moping. He has completed his funeral duties and left his grieving mother in the hands of her extended family.

"Are you alright?" I ask.

"Yes," he lies.

"I'm sorry that you lost your father," I say, sensing that there is something else bothering him.

"Thank you," he replies, "my father was good man."

"Yes, he was," I agree, "He was deserving of such a beautiful funeral."

"True. But he deserves more than that," he says cryptically.

"Like what?" I ask.

"In Malawian culture," he explains, "we build headstones at graves to honor dead relatives."

"Oh. So you are going to build a headstone?"

"We cannot," he gripes sullenly, "We don't have money."

It's an obvious cue, a plea for action. Here we go again, I think — more financial troubles and more requests for assistance from the *azungu*. First, it was the opportunity to invest in his clothing business, which I turned down, nearly spoiling our friendship. Now, it's a funeral expense. I want to help him, I really do, but dampening my enthusiasm is the realization that if I help one friend with one request for money, the flood gates might open. Also in the back of my mind are the Division Education Manager's scandalous accusations about Mr. Zimbota's financial improprieties, which have never been clarified to my satisfaction. Money management is the only thing about him that I don't trust.

On the other hand, it's only money. Pieces of paper, no matter how valuable, should never come between friends. The worst thing that can happen is that he doesn't pay me back, which isn't all that bad in the grand scheme of things. Yet, if Mr. Zimbota repays the money, and proves me wrong, it could be a turning point in our relationship. Doesn't he — the man who for so long has fed, mentored and watched over me — deserve an opportunity to shatter a stereotype that blacks don't repay? He does — nothing ventured, nothing gained, right?

"I can help you pay for the headstone," I say.

"Thank you," he replies, "I'll pay you back."

"Hmm," I utter, wincing in doubt, "Are you sure? I've heard that before, from other people, but I've rarely seen it happen."

"Yes," he sighs defensively, "You should trust me."

"What about the things the Education Manager has said about you?"

"They are lies!" he shouts, "I didn't steal school's money!"

His frustration boils over, flushing his face and shattering his signature composure. I've never seen him this angry or passionate about anything. It could be a defensive, kneejerk reaction to a painful but true accusation, like a defendant pleading not guilty after his crime has been caught on tape. But, it could also be something else entirely, an earnest outburst of emotion over a slanderous and unwarranted accusation. For the first time, I'm convinced it's the latter. He's telling the truth. His red face is all the assurance I need.

"Here is the money," I say, opening my wallet and handing him a wad of cash.

"Thank you," he nods, as a wave of relief relaxes his face.

"Oh, and Mr. Zimbota," I call, as he steps away, "I trust you."

"You have done good thing," he says, "I will pay you next month."

And, beaming with pride, he does.

"Thank you for helping me," he says, after returning the money.

"I'm sorry that I didn't do it earlier," I reply.

"No problem," he smiles, "First, you needed to learn."

"Yes," I retort, "and you needed to teach."

"Teach what?" he asks.

"Teach me to overcome my fear of being cheated. It was a process."

"But together," he grins, "We showed that white people are not selfish and black people repay money!"

"Yes, we did."

Yet, Mr. Zimbota and I are not alone, not by a long shot. As we are debunking racial myths in the hinterlands of Malawi, another man, commanding a much larger bully pulpit, is leading an international renaissance of tolerance and acceptance. He, the progeny of a pale, white American mother and an eggplant-dark African father, is shattering glass ceilings and changing minds, gunning for the highest of all prizes — the American Presidency. Even in the African bush, beyond the reach of newspapers and televisions, where international press coverage of his speeches crackles over dusty radio speakers, he deserves much of the credit for the strides that I make toward racial reconciliation. For the first time in my life, I feel the weight of global destiny — his and ours — coalesce, as the world bears witness to the realization of King's vision in the flesh.

****

Mr. Namanya, the Deputy Headmaster, finds me outside the staffroom.

"Mr. Michael," he says.

"Yes," I moan drowsily, sitting comfortably in the sun as another school day begins, "What do you want?"

"I hear on radio that America has black candidate."

I nod.

"His name is Barack Obama," he explains, "Obama is a Bantu name, and all of us," he points to the students and teachers, "are from Bantu tribes."

"Are you excited?" I ask.

"Yes," he shrieks, "We are behind Obama one-hundred percent, but he won't win."

"Why?" I inquire.

"Because he runs against Hillary," he explains, "She will win because she is white."

I'm not convinced he's right, but Mr. Namanya's interest in American politics inspires me. Sifting through piles of Newsweek magazines provided (usually a few weeks late) by Peace Corps, I find many articles describing Obama's background and rise to prominence. The next day, I bring a stack of them to the staffroom, hoping to put them to use starting conversations instead of cooking fires. I show Mr. Namanya one article in particular about Obama's father growing up in rural Kenya.

"See, Obama has white blood, too," I point, "His mother was a white woman from Kansas."

"What is Kansas?" he asks.

"It's an American state with a lot of white people," I smile.

"Obama comes from white people?" he wonders, clearly confused.

"No," I reply, "Barack is multi-racial and multi-national. He has lived in many different villages in America and many different countries around the world."

"Did he live in Africa?" Mr. Namanya wonders.

"No," I admit, "but he visited his father's family in Kenya. Look, here's a picture of Barack with his grandmother."

"He is very light. She is dark, like me," he comments.

I clumsily tack the article and picture to a wall outside the staffroom, on a makeshift message board for student announcements. Underneath it I write, "Did you know that Barak Obama's father is from Africa?" Students immediately congregate to see what I have done, triggering a miniature riot of pushing and shoving.

"A black man might become President of the United States," I tell them.

"What?" they say.

"His father was a goat shepherd in Kenya," I continue.

They are unimpressed, perhaps disappointed that I'm not posting their grades.

"Will we be tested on this?" one asks, a little twerp who likes to challenge me.

"No," I sneer playfully, a bit taken aback by the shortsightedness of his question.

"Then why does it matter?" he inquires.

"Because if Obama can become President, so can you!" I explain, immediately realizing how absurd that must sound to a kid who sleeps on a mud floor and eats one meal per day, "I want you to believe in yourselves."

During an assembly a few weeks later, I take the stage, still trying to sell the message.

"Mr. Buckler has announcement," Mr. Namanya says, quieting the crowd.

"Barack Obama," I report, "has defeated Hillary Clinton to become the Democratic Party candidate for President of the United States."

The crowd dances and cheers.

"Obama, Obama, Obama...," the Boys chant.

"This is great day," Mr. Namanya sermonizes, as student voices fade into silence,

"A black man, an African, has won. We should be so proud."

"And if he defeats John McCain," I interject, "he will become President!"

"Yes," the Head Boy adds, "we will be so happy."

Yet, over dinner that night, the Boys share how the students really feel.

"What do the students think of the election now?" I ask them, gloating.

"Don't worry, sir, they are excited," Alfred replies.

"I'm not worried," I say, "I'm just wondering how they feel."

"They feel good," Myson explains, "but they cannot believe that black man will win. It will be tough road."

"Why?" I ask, "Obama is leading in the polls."

"Because there are so, so many white people in America," Gift says, "and they will vote for white man."

"You might be right," I admit, "I guess time will tell."

In the meantime, I work to prove them wrong. At Peace Corps events, I distribute absentee ballots and answer questions about them, appreciating that every vote matters (as we learned during the 2000 Presidential race). If all goes well, our ballots will never be counted, but if there was ever an election that inspired my participation, this is the one. When election night rolls around, I spend it with Mark Visocky, a USAID employee who invites Volunteers to his home in Lilongwe for food and spirited discussions about development policy. He's the perfect companion for what's coming.

Mark and I retire early and rise at the crack of dawn for breaking news coverage. With my hand shaking wildly, I can barely operate the remote control to turn on the satellite television system. But, as I do, the announcement I've been waiting for my whole life fills the screen: "Barak Obama will become the forty-fourth President of the United States." I lose control, as rosy cheeks feel the soft tickle of tears. "It means so much," I explain to Mark, "not because of Obama's greatness, but ours as a country. We have been through so much and come so far." He nods in agreement.

Back in Khwalala, after I've had a few days to process the enormity of what has happened, I chat with the Boys about Obama's victory. They do a great job of placing it in perspective.

"How do you feel?" I inquire.

"We are so excited," they exclaim, "We think that Africa has bright days in future."

"So, now you understand," I continue, "Race shouldn't matter."

"Yes," Alfred replies, "Black people can become President of United States!"

"Sure, but that's not all," I continue, "whites and blacks can marry and have children."

"True!" Myson exclaims, "I want American wife."

"What else?" I ask, "What else has changed?"

"Well," Gift answers, "Because of you, we no longer believe that white vampires roam villages at night eating black children. You haven't eaten any children."

"Thanks for noticing," I quip, "so you realize that all racial stereotypes are problematic."

"Gift and I do," Myson jokes, "but not Alfred."

"What?" I retort, "I don't understand."

"Alfred is scared, sir."

"Why?" I ask, turning to Alfred.

"Because Chinese man came to village yesterday," he begins.

"So what? Are you afraid of Chinese people."

Alfred looks down, ashamed of what he is about to say.

"Yes," he answers.

"Why?" I ask.

"Because Chinese like to eat children," he whispers.

"That's ridiculous!" I shout.

I shouldn't be overreacting, but it's hard not to. I tell them that people from all over the world are basically the same (*"Tili chimodzimodzi"*) and that "we are one in the eyes of God." They watch me befriend people from a variety of races and cultural backgrounds, building valuable relationships. But it's not enough for them, because they never put the lessons into practice. In order to change, Alfred needs to meet a Chinese person.

"Alfred," I say, "I'm going to invite that Chinese person over to dinner."

"Yes, sir," he quivers, already dreading the occasion.

"And, since we will be eating a Malawian, you will be the main course," I wink.

He smiles, appreciating my sarcasm, as Myson and Gift keel over in laughter.

XII

DARK DAYS

As many of you know, I had a health scare at my school. It was a traumatic experience that left me shaken and yearning for the comforts of family and friends. I want to come home.

— Letter Home, July 2008

My grandmother, Gracky, always told me to make the most of a bad situation. When I was a child, she empathized when my younger brother, Bob, antagonized me until I pushed or punched him, triggering his halfhearted cries and drawing the ire (and often the spanking) of my parents.

"What's wrong?" she asked me one day after I was disciplined for "rough play."

"It's Bob," I cried, "He hits me, but when I hit him back, he screams bloody murder, and my parents get angry."

"Bob is the baby," she explained, "Your parents are favoring him because he is younger and weaker."

"So, what should I do? Stay away from him?"

"No," she explained, "You need to outsmart him. The solution is to cry first, before Bob does. Beat him to the punch."

When Bob upset me, I didn't feel like crying, and manufacturing tears felt disingenuous, but Gracky's approach was worth a try. And, sure enough, it worked. Whenever Bob hit or kicked me, I delivered Oscar-worthy outbursts, and Bob stopped the nonsense after receiving a few spankings of his own.

Gracky was similarly innovative with her funeral, one of the saddest days of my life. Before passing, she was very specific about how she wanted it: a Quaker celebration with friends and family members gathered not to mope, but tell personal stories about her. Comfortable, casual attire was encouraged, and Bob wore floral-patterned shorts, the sort of tacky island garb that sits in your closet awaiting a Caribbean vacation. Looking like Panama Jack, he stood before the congregation and told all the R-rated jokes Gracky had taught us over the years. Surely, Gracky was smiling from above. Everyone else was.

In Malawi, midway through my second year, I hit a wall and need some guidance from Gracky. The challenges of everyday life are wearing on me like never before, their charms having faded long ago. I'm not feeling healthy, physically or psychologically, and it shows in my demeanor. Facing unmotivated classes, I sometimes lose my temper and raise my voice, sermonizing students to stop wasting my time. "You work too hard," Mr. Zimbota says after hearing one of my rants, "maybe you should rest."

But when I try to rest, it doesn't go well. At night, instead of snoozing soundly, I talk through stress in my sleep. The boys hear my babbling and find it entertaining.

"Mr. Buckler, last night you spoke about certain news for more than five minutes," Myson observes one morning.

"Wow, was it really that long?" I ask, embarrassed.

"Oh, yes. Sir, maybe it's because you eat by door last night," he suggests, citing a traditional belief that sitting under a doorway causes bad dreams.

Interesting theory, but I'm pretty sure that other things are to blame.

Deprivation is not a pleasant state of existence. In the village, removed from creature comforts, food is simple, communication is difficult, intimate relationships are few, houses are austere, and roads are one-lane dirt tracks. Electrical outlets, cars, air conditioning, overhead lighting, showers, heaters, gyms and computers are virtually nonexistent. And, to preserve their reputations, most Volunteers deprive themselves of vices like alcohol and cigarettes. Though beautiful in its simplicity, life as a Peace Corps Volunteer becomes a grind of homogeneity, a thirsting for chromatic subversion.

Over time, the "novelties" of third-world village living exact a steep psychological price. I, for one, emote like a yo-yo, enduring a roller coaster ride of emotional extremes that drives many Volunteers to withdraw, lash out or leave, whatever smoothes the bumps and corrals the cycle. Spiraling downward fast, I feel like a guitar that's always out of tune, playing an internal melody of Memphis blues. Half of the Volunteers seem to be on some sort of anti-depressant medication. I wonder whether I should join their ranks.

In addition to mental strife, there are physical health scares. A handful of Volunteers contract malaria, the nefarious titleholder of biggest killer in Africa. Tuberculosis is a movie disease until it infects a burly six-foot-seven Viking-like Volunteer from North Carolina, reducing him to a coughing skeleton. Another friend is totally incapacitated by schistosomiasis, a snail parasite commonly found in certain parts of Lake Malawi. Thankfully, everyone returns to full health, but mortality (whether your own or someone else's) is always front and center, lurking in the shadows, threatening to strike.

Still, none of us is sent home in a body bag because the medical care is superb given the circumstances. Though village clinics and health centers are sketchy, the Peace Corps staffs a medical unit in Lilongwe with two top-notch doctors and one motherly nurse, Evelyn. In addition to scheduled checkups, walk-in treatment is available round-the-clock. Most medical problems are resolved in Malawi, and Volunteers with conditions requiring special tests or surgeries are airlifted to South Africa for first-world facilities. In many ways, our medical care in Africa is better than in the States.

* * * *

My first major health issue in Malawi is subterranean. As I walk in Lilongwe shortly after dark with Allison Lipper (a pint-sized, brainy Volunteer from New Jersey), our intriguing conversation about romantic relationships in Peace Corps distracts me from the dangers of my surroundings. Nothing seems amiss until I take a step forward that doesn't find the ground and suddenly feel myself plunging into darkness. In slow motion, my body slides down a rough, brick wall and grinds to a halt. Allison's desperate, panicked pleas from above are the only reminders that I am alive and not alone.

"Mike, Mike, can you hear me? Are you alright?" she screams.

Silence follows. A large transport truck rumbles down the road. I hear noises from its squeaky struts and swinging chains coming from above. The earth around me vibrates to the tune of its belching engine.

"Mike, please say something," she tries again, "I can't see you."

"I think I'm alright," I groan.

"How do you feel?"

"Well my body hurts," I reply, "and I'm not sure where I am. It's very strange."

"What happened?" she asks.

What happened is that I fell into a twelve-foot sewer hole. One of many dug (but not covered) by the city to access water pipes, it is affectionately known as an *azungu* (white people) trap, suggesting that I wasn't the first foreigner to fall into one. Immediately next to me in the hole is a pipe joint with swollen, metallic rivets. Somehow, I have missed its chilling, pointy apex by inches, avoiding serious injury. Stewing over my brush with doom, I peer upward into the night sky and, using the pipe joint as a foothold and brickwork joints as handholds, painstakingly climb toward early evening stars.

A labored walk back to the Peace Corps house follows. There, I assess my injuries — swollen knee, lacerations on my chin and arms, some bruised ribs, and a very sore back that absorbed most of the impact — and take a shower to calm my nerves and clean out the dirt-packed scrapes and cuts. Drying my body, I suddenly feel changed, determined to seize every moment of every day, before it's too late. Tonight, I want to kiss a girl — it has been way too long — and the time is right. One of my best friends, a fellow Volunteer from Rochester, NY, has been making some romantic overtures. There's no time to waste.

After freshening up, I find her in the kitchen and make my intentions known. Naturally, she's worried about me and hesitant to do anything that might worsen my injuries, but in the uncertain world of Peace Corps service, there's no time like the present, especially when it comes to romance. We leave the house and find a quiet spot to pet each other playfully over sips of brandy. As a full moon rises against the starry sky, casting a soft light on her face, I kiss her sweetly. After it's over, I wonder why I needed to fall into a hole and injure myself to complete such a beautiful and natural act. Man, I'm dense.

The next day, I am summoned to the Peace Corps medical office, where Dr. Max is on duty. A native Zimbabwean, he was lucky to be raised in the safe environs of Zambia in the 1960s, removed from a thirteen-year guerilla war raging against colonial powers in his motherland (known as the Republic of Rhodesia or Southern Rhodesia before independence).

"My father was a prominent businessman," he explained during my last office visit.

"What type of businessman?"

"By day, he operated a small bakery, but that wasn't all."

"What else did he do?" I asked.

"He would leave us for days at a time," Dr. Max replied, "coming and going in the dark of night."

"Was he having an affair?"

"No, something very different" Dr. Max explained, "He was smuggling money and guns to resistance fighters in Zimbabwe. He was trying to make things better for his country and people."

After university in the U.K. and medical school in America, Dr. Max returned to Southeastern Africa to make things better, too. He's making me better today.

"Michael, you look like a mob beat you up," he jokes after surveying my battered body.

"I do?"

"Yeah, but don't worry," he smiles, "You'll be back to normal within a few days," warmth and empathy radiating from his pudgy, dough-boy face.

"Good as new," I agree, trying to play it cool, like I didn't almost perish in a pit.

"You are a very lucky guy," Dr. Max comments, writing something in my medical chart, "What happened could have been much more serious."

"Yes," I reply, "It's rough out there."

"I know. I really admire what you guys do," Max says, "Peace Corps is one of the best things about America."

"Glad we have your endorsement," I quip.

"Speaking of Peace Corps, I have another Volunteer to see," Max says suddenly, "She's been having a hard time and needs a shoulder to cry on. Now, get out of here."

* * * *

She's not alone. Crying sessions with Peace Corps doctors comfort many a distraught Volunteer. Eating a high carbohydrate diet, women tend to gain weight and never stop hearing "compliments" from Malawian well-wishers about how "fat" they are. Other annoyances are equally off-putting, such as stares and shouts, begging and bullying, cheating and stealing, broken promises, repeated communication breakdowns, and overall dysfunction, one-thousand cuts slowly bleeding you to death. It's amazing what a hug can do for someone who hasn't been touched in weeks.

When you're sick of village immersion, downtime with fellow Volunteers is the best medicine. After realizing that isolation and lack of stimulation compromise mental and emotional health, causing Volunteers to opt for Early Termination (ET), Peace Corps Malawi leadership begins clustering us within the same geographical areas. I routinely ride my bike to find familiar American faces — Eric has electricity, Miata has SPAM, Linda is the world's best hostess, and Nikki and I reminisce about our beloved Portland, Oregon. Without those impromptu therapy sessions, I would probably crack.

Another uplifting distraction is a trip to the city. Needing a break, Volunteers typically make the trek every two or three weeks. Unmistakable in grungy clothes, sandals and sunglasses, they pull into town and lash their bodies to round-the-clock feeding troughs of hedonistic delights. Famine behind them, it is time for an adrenaline-fueled smorgasbord of food, sex, drugs, Internet, alcohol, and dance clubs. (Hey, don't judge!) Each Volunteer indulges one or more vices (whether ice cream or poker), and debauchery that most people enjoy over a span of several weeks, Volunteers pack into a weekend.

Houses rented by Peace Corps host the urban forays. Each is a large, electrified, colonial-style villa protected by barbed-wire fences and security guards — a versatile hostel-bunker complete with beds, cubbies, computers, refrigerators, full kitchens, common areas, DVD players and televisions. By design, these dwellings allow Volunteers to enjoy overnight respites, restock on grocery items, attend meetings, and work on development projects. They are our American-style homes away from home.

And social events at Peace Corps houses are a huge draw. As Volunteers amass, the air radiates with frenetic energy. Those arriving early get beds, while latecomers rummage for couches or floor space, or pitch tents in the yard. Noise reverberates down the cement halls as people talk too loudly and play their music (an amalgam of eclectic genres) over each other. For older Volunteers, it's a reminder of how much things have changed since college. For younger Volunteers, it's a reminder of how little things changed since college. For everyone, it's a social experiment in communal living and group patience.

Naturally, in such close quarters, tensions arise. One memorable evening, four friends decide to stay up until 4:30 a.m., drinking and blasting songs. The music is really good, but even so, it's wakes me up at 3:30 a.m. Full of piss and vinegar, I dial one of the culprits from my bed.

"You guys are being jerks," I say, "Turn that noise down!"

"Ah...sorry man," he replies.

"But, before you do," I add, "would you please play a Tom Petty tune?"

"Sure, we like taking requests."

Laughing, he gets the message and plays the song, appreciating the creative reprimand. The incident, which could have gotten ugly, earns a mild rating on the drama meter.

But some weekends in town go down like daytime soap operas, complete with vixens, villains, victims and lots of bad makeup and hair. To capture this strange environment, we expand our vocabularies to include: "groupies" — drunken people who corner you into long conversations; and "Peace Corps goggles" — an alcohol-induced condition that dramatically improves the attractiveness of other Volunteers. Under such conditions, the storylines are predictable: torrid romances, drunken shenanigans, and bitter rivalries.

Sexual behaviors, in particular, are unhealthy. If love is a coffee bean (it is for me in the morning), carefully grown on a quiet hillside, harvested with loving hands, and brewed to create a perfect, aromatic cup of heaven, relationships in

Peace Corps Malawi are like cans of instant coffee grounds that you buy in bulk at a warehouse store — fast, easy and convenient, but not entirely satisfying. With a few notable exceptions, unions seem to spout like weeds and linger like shooting stars, born of desperation and convenience, not intimacy and mutual respect. But, as the saying goes, beggars cannot be choosers.

Luckily, the STD risk within Peace Corps Malawi is relatively low. But things get messy when affection-starved Volunteers venture into the general populace and face one of the highest HIV rates in the world. Those who take risks (e.g., unprotected sex) are placed on PEP (Post-Exposure Prophylaxis), and endure a month of energy zapping, nauseating misery. Whenever someone loses twenty pounds in four weeks, we suspect that PEP is to blame. Thankfully, to the best of my knowledge, no Volunteer tests HIV-positive during my tour, though several nearly have heart attacks waiting for their negative results.

Speaking of heart attacks, Peace Corps bureaucrats in Washington, D.C., cause a stir by threatening to eliminate the houses as an unnecessary expense. Thankfully, the move is resisted by staffers in the Peace Corps Malawi office. They know that Volunteers cherish the houses as safe havens to work on development projects, enjoy group dinners, and hold meetings for various charitable ventures. They understand that without a fundamental philosophical shift, Peace Corps assignments will continue to be "the hardest jobs you'll ever love," and that Volunteers will find outlets (healthy and unhealthy) to process their difficulties. Houses or no houses, we aren't living in Kansas.

****

"Home is where the heart is," said Pliny the Elder. Every day I fantasize about returning home to America, dwelling upon the most curious nuances. Sure, laundry machines and Internet banking are nice, but you don't pine for them like you do the little things, like being able to say, "I love you," before retiring to bed, or receiving a long distance call and being able to suggest, "I'm tied up at the moment. Can I call you right back?" Intimate touches from lovers tease your mind like taffy, as do the sweet smell of pancakes on a slow, Sunday morning. I can almost taste the pancakes.

Malawians get it. As they say, "Children are wealth," an allusion not to the nefarious child trafficking trade, but to the importance of family. Africans operate communally in networks of familial support that reach far and wide like river tributaries. On his meager government salary, Mr. Zimbota supports forty people, paying school fees here and buying shoes there. In *Ishmael*, Daniel Quinn wrote that African families are like a hand, of which each member is a finger. Individualism, a distinct sense of self, is secondary.

Yet, for better or worse, I used to be the opposite. Feeling suffocated by my parents and their old-fashioned lifestyle, I neglected familial ties, hitching my wagon to the sweet, ethereal perfumes of friends and lovers. Geographical distance, professional responsibilities, and economic prosperity obscured the necessity of family, inspiring an artificial feeling of self-sufficiency. My parents and I were living separate lives, mutually free (in my mind) from burdens of accountability. But I was wrong — dead wrong. Turns out, my folks were deeply hurt, taking my aloofness personally and praying it was short-lived.

Needless to say, the prodigal son came around. I learned the hard way that when life takes a sour turn, which it inevitably does, many of your so-called friends peel away and jump ship. Their absence exposes the steadfastly faithful presence of the people who reared you and fought with you over coloring books and toy fire trucks, never abandoning you and patiently awaiting your return. For me, it took the sting of a humiliating divorce. But now, at the wise-old age of thirty-five, I appreciate what Malawians knew all along — you can have all the admirers and material wealth in the world, but without family, you are poor. That brings me to dear old Mom.

From my earliest cognitive moments, Mom and I butted heads. Equally stubborn, we had wildly divergent outlooks. I was "live and let live," while Mom was "everything has its proper role and place." I was a skeptical risk taker; Mom was a gullible worrier. I liked to process and persuade; Mom tended to intuit and react. I was short-winded and impetuous; Mom was wordy and deliberate. I was an engineer and a lawyer; Mom was a social worker and a teacher. Mom wanted me to come home, open a modest law practice, and make babies; I wanted to run around the world inoculating other people's babies.

Yet, in spite of these differences, I never question Mom's love and devotion. Mom sends letters and care packages to Malawi, and calls regularly. With my father, Mom organizes a group to commiserate with the parents of other Peace Corps Volunteers. Then, Mom does the impossible: in an Amazonian act of love and sacrifice, she boards a plane and visits me. Let's be clear — Mom has no desire to visit Malawi (none whatsoever), but that doesn't matter — her son is living there amid lots of yucky stuff and, by golly, Mom is coming armed with Lysol (literally and figuratively). Never underestimate a Mom.

After decades of strife and estrangement, it is time to Africanize. In that vein, I write Mom a poem:

The author of this tribute is your son,
A man largely of your creation.
Cradled in your womb,
Suckled by your breast,
Nourished by your meals,
Empowered by your steadfast support.
Aware and appreciative, you should know, of your sacrifice,
Telltale signs of your devotion abound,

My successes and strengths testaments to your efforts,
I want you to share in them.
Too often your importance goes unacknowledged,
Fear and insecurity hijack my tongue,
Twisting praise into criticism,
Rebukes supplant overtures of love.
A deep bond exists between us,
Your son loves you very much,
Is proud to call you mother,
Can never repay you.
Once a mother, always a mother,
I honor you now and forever.

I want to be part of the Buckler hand again. I count down the days until I step off the plane and give Mom a big hug — a blessed airport reunion. I have four months to go. As it turns out, they would feel like the longest four months of my life.

"I've done everything I set out to accomplish," I tell Eric Cornish, over an impromptu lunch, a few days after writing the poem.

"Really," he replies, "I wish that I could say that."

"It has been a great ride," I continue, "and I stand by my accomplishments, but now I'm just spinning my wheels."

"I know the feeling," he says, "Hang in there."

"Thanks man, but I'm just done," I respond, "I want to see my family and pet my dog, Cameron."

"Then go home early," he says abruptly, "You wouldn't be the first one."

He's right — Volunteers leave for all sorts of reasons. Some decide that they've had enough, or would rather be in grad school, and opt for ET — Early Termination. Others are forced out by Peace Corps. Those breaking a golden rule, like traveling outside a host country without approval, are given an AS — Administrative Separation, while Volunteers with medical conditions that endanger their wellbeing or compromise their service receive a MS — Medical Separation. In Malawi, for one reason or another, about one-third of the Volunteers don't complete the two-year service commitment.

"I want to leave," I reply, "but I feel guilty about it."

"Why?" he asks, "You've been a great Volunteer."

"I don't want to be a quitter," I explain, "I need a better reason to leave than boredom and homesickness."

"Like what?"

"The most graceful exit is a health problem," I suggest jokingly.

"Be careful what you wish for," he foreshadows.

A few weeks later, fate calls my bluff.

It happens so fast. During a frustrating conversation with a colleague at school, I suddenly feel dizzy and cannot breathe, struggling like there is a heavy weight resting on my chest. Fearing that I am having a heart attack and won't live much longer (common symptoms of a panic attack), I sit down, relax, pray, and slowly recover. Malawian onlookers look mortified and helpless, fearing the worst. It is, by far, the scariest medical problem I have experienced in my life.

Following the protocol taught during training, I call Peace Corps doctors. They instruct me to stop taking Larium (a.k.a., Mefloquine), a malaria prophylaxis known for causing anxiety. They also provide a comforting, albeit distant, presence, and after listening to my symptoms, assure me that everything is probably fine. After performing an EKG in Lilongwe, they conclude that I am generally healthy but probably under too much stress. "Maybe the thought of leaving Malawi is overwhelming for you," they speculate. It's an interesting theory, but I'm not so sure.

Indeed, the evidence suggests the opposite — staying in Malawi is the problem. After the initial panic attack, others follow, becoming progressively less frequent and intense, as the malaria drug slowly dissipates from my system (takes about six weeks). Fearing the worst (a miserable last few months or a forced trip home), I try to alter my perspective by falling back in love with my host country and becoming less driven and expectant. As Dr. Erfan (the other Peace Corps doctor) explains, "Try it! You might not be as motivated, but you'll be happier." And he's right — the strategy helps, and I steadily improve.

Yet, like any good patient, I don't follow all of the doctor's orders.

"Do you drink coffee?" Dr. Erfan asks me over the phone.

"Yes, everyday," I reply guardedly, tempted to lie about my habit.

"Stop drinking it," he advises, "and tell me whether you feel better."

I hang up the phone in a foul mood. Dreading a future of lethargic mornings and caffeine-withdrawal headaches, I stomp around my house preparing to banish my containers of instant coffee granules to food purgatory. Then, suddenly, I receive an unmistakable sign that I should continue the caffeinated love affair.

It is literally a sign — a piece of paper with writing. Myson posted it on the wall several months earlier as a household proclamation. Entitled, "Foods Needed to Avoid Dying," it is a meticulous listing of the edibles that each of us needs to survive. Gift's is corn porridge, Alfred's is peas, Myson's is beans, and mine are eggplant (rumored among Malawians to cause elephantiasis of the testicles) and COFFEE. Performing mental *jujitsu*, I disassociate Myson from his humble roots, promoting him to Nostradamus-like prognosticator, and as soon as I do, drinking coffee makes sense again. My logic is foolproof: Myson the Magnificent says that I will die without coffee; I don't want to die; therefore, I must continue drinking coffee. Simple, don't you think?

Yet, the panic attacks keep coming. Each time one arises, I agonize over the reality that sound medical care is hours, if not days, away. The attacks also remind me that packing my bags and quitting is better than taking foolish risks with my life. "If I die in a Malawian village," I wonder, "how many days will pass before my family is notified?" Fighting thoughts like this, each day becomes a struggle for sanity and motivation. If I want to fulfill my Peace Corps commitment, something needs to change.

And it's a perfect time to make a big adjustment: relinquishing my teaching responsibilities. During this time of year, half of the students sit for a national examination and want self-directed time to prepare. Likewise, teaching colleagues travel to proctor examinations at other schools, leaving behind a skeleton staff. Knowing the situation, the remaining students (freshman and juniors) often don't come to school, and even when they do, the hot African sun and empty bellies (caused by end-of-the-year food shortages) conspire to transform them from eager pupils into sleepy nincompoops.

But there's another (perhaps better) reason to bow out of the teaching profession at this juncture. Peace Corps is about building capacity and empowering self-sufficiency, not creating dependencies. I eventually need to hand over all of my responsibilities to Malawians, and teaching is just the first domino to fall. It has been fun at times, and challenging at others, but within this insufferable end-of-the-year environment, it is high time to distance myself from Malawi's educational crisis, and turn my attention to other pursuits — community projects, leisure pleasures and goodbyes.

* * * *

Unfortunately, one of those pursuits — perhaps the biggest one — suddenly hits the skids.

"We have some problems," Mr. Zimbota says, as I enter the staff room.

"What?" I ask.

"The Education Manager visited yesterday," he elaborates, as the other teachers stare at the floor, "and she rejected our plans for girls' boarding school."

"But we sent her the proposal months ago, and she supported the project," I cry in disbelief.

"Yes," he nods.

"As an advocate for female empowerment, how can she do this?"

"She has changed her mind," he replies, "but we cannot accept it. You must discuss with her and find a way forward."

"I will try my best," I promise.

It's amazing that I managed to hear this disappointing news without experiencing a panic attack. I'm not happy, I'm not sad, I'm just numb. Comfortably numb. It's a good sign.

The next day, I meet with the Education Manager at Division Headquarters, a one-story, communistic office building located in a town about forty miles away.

Strolling across the front lawn, past a tattered Malawian flag fluttering despondently in the late-morning breeze, I find her hard at work. A tall and commanding middle-aged women, she welcomes me into her dark, dank office, and after some small talk, gets right to the point.

"I cannot let you build your boarding school," she says.

"Why?" I wonder.

"There must be separate areas on campus for boarding and learning. Your plan mixes the two. I don't want girls hanging their underwear in the open next to classrooms."

Months of toil (blood, sweat, and tears) wash across my disappointed face.

"I'm sorry," she says, seeing my color disappear, "but the girls must have their own, private space."

"Where?" I ask.

"Possibly outside the school fence," she explains, "That's where my hostel was located when I was a secondary school student."

"Why didn't community members see this coming?" I mutter.

"They should have," she says in a maternal way, "It would have been the culturally appropriate thing to do."

Her thoughtful words are persuasive. Like a spell, they lull me into a trance of contrition. It all makes sense — she is right, and Khwalala is wrong. But something isn't adding up.

Hey, not so fast, lady! Don't blame the community when you have some explaining to do. For starters, I want to know whether your justification for discontinuing our project is legitimate or the latest chapter in a longstanding feud with Mr. Zimbota. I also want to ask you why you didn't raise this concern during the nascent stages of the project, before the community became invested. Of course, I ask neither. It won't do any good — the project is on life support, its prospects fading like a dying candle. And, as a disgruntled aid worker, I'm on the verge of calling it quits and kissing Malawi goodbye.

Grasping for inspiration, I have an epiphany.

"One more thing, if you don't mind."

"What is it?" she sighs, wanting me to drop the issue and go away.

"What if we changed our plans by using one less building and erecting a fence around the boarding facility, giving the girls their own private corner of campus?"

"Hmm," she responds after contemplating for a few moments, "I'm not making any promises, but that might work...maybe...if it's done right."

"Very good," I cheer, "I'll tell the school and the community that there is hope."

"Not so fast," she counters, "I'll send an inspector to your school this week to evaluate this idea and write a report."

"Wonderful," I say, "we look forward to his visit."

"Sure, sure," she smirks, "and I look forward to his report."

The Education Manager is being conservative for good reason. A government post like hers is precious, and you don't achieve job security in Malawi by making waves. The Malawian Ministry of Education and African Development Bank (ADB) are spending gobs of money renovating dilapidated village schools like Khwalala C.D.S.S. into palatial campuses, presumably for the benefit of day students. She doesn't want to be the first Education Manager in Malawi to condone boarding facilities at a newly-renovated day school. It's classic cover-your-ass policy making. I understand, sort of.

"Thanks for your time," I say to the Education Manager.

"Oh, Michael, it was a pleasure. Please come see me anytime. You are most welcome here."

"I think that we have found a solution," I add, shaking her hand.

"Maybe," she smiles, "but don't get your hopes up."

In Khwalala, a few hours later, I report the news. The teachers are downright giddy.

"We go forward, with or without her," they agree.

"I like your enthusiasm," I say, "but we need her support, right?"

"She cannot ruin our most important community project. Nothing will stop us!"

"Well," I sigh, "We need to reevaluate the situation in a couple of weeks, when we have more information."

"Very well."

And, in two weeks' time, we have news — some good, some bad. The good news is that the Education Manager is off our backs, at least for now. Her inspector never comes to the school to write a report, which we interpret as a good sign. The project has been taken off life support, and is breathing on its own. But it's still in intensive care because the Education Manager isn't our only problem.

Money is. After several months of waiting and inquiring, we haven't received an answer from Peace Corps about whether the project will be funded. Moreover, much closer to home, the Group Village Headman is grumbling again about the project, but at least now we know why. Turns out that he is not only a chief, but a businessman — the owner of some local tenements rented by students. As such, he stands to lose money when our boarding facility opens, and every dollar of income counts (now more than ever) as the region feels the effects of the global economic meltdown.

Bad financial news travels downhill from wealthy to poor, gaining momentum along the way. It's a mistake to think that Malawians are spared because they grow their own food. The reality is that a dearth of manufacturing in Malawi drives the importation of everything critical for survival and development (e.g., fuel, seeds, fertilizer). In my village, for example, the prices of most items rise by thirty percent. Pressure mounts as people scramble to meet their basic needs, and drop-out rates soar as students face an untenable choice: food or education.

Making matters worse, our boarding plans face another barrier — the incompetent ADB. Its much-ballyhooed renovation of Khwalala C.D.S.S. began in 2005.

The work was supposed to be finished in less than two years, and we are about to enter year four of the project, with no end in sight.

The original contractor chosen by the ADB was a cocksure, young Malawian named Felix. Like a lion patrolling a savannah, he drove his SUV wildly through the villages, sipping soda and moonshine and bragging about how he was mentioned in a hit Malawian song. The son of a successful contractor, he complained about his workers and nonchalantly admitted that he had never managed a construction project before, much less a school renovation. Yet, for some inexplicable reason, he had been entrusted by the ADB with three of these multi-million dollar projects. Something smelled fishy to me.

So, it comes as no surprise when the renovation implodes. For months, workers aren't paid, materials don't arrive on time, and costs don't jive with the budget. Then, the project suddenly grinds to a halt, and workers disappear. At the school, we hear nothing but excuses like, "there's a cement shortage because South Africans are building stadiums for the World Cup," a dubious claim given that other construction projects in the area haven't skipped a beat. Finally, the truth emerges — the ADB has fired Felix for financial improprieties and is seeking a replacement. All we can do is wait.

Amid this strife (money problems and ADB incompetence), the Education Manager decides to transfer Mr. Zimbota to another school. He arrived seven years earlier when the school had one building, but now that it is on the brink of becoming one of the nicest schools in the region, a better-educated administrator is set to replace him, a requirement of the ADB contract. Hearing the news, I'm bereft. He has been a close friend and strong supporter of mine from the beginning, and I want him to stay, at least until the fate of the boarding facility is decided. He tells me that he wants to stay, too.

So, I fight for him. I write emails to the Education Manager (his old nemesis) and MP Kaliati (his old friend), arguing that he wants to stay and that replacing him will spell disaster for our projects. Within a few weeks, the Education Manager relents, but not without a devastating catch. Mr. Zimbota will stay at the school, not as Headmaster, but as an ordinary teacher, a humiliating demotion for a person used to being the boss. I find him moping around campus after receiving the news.

"Are you alright?" I ask.

"No," he admits, "I am very unhappy."

"Why? I thought that you wanted to stay here."

"I do want to stay," he replies sorrowfully.

"Then, what's the problem?"

"I am no longer headmaster," he explains, "Other men no longer respect me. They laugh at me behind my back."

"I'm sorry," I say, "I didn't know this would happen."

"Please leave now," he snaps, "I want to be alone."

Maybe trying to "help" him was a mistake. Maybe all of this was a mistake.

I walk to the staff room. Finding the other teachers, I initiate a conversation about how they can assist with the boarding project, if it goes forward. Yet, the discussion deteriorates into bickering over project titles, responsibilities and whether teachers will be paid for their assistance — petty antics that will surely poison our chances of success.

"We've already been over this," I address them.

"We have?" they ask, genuinely surprised.

"Yes," I remind them, "You know that no one is getting paid for helping the school, and responsibilities will be assigned if and when we get funding."

"But we always get paid allowances for extra work," one says, smirking.

"For once," I yell, "try to think about what's best for the school, not your own wallet."

Hot and flushed, I feel a panic attack coming on. Excusing myself before the attack escalates, I start walking toward my house. In the fresh air and sun, away from vitriol and dysfunction, I feel better, and by the time I reach my front door, the attack has subsided.

Alone in the house, I take stock of my life. Though I feel slightly better (if not disconnected) without teaching responsibilities, I am still tired, frustrated and questioning the value of my volunteerism, now more than ever. Making matters worse, the doctors cannot explain the panic attacks. Whether they are a physical response to psychological turmoil or a purely physical condition is unclear. Whether they are harmless or dangerous is also a mystery. Hitting rock bottom, seemingly unable to take another day of this torture, I retrieve my dusty travel bags from storage and start packing. It's a surrender.

A few minutes later, I hear a soft knock. I walk to my front door and open it, finding one of Mr. Zimbota's daughters on the porch, smiling as usual.

"Uncle, I have food for you from my mother," she says.

"Thank you very much," I reply, "It looks delicious."

"Mother wants you to be fat and healthy," she explains, joking about my slender physique.

"I promise to eat it all and get very, very fat!"

She places the food on my table and disappears. I twist the lid off the container and inhale the savory smells of *nsima* and fresh peas mixed with peanut flour. Nobody makes *nsima* like her mother — nobody. I sigh and reseal the lid, writhing over what to do next. No matter how desperate I am to escape Malawi and its problems, leaving these people will be grueling.

XIII

PAY DIRT

Hello, America! You're probably surprised to be receiving an email from me today. We didn't get Internet access in the village, but other circumstances did change abruptly yesterday, as they often do, necessitating my trip to town. As we say in Malawi, "Zimachitika" (meaning "things happen").

— Email Home, August 2008

I slowly eat the *nsima* and peas, agonizing over what to do. Betraying my mind like poison, they fill my stomach but drain my soul, a humiliating last supper of what ifs. And the aftermath is worse: painful, metallic burps punish my thoughts of leaving with a serrated dagger of heartburn. Struggling for mental and digestive peace, I compose a checklist with two columns — reasons to stay in Malawi on the left and reasons to go on the right. Closing my eyes, I review the list. The column on the right is longer, but the left-hand column contains a trump card.

I never attained Eagle Scout. Flanked by my father, I was a full-fledged Cub Scout, Webelos and Boy Scout, merrily camping and hiking my way through elementary and middle schools. By early high school, I was a Life Scout, three merit badges away from the rarefied apex of Scouting. I even started a community service project required to reach Eagle, renovating a one-room school house for historical preservation. After years of commitment, the prize was mine for the taking. It was supposed to be my finest hour.

Yet, it wasn't. I squandered the opportunity, letting it "die a natural death," as Mr. Zimbota likes to say. The explanations (excuses really) were many: I was consumed by high school life; I was lazy; many of the boys in Troop 1321 seemed unwelcoming and sophomoric; and the leadership (several current or former military personnel) was rigid and insensitive. But, in the final analysis, I know that I was responsible — I just didn't want it badly enough. I let it pass, and I can never get it back.

My father didn't have that luxury. A lifelong dyslexic, he finished his scouting career at the rank of First Class not because he didn't want to become an Eagle Scout, but because his handicap prevented him from learning Morse Code, a requirement for advancement. Likewise, later in life, he abandoned a Ph.D. program when he couldn't satisfy the foreign language requisites. So, when I blithely discarded my shot at Scouting immortality, an occasion to atone for his perceived shortcomings, he was hurt. In hindsight, so was I.

History isn't going to repeat itself in Malawi! Though my health is a constant worry, and the opportunity to work on Obama's presidential campaign is enticing, I cannot walk away. I care too much about the Boys, knowing that if I jump ship, they will be evicted from my house and scattered into the villages. I'm also too stubborn to quit. No one wants to drop out at Mile 26 of a marathon, steps before reaching the finish line. I've made a commitment to myself, my family and my country, and I intend to fulfill it.

When one of the Boys modifies a routine, he declares, "I'm changing the channel," a reference to the television set he dreams of owning. For example, each of them bathes in the morning, and I bathe at night. After they inquire about this behavioral difference (none go unnoticed), I explain that I like to go to bed squeaky clean and that during the cold season, evenings are usually warmer (and, thus, better for bathing) than mornings. Always trying to emulate me, Alfred decides to follow suit, announcing, "I'm changing the channel, sir. Nighttime baths for me!" And, although he returns to the Alfred channel of morning baths after only a few days on the Mike channel, his willingness to try something new inspires me to act. To stay in Malawi, I need to change the channel, too.

My plan for persevering is simple. For the next several months, I will have as much fun as possible, doing things my way, on my time, and resisting the temptation to feel guilty about any of it. To wit, I will ride my bike often, get extra sleep, travel regularly, socialize more, work less, spend extra nights in Blantyre with friends, lead more hikes on Mulanje Mountain, and treat myself to culinary delights (and red wine). There is just one ironclad rule — I cannot leave early, PERIOD. I'm about to change the channel, but will it work?

* * * *

A few days later, a female student raps on the staff room door. I motion her in.

"Have you heard any news about girls' boarding school?" she asks.

"No, sorry," I say, "I'm still waiting for word."

"I want to study extra harder and become nurse."

"You can," I encourage her, "You are already one of my best students."

"Thank you," she blushes, "But I can do better if I live at school."

"I understand," I reply, "but first the donor needs to gives us money."

"Oh," she murmurs, "that will take many months?"

"Possibly," I reply apologetically, "but maybe the donor will help us soon."

"Yes, sir, I will pray about that," she promises.

"Thank you," I say, "and I'll let you know if your prayers are answered."

We submitted the funding proposal in November 2007, and it's already August 2008. I'm out of here in three months, which doesn't give us much time. I'm not hopeful.

A few days later, in a dramatic shift of events, Peace Corps approves the funding. Yet, during the eight-month approval process, the cost of several budgetary items (e.g., building materials) has escalated dramatically. Community members, elated that the proposal was approved, are reluctant to remedy the shortfall by slashing supplies of necessary items like cement or reducing the number of girls invited to board. They are frustrated about why it took so long for the funding to come in the first place.

To bridge the financial gap, I turn to friends and family in the States for help. Having worked on eighty-million-dollar patent infringement cases, I'm beside myself pleading for one-thousand dollars to complete a seven-thousand-dollar project, surely less than Peace Corps Malawi spends on gas each month. Nevertheless, it works — stateside supporters come to our rescue by quickly ponying up the funds. We're getting somewhere.

Yet, before we get ahead of ourselves, there is a landmine to diffuse. I need assurances that once the project is underway, the Ministry of Education won't balk and shut it down, squandering our hopes and hard work. I fear that the Ministry will take an "official" position that boarding facilities are inappropriate at schools that have been renovated by the ADB. To preempt this nightmare, Dora Mwalwenje (my Peace Corps boss) calls an old friend at the Ministry and verbally confirms (nothing in writing, of course) that this is not the case: we have a green light to proceed with the project. We are finally in business.

But it's not my business — it's theirs. Eschewing a leadership role, I decide that the project will succeed only if Malawians grab the baton and run. Malawi, their poor country, wants and needs a girls' boarding facility. Malawian children are the direct beneficiaries. Malawian contractors and laborers will be hired to complete the work. And if the boarding facility doesn't open early next year like it's supposed to, the likely cause will be a delay in the ADB renovation, which has been mismanaged by Malawians.

So, before receiving a cent of grant money, I call a meeting of community leaders.

"This is your project," I tell them.

"Yes, of course," they nod casually, failing to appreciate the implications.

"You make the decisions, and you are solely responsible for its success or failure."

"Oh," they twitter, starting to comprehend the magnitude of my words.

"Are you absolutely sure that you want this opportunity?" I ask.

The room goes slient. After a few seconds, which feel like an eternity, the village headman stands and faces the group. He adjusts his collared shirt and pants, and clears his voice, grand theater that leaves me waiting on pins and needles. The community wants the project, but he doesn't. What's about to come out of his mouth is anyone's guess.

"Yes," he speaks for the group.

"You want the project?" I confirm, checking my ears.

"We told you that we want it months ago, and we still do. When do we get money?"

"*Mudzalandira ndalama posachedwa*," I tell them, "You will receive the money soon."

And they do.

With money in hand, they spring into action. A volunteer committee forms, composed of a cross-section of interested villagers — teachers, students, school committee members, parents and chiefs. It is tasked with hiring a contractor and a carpenter, making logistical decisions and resolving any problems that arise. Once the project is complete, the committee will manage the facility by performing routine maintenance and setting administrative policies like boarding fees. Its first order of business, however, is finding someone to tackle the precarious task of acquiring building supplies in Blantyre.

Mr. Nyambalo is the lucky duck who gets to travel to Blantyre with me and a backpack of cash. Emerging from village capillaries (bike paths and corn-stalk alleys), we join other town-goers on musical-chair minibuses, which rumble through the dirt-track veins of rural transport, bound for town. Ferrying people to the main chamber of Malawian commerce, the minibuses proceed with magnetic persistence, dropping off expectant shoppers, reloading, and returning with satisfied buyers and their goods. Every day, over multiple trips, the cycle repeats itself. Blantyre, as the saying goes, is where the action is.

The city's heart pulsates to our arrival. Streams of people pour down boulevards and squeeze through claustrophobic corridors. Tripping over cracked sidewalks and curbs, slipping on discarded food wrappers, they swell forward through a dense array of shops offering everything importable, from food warmers to automobile tires. Stretched across the chest of an adjacent hillside, a massive open-air market sits precariously in the mud, poised to slide down the slope. For the time being, we stay on the pavement.

Mr. Nyambalo and I poke past the crowds and enter a hardware store. The owner, a thirty-something Arab businessman, shouts prices in a rapid-fire tongue, as each customer inquiry is nibbled and spit out in turn. Between bites, he pauses to puff on a designer cigarette limply hanging from the furrow of his cracked lips. Money and goods flow across the plywood countertop to the allegro symphony of cowboy capitalism. The owner looks up and recognizes me immediately.

"How are you, my teacher friend?" he asks.

"Fine, thank you," I reply, "I'm here to buy things for my school. Remember the quotation you wrote me?"

"Yes, but hold on," he warns, "all of those prices have gone up thirty percent. I just got back from China and Dubai. Costs are skyrocketing worldwide."

"I know. We'll buy as much as we can, but you need to give us your best prices — it's for a girls' boarding school."

He scrambles for a notepad and scribbles.

"I have everything you need, and here are the lowest prices I can give you," he says, handing me a fresh quotation.

"What about transporting this stuff?" I ask.

"Yes, sir, we have that screw in two sizes," he shouts over me to another customer.

"You told me that we could use your truck to haul these things to our village," I say, raising my voice to compete for his attention, "Is that still possible?"

"I would offer you my truck, but it's broken."

"Really?" I squawk, "What will we do for transport?"

"Don't worry," he winks, "A friend of mine will bring his truck here this afternoon to haul your stuff, but you must pay him in cash — no trace, right bro?"

"Ok, let's do it," I say, handing him cash for all the boarding school materials and supplies.

"Very good," he exclaims, "I'll make it happen."

"Thank you," I nod.

"This money is good, right?" he shouts, as I walk out the door.

"The money came straight from my account," I reply, "You can check at the bank."

He does before arranging our order.

With a few hours to kill, Mr. Nyambalo and I sit on a bench outside the hardware store. Tucking our feet underneath to avoid the sidewalk stampede of hucksters and beggars, we watch the day unfold in sun clicks and cloud breaks. Although we make a paranoid pact not to let the owner of the hardware store out of our sights, our stomachs get the best of us after a few hours, and we walk deep into the hillside market to aromatic plywood shanties, whose proprietors serve two-dollar plates of rice and beans topped with chicken.

"I hope truck comes this afternoon," he says, in between bites.

"Me, too," I agree, knowing that the chances are 50-50.

"What will happen if it doesn't come?" he asks.

"Good question. I have no idea what we will do."

Around 3 p.m., the truck shows. It's a behemoth whose long, planar trailer is stacked and bound for the bumpy road ahead. A quick glance reveals that most of the big items are present — cement bags, mattresses, lumber, wood stoves, and steel sheets — and once the invoice is double-checked against all the cargo, the truck starts down the road with Mr. Nyambalo, en route to Khwalala. I stay in town to celebrate the achievement and wash my hands of the aftermath, content to assist on an informal basis, providing lump-sum infusions of cash and watching the budget, but not managing the day-to-day affairs.

The boarding school committee, Mr. Nyambalo reports, springs into action. They call on the community to provide the funds and labor that have been promised: the school donates ten-thousand bricks, parents pool their meager savings to transport the bricks from a local kiln to campus, and students carry sand from the river on their heads, one bucket at a time. Their efforts satisfy the "community contribution" requirement, an effective differentiator of good and bad projects that is based on the simple premise that people don't like to waste their precious resources on pointless endeavors.

Paid workers come through, too. The contractor digs foundations and, brick by brick, walls rise, cement lines are smoothed, and roof beams are erected. Then, without missing a beat, he builds a washing station and coats all of his creations in white paint. Not to be outdone, a carpenter labors with hand tools, beside a snowdrift of wood shavings, to build sixteen bunk beds. The campus smells of cedar, his hardwood of choice, painstakingly harvested from Mulanje Mountain groves. I'm told that the scent is lovely, but I cannot smell it. My nose is saturated with another fragrance — the sweet perfume of success.

Why success and not failure? In hindsight, surrendering control wasn't easy for me. Yet, empowering community members, by showing confidence in their abilities and respecting their decisions, was profoundly effective. I provided some much-needed discipline and structure, but gave them the freedom to fail, on their terms. Consequently, they soared, and starting sometime in 2009, thirty-two girls should have an opportunity to live at school, finally spared the long commutes, unsanitary living conditions, and household chores that undermine their educations. Together, we made a difference.

Yet, due to circumstances beyond our control, I won't see the finished product.

The ADB renovation (eighty-five percent complete for months) is comatose, and the ballyhooed replacement contractor is still being found. As the days tick by, it becomes impossible, before my departure, for the ADB to uphold its end of the bargain and finish the new library, allowing our contractor to renovate the old one into a girls' hostel. Tragically, our little project, a development experiment that succeeded against all the odds, is on hold not because villagers have screwed the pooch (indeed they had triumphed), but due to a billion-dollar financial institution dropping the ball, a recurring story in Africa.

* * * *

On the heels of our boarding school success, I'm a burned-out, lame duck Volunteer without any responsibilities. Desperate for a sense of purpose during my last month, I decide to tie up loose ends before it's too late. There are places to visit, people to thank and goodbyes to deliver. With one foot firmly planted in Malawi, the other steps toward America, marking the beginning of a slow transition from sandal-strapped Peace Corps journeyman and Malawi celebrity to American average Joe.

Yet, before checking out completely, I keep a promise to my students. It's the culmination of months of planning.

"What are our goals?" I remember asking the Wildlife Club at our first meeting two years ago.

"Goals?" Myson said, raising his hand, "What do you mean?"

"Hmm," I said, searching for another word, "*Zolinga!*"

"Yes, yes," Myson replied, "We understand now."

"Ok, what are our *zolinga* for the year?" I asked again.

The students looked at each other and started whispering. Answering for the group, Alfred cleared his throat and stood erect, using every last inch of his five-foot body.

"We want to continue working extra harder to plant and water trees," he said.

"Wonderful," I replied, "Do you have other *zolinga?*"

"Yes," he proclaimed, never lacking in confidence or ambition, "Most especially, we want to take trip to Liwonde."

"Very good," I answered, "If you work very hard this year and next, and many trees survive, I will help you reach Liwonde."

The students clapped and promised to honor their environmental commitments by guarding the trees with their lives. Of course, whether they would remained to be seen.

Liwonde is shorthand for Liwonde National Park, the dream destination of every Malawian secondary school student. The Park is only about seventy miles from Khwalala, and as a student group, we can stay there free of charge. Getting there, however, is virtually impossible for students given the high cost of transport. During Wildlife Club meetings held over the past two years, I have learned that none of the students has the resources to pay a full fare (seven U.S. dollars), but each is willing to contribute food and pay half a fare. For the kids to go, I will need to pay the remainder.

The health of the trees is the key that can unlock my wallet, opening a magical door of Narnia that stands between village students and the crown jewel of the Malawian National Park System. Back in 2007, to maximize their chances of success, Alfred and I wrote a watering schedule that gave each Wildlife Club member responsibility over a particular section of campus, ensuring that every tree got watered every few days. By the end of 2008, the schedule is unreadable — ripped from wind whippings and washed out from sun damage — but it doesn't matter because each kid knows his or her assignment by heart.

"Are the students watering the trees?" I ask Alfred.

"I think so," he replies.

"You think so?" I retort, "As President, you are responsible for them. You are the leader."

"Yes, sir," he says, "They water every morning before school. I watch them."

He's right: the proof is in the pudding. By October 2008, adolescent trees dot campus like green speaker posts at a drive-in theater. Most have fared well during the long dry seasons, and a few of the hybrid mangoes are even producing fruit. The students have kept their side of the bargain, and it's time for me to keep mine.

True to my word, I book a bus and plan a three-day excursion to Liwonde National Park. When the bus arrives in Khwalala to take us away, I begin to appreciate the magnitude of the occasion: passengers arrive dressed in their finest clothes and scores of villagers assemble to wish us a nice journey. Students decorate the bus's exterior panels with colorful signage advertising our school and the purpose of our trip. It reads: "Khwalala C.D.S.S. — Mulanje District. JOURNEY TO LIWONDE NATIONAL PARK!"

On the finest of driving days, we set off. The first stop is Blantyre, which several students have never seen before, despite its proximity. As we tool around the city, the teachers point out landmarks like tour guides, and the kids seem elated. But after we stop for fuel at a gas station, several of them rush out to buy hard candy.

"What are they doing?" I ask Mr. Namanya, pointing outside the bus. "Where?" he replies, disoriented from a catnap.

"Why are those students buying hard candy instead of real food?"

"Oh," he laughs, "Their stomachs hurt because they have not travelled by bus before. They eat sweets to vomit."

"Oh," I say, "Thanks for the warning."

From Blantyre, we drive for two hours before reaching the Park. Arriving (to my great relief) without expelling a single drop of vomit, we find our lodging just inside the Park gates. It is a small compound of hostels and classrooms built by the government for school trips, complete with bunk beds, mattresses, flushing toilets (a curious novelty for all of the students and some of the teachers), an outdoor kitchen and an entertainment system to watch nature movies. It's not the Ritz Carleton, but it might as well be.

The next day, as we drive the length of the Park with a machine-gun wielding guide, the students are in awe. Too giddy to sit, they spend most of trip standing, pointing and shouting. With mouths agape, they furiously scribble notes about park animals (e.g., elephants, monkeys, warthogs) in their exercise books.

"Mr. Buckler," a girl screams at me, "Do you see that animal?"

"Ah, yes," I reply, struggling to match her enthusiasm on this, my third, trip to the Park.

"It is waterbuck," she continues, "I know this because it have white ring on its *thako*."

"Mary, you are supposed to use English," I remind her, "The English word for *thako* is butt or behind or rump."

"Yes, sir," she blushes.

By the end of the day, the kids are exhausted from information overload.

On the trip home the following day, the learning continues. Just outside the Park, students marvel at the power of the Shire River as it churns through dam turbines (incidentally, all power in Malawi is hydroelectric). Zomba is also on the way home, and we cannot pass without visiting Domasi Teacher College, where one of our teachers is a part-time student, and Chancellor College, the premier university in Malawi. Both schools are concrete examples of the gold waiting at the end of the rainbow. These kids have dreams of making it big, but until today, they were intangible wisps of imagination.

A few hours later, the group returns safely to Khwalala. Tired but giddy, they brag to friends about the odyssey, possessing a newfound perspective on their country and opportunities available within it. Before going, I fretted over whether the expense was justified (given all the ways money can help) and the message my contribution would send to the community. Yet, in the end, it was money well spent on an educational experience that Malawians wanted, and partially financed, for themselves — a marriage of Malawian initiative and foreign assistance. My work is done.

But, the fun is just beginning. Weeks before my flight home, I treat myself to the backpacking trip of a lifetime. It all began two years ago when I was reading Outside Magazine and stumbled upon an article about the "World's Wildest Bars." It described a remote lodge on the northern shore of "vast and forest-rimmed Lake Malawi" with "a bar and restaurant built into a rock cave near a waterfall." The lodge was reachable only on foot or via boat, and boasted vodka-filled watermelons "kept chilled in a kerosene icebox." The article whetted my appetite for adventure, and after other intrepid Volunteers sampled the lodge's treasures, I couldn't wait to experience them for myself.

Jared Belden (another Volunteer) agrees to be my travel partner. Built like a Cadillac Fleetwood, his body is lean but dense, like scaffolding longing to support the weight of a tool belt and cement bags. Passive and shy by nature, with a

tendency to hunch, he's almost ashamed of it. Yet, he's not ashamed of his mind —
a Rolls Royce fountain of published poems. Had he not been assigned to a school
in Northern Malawi, we probably would have become bosom buddies. Oh well,
better late than never.

We start our hike in the mountains outside of Mzuzu, near the town of Chik-
wina. A windy, tree-canopied descent to the lake shore consumes the entire first
day. Reaching Usisya Lodge in the early afternoon, we rest our sore bodies by the
water's edge. Thinking we have the place to ourselves, we are surprised by the
appearance of two youngish, white people. They are Hope Thornton, a longtime
American aid worker in Malawi, and her British boyfriend, both teachers at a local
community center.

"Are you guys Peace Corps?" Hope asks.

"Yeah, how could you tell?" I joke.

"Oh, just guessing," she replies, "When will you finish your service?"

"In a few weeks," Jared answers.

"Oh, that's fantastic," she exclaims.

She's a beautiful woman, or so it seems. I'm tired and dehydrated, so she could
be a mirage, but a mirage wouldn't look that good or sound that sweet, right?
Touching her to confirm her authenticity would be inappropriate, but I'm pretty
sure that she's real — yeah, definitely real. She's as real as her dour boyfriend,
whom I wish were a mirage. He scrutinizes our overtures with skeptical eyes, like
he's sizing up the competition.

"Have a seat and join us for a few minutes," I suggest.

"I can't, sorry. I need to help my boyfriend make dinner, but I want to ask you
something first."

"What's that?" I inquire.

"Are you looking for work after Peace Corps?"

"Sure am," I answer.

"You should contact Putney Student Travel, a Vermont-based organization
that sends kids on trips all over the world, including Malawi."

"Sounds cool," I reply.

"Yeah," she says, turning to leave, "I heard you speaking with the cooks earlier.
Your language skills are impressive."

"Thanks," I say, "but before you go, tell me which organization you work for? I
want to work for that one."

"Good night," she laughs, walking away.

A seed is planted. A boyish crush goes unrequited. Another day passes.

Just our luck, the following morning is hot and sticky. Making matters worse,
the rest of the hike runs along the grassy lakeshore, fully exposed to the scorch-
ing sun. The going is tough, but after another six hours of hiking, we stagger into
Ruarwe and find the Where Are We? Lodge, feeling like we have reached El
Dorado — our City of Gold in Malawi. Tucked in a serene cove, alongside idyl-
lic waterfalls cascading down from overarching mountains, the Lodge welcomes

us with a gracious staff and fully stocked beer refrigerator. The only letdown: no vodka-filled watermelons.

I understand why Outside Magazine was so impressed. In addition to the legendary bar and restaurant, the Lodge is a village of charming villas. Connecting everything are paths stretched across verdantly landscaped courtyards and cut through the stone hearts of breathtaking cliffs. The meals are large and prepared with a culinary skill that you wouldn't expect to find so far off the beaten path, and the prices are reasonable, even for a Peace Corps Volunteer. It's a playground for adults, a boatload of whom arrive every week on the famous Ilala — a rustic steamer that circumnavigates Lake Malawi.

Yet, after a restful and indulgent evening in Ruarwe, dawn brings a new day of pain. Leaving Where Are We? Lodge with profound regret, we march along a parade route of villages, getting barraged with requests for money. Trudging in extreme heat, steady streams of sweat pour from our flushed bodies like wax dripping from a candle, as the rocky, uneven terrain mocks our wrenched toe nails and bloody foot blisters. Still, we doggedly persist. Surviving a third six-hour day of hiking, we reach Chalo Village.

As expected, Jared and I are pampered in Chalo. We are given places to sleep and offered heaping piles of food. We are also informed that a boat taxi will be leaving the next morning and can drop us at our next destination, rescuing us from another day of podiatric pain. After a good night's sleep, and a beautiful boat ride, we arrive at Chiweta to the telltale signs of Malawian civilization — decrepit roads, unreliable electricity, and spotty phone service. Outside Magazine was right — it was a wild trip.

Around midday, Jared and I bid farewell. We are going in different directions like opposite ends of a compass needle. I point south, aiming for Khwalala, a two-day drive, and he stays in the north, headed back to his school. The fun is over, and soon we will begin the heartrending work of saying goodbyes, packing belongings and moving out.

"Good luck, Jared," I say.

"Thanks," he smiles.

"It was a pleasure, and I hope to see you again sometime, somewhere," I add, feeling the sting of parting with yet another amazing person after a brief but intense collaboration — a habit in Peace Corps.

"I had a wonderful time," he replies, "Good luck finishing your work and leaving the village. We're going home soon!"

Oh, yeah, we are, aren't we?

* * * *

Entering the homestretch in Khwalala Village, change knocks at the door, steadily inching toward crescendo. Like a broken record, it repeats a simple message: the status quo is a ruse, a convenient fiction — everything is impermanent.

Nothing is spared — not the memories we desperately clutch, nor the neurons that capture and preserve them. Not even the strongest metals, densest plastics or fiercest mountains. Certainly not me or my life plan or, better yet, life's plan for me. I try not to listen, but change is in the air.

Every day someone reminds me that I'm leaving. I feel like a once-dominant pitcher whose fastball has lost its zip being ushered into retirement by sentimental fans. Malawians aren't good at goodbyes, so they withdraw and sulk, or beg you to stay for another year of service. The Boys fret every time I ride my bike to a neighboring village, fearing that I won't return. And when I hiked the northern lakeshore with Jared, they acted like someone had died. Naturally, I worry about how they will react when my real departure date comes. No sense in wondering — I'll know soon enough.

Maybe it would comfort them to know that despite wanting to leave, and continuing to struggle with panic attacks, I'm tempted to extend my service. Did I really just say that? Why on God's earth would I stay? Well, the simple truth is that I yearn for the simple things — a third mango season, and another year of swimming among schools of refreshingly pleasant and content human beings. I also want to witness the drama of a Malawian election, scheduled for June 2009. After two years of immersion, I finally feel integrated and effective, at the top of my game. The deep, baritone beats of an African drum corps rattle my brain — stay, stay, stay…stay, stay, stay…stay, stay, stay.

But, it isn't to be. Go, I think. Go, I feel. Go, I know. Though I vacillate like a small boat on stormy seas, I recognize that without independent wealth and a masochistic disorder, one cannot remain a Peace Corps Volunteer forever. Two years earlier, I felt something calling me away to Africa. I followed, and the experience has been magical. For the last several months, that same voice, whispering from the depths of my internal compass, has been hailing me home. Once again, I should heed.

Back at my house, I inventory my possessions. After setting aside expensive camping gear and favorite items of clothing, I divide the rest among my closest Malawian friends, creating a gift bag for each one. Malawians frequently ask, "What are you giving me as remembrance?" which sounds presumptuous to Western ears. A bit taken aback, I usually reply with sarcasm: "Nothing" or "What are you going to give me?" But this *adios* is permanent, and I know that a gift from me will be cherished for a lifetime.

Yet, gift giving is tricky business. Who among my friends gets what, and how much, will be critiqued, and the results could spark an uproar of jealousy. So, instead of giving away my cell phone and bicycle (both expensive, highly prized possessions), I decide to sell them. The buyer of both is the alcoholic teacher at my school with whom I have squabbled on occasion over the years. The gesture not only puts money in my pocket, but reconciles a strained relationship, proving that it's never too late to do the right thing.

"At first, people were speaking badly of me," he says, tears filling his eyes.

"Yes, I know," I reply.

"They said that *azungu* didn't like me because I was bad man."

"They knew that I didn't like your drinking."

"But then you sold me your things," he says with a smile.

"Did that change anything?" I ask, surprised that it could.

"Yes," he answers, "It showed that we are now friends."

And he's right. After tiptoeing around the conflict for the last two years, quietly encouraging me to made amends with my troubled colleague, the other teachers appreciate my olive branch, despite the late hour. They are noticeably happier.

At a secret faculty meeting, they decide to organize a farewell party for me. Not privy to the planning details, I'm told only the time and date. And, on the big day, I find myself sitting in a chair at the front of a classroom full of people. Next to me, in a similar position of prominence, is the Group Village Headman. Other distinguished guests — lower chiefs, teaching colleagues, and politicians — sit along the walls, and several students fan out in the middle of the room, jostling for a good view of the action. Two Peace Corps Volunteers are also there, taking pictures and providing emotional support.

Mr. Kachingwe directs the program. It starts with sedate, longwinded speeches from distinguished community members. Then, there are gifts — a paper mache hat from a student and a wooden carving of Malawi from Mr. Zimbota — and an *a capella* performance from the Boys. At the end, after I say a few words of thanks and gratitude, female students descend upon us like angels, carrying heaping plates of *nsima*, cabbage and chicken, as a DJ plays Shape of my Heart by the Backstreet Boys. Overall, the event is bizarre, awkward and wonderful, which pretty much sums up my two years in Malawi.

After the meal, we hold a school dance. I finance it as a goodbye to the students. While they salaciously strut, groove and grind in the shadows of a congested classroom, I sit outside with the teachers, getting loopy on makeshift cocktails of soda and Powers No. 1, a cheap sugarcane liquor fancied by Peace Corps Volunteers.

"Why did we wait for two years to drink together?" I ask my colleagues.

"Because we don't drink, remember?" Mr. Namanya winks, two sheets to the wind.

Oh, good point. And, while we're suspending reality, I would like the record to reflect that the Backstreet Boys were not played at my farewell party.

Speaking of farewells, I have many goodbyes. Goodbye trees and girls' boarding school — may you endure as reminders that good things can happen when people work together to improve their communities. Goodbye Boys, the best housemates I've ever had — may you realize your dreams. Goodbye *nsima* — I will cook you in America, but you won't taste the same. Goodbye Peace Corps — it took me a while to find you, and the going was tough at times, but I've never been prouder of anything in my life. Goodbye Mr. Zimbota — I cannot continue without crying. Goodbye Malawi — you will always have *malo ofunika* (an important place) in my heart.

I move out the next day. My helpers, Mr. Zimbota and the Boys, rise early to transport my suitcases to town via *matola* (absurdly dangerous open pickup trucks stuffed with people). I, on the other hand, pedal out of Khwalala on a bicycle, riding a fitting farewell tour of thank-yous. Once everyone arrives at the Peace Corps house in Blantyre, I make a gourmet lunch for the crew. Being selfish, I keep them there as long as possible, but after Mr. Zimbota reminds me of the late time, I bid them farewell with bear hugs and promises of future meetings, assuring them that this is not a final goodbye.

"Michael, we will be missing you," Mr. Zimbota and the Boys say.

"Thank you," I reply teary-eyed, "I will call you and send text messages. We will always be family."

"Yes," they agree, "and when you go home, please tell people about us. Tell them about Malawi."

"I will," I promise, "I want to write a book."

"About what?" Mr. Zimbota asks.

I pause and compose myself.

"About how I came here to help you and to teach you about the world," I explain.

"Yes, you have taught us many things," he interjects before I can finish.

"Perhaps," I say, "but I think I've learned far more than I've taught. I will never be the same."

"We will never be the same, either," he says.

Mr. Zimbota extends his dark brown hand. It's the hand of a man who, over two years, has befriended me, taught with me, defended me, fed me, traveled with me, mentored me, nursed me back to health, scolded me, listened to me, rooted for me, bid farewell to me and, perhaps most important of all, never betrayed me. In short, it's the hand of a dear, lifelong friend. I hesitate before grabbing it, wanting to take it with me wherever I go, but knowing that it's desperately needed here in Africa. After we exchange a firm handshake of mutual respect, Mr. Zimbota gathers the Boys and slowly walks away.

A week later, leaving Malawian airspace on a shimmering South African Airways jet doesn't feel like an authentic *bon voyage*. That's because a Peace Corps doctor is on the plane with me, en route to South Africa with his family. Knowing that it is his birthday, I approach a flight attendant about making a brief announcement to the passengers and crew. A few minutes later, about twenty-thousand feet over Khwalala Village, she rings over the intercom, "South African Airways wants to wish Dr. Erfan a very happy birthday." It is my last act as a Peace Corps Volunteer.

XIV

REFLECTIONS

According to an African legend, "when the first man was made, he wandered alone in the great forest and on the plains, and he worried very much because he could not remember yesterday and so he could not imagine tomorrow." God, as the story goes, changed that by giving us memories. If the past is always part of the present, Malawi will never leave me, and I will never leave Malawi.

— Letter Home, November 2008

I squirm on the long flight from South Africa to Virginia, preparing for a torrent of emotion at Dulles International Airport. Deplaning anxiously, trying to ignore my racing heart and damp eyes, I glide through customs and emerge to find...well...NOTHING. No banners, no balloons, no cries of jubilation from familiar people. Thirty minutes later, my family trickles in, gaily chatting about my five-month-old niece, Morgan, and reiterating a warning from her pediatrician that I shouldn't touch her for at least two weeks, lest she be exposed to my residual African cooties!

Needless to say, it is a rather abrupt introduction to a phenomenon known as "readjustment." It usually starts with trivial discomforts, like sensory overload at a mall or grocery store. But, over time, a deeper reality emerges: you are changed forever and nothing you experience, here or aboard, will ever look or feel the same to you, not even the loved ones you left behind. You will forever straddle cultural, linguistic and geographical divides as a citizen of the world, traveling anywhere with relative ease, yet never feeling truly at home, except in the company of other Peace Corps Volunteers.

You also realize that, in the words of a returned Volunteer, "people at home don't care that much about your experience." While you were living your life abroad, they were living theirs in the good ole U.S. of A. Fresh off the plane, you're a novelty, peppered with the same three questions, "How do you feel? What was the first thing you wanted when you came back? What do you miss the most about [fill in host country]?" But your status plummets from exotic to mundane fast, at which point you face the sobering task of rebuilding an American life from the ground up.

Still, I readjust better than most. After leaving strong roots like friends, family and a six-figure salary, adjusting to life in a Malawian village was harrowing. Younger Volunteers, fresh from college or a first job, seemed more adaptable. Coming back, on the other hand, doesn't seem as daunting to me. Thanks to Malawi, I have a fresh appreciation for the opportunities available in America. And with graduate school behind me, I'm prepared to hit the ground running and find a mid-level job in international development. Now, if only the economy would cooperate.

Easing the transition are frequent Internet phone calls to friends in Malawi. Over many hours of voice echoes, speech delays and garbled sentences, I learn that all three of the Boys are thriving. Having watched them study hard for the college entrance examination (a.k.a. MSCE), religiously attending classes and spending every weekday afternoon with a math tutor, I am overjoyed to receive the following text message in February 2009:

> Mike we a'r hapy 2 pass MSCEplease call in order 2 know our progms.
> Bucklers in Mw please call 2morrow any time_bucklers hav done well.

Halfway through a D.C. winter, I bask in sunny news from Africa — all three

Boys have passed! Armed with these valuable credentials, Myson wants to become a businessman, Gift a nurse, and Alfred a teacher. Yet, although each has the ambition and intellect to achieve his goals, none can afford the cost of higher education. And there's no wealthy relative, government student loan program, or United Negro College Fund to save the day. So, I decide to write this book and tell their stories, hoping that royalties and donations from readers will be enough to give each of them the educational opportunity of a lifetime.

Adult friends in Malawi also have big news. MP Kaliati retained her parliamentary seat during the third democratic election in Malawian history, but it wasn't easy. After showing poorly in Khwalala, she punished the village by attacking its intellectual center — the school. First, she transferred teachers, sending Mr. Zimbota (a Kaliati friend) to a school with electricity and banishing Mr. Namanya (a Kaliati foe) to a wretched one. Next, to drive home her point, she blocked funding to continue the ADB's campus renovation, exacting revenge by hijacking the educations of innocent students.

Still, even Kaliati's wrath has its limits. My replacement — Timothy O'Brien, a Peace Corps Volunteer from Connecticut, reports that Khwalala, slow and dysfunctional as usual, is doing surprisingly well. With the school in the capable hands of two diaper dandies — Mr. Kachingwe and Mr. Nyambalo, students are attending, teachers are working hard, and test scores are up. In record time, a teacher house was constructed with community money, and a second is on the way. Finally, the trees continue to thrive and feed students as living, breathing testaments to my development efforts.

Yet, before I can adjust to these changes, Myson sends a message that Mr. Zimbota is gravely ill. He is confined to bed, I'm told, writhing in pain. When I call his phone, he answers and assures me that he will recover, but he's not the Mr. Zimbota I remember. Intoxicated from pain killers, he speaks with slurred words and long pauses, which I'm told is a vast improvement. Satisfied that he is healing, I wait three days to ascertain his progress. But, when I call again, his wife answers. Mr. Zimbota, she explains in a brave voice, died last night, leaving behind three beautiful daughters. More orphans for Malawi.

Stateside, life goes on — painfully at first and, then, a little easier each day. I settle in Washington, D.C., among supportive Peace Corps friends who served in Eastern Africa. To cope with reverse culture shock and Mr. Zimbota's untimely death, I cook *nsima*, decorate my apartment with African fabrics, and write... edit...write. My parents read a draft of the book and suggest that I describe their parenting style as "involved," not "overbearing." While they censor my writing and encourage me to find secure employment, the economy moans, laying off friends and decimating stock portfolios. Consequently, my search for an international development job is a bit, um, discouraging.

* * * *

For the first time in my life, I am what the Labor Department calls "fractionally unemployed: voluntarily in between jobs." It's nice for awhile, but after months of late-morning breakfasts, unshaven days and unanswered employment applications, I plummet to "discouraged worker: person who has given up looking for a job." Before I go crazy, I need to get out of the house and do something. So, I look for opportunities to satisfy the third goal of Peace Corps: helping promote a better understanding of other peoples on the part of Americans. One night, over beers and pizza, a teacher friend invites me to speak to her students, who are studying African cultures.

"What do you want me to talk about?" I ask.

"You can choose the content," my friend responds, "but maybe you could show some pictures and answer questions."

"Sounds pretty broad," I say, "Can you be more specific?"

"Well," she replies, "I'm particularly interested in hearing about what your life was like in Africa."

"No problem. I can do that."

Heeding her advice, I get started. I collect some pictures from Malawi and rifle through my Peace Corps journal for interesting vignettes, expecting the task to be brief. But distilling two years of life into a twenty-minute computer presentation is like writing Cliff Notes for *War and Peace*, so hours of work become days, and before I am done, a week has passed. With the substantive stuff out of the way, I turn to the frivolous chores, like getting a haircut and unearthing my finest pair of khakis pants. Looking respectable again, I march into the school and find my friend hard at work.

"Today, we have a very special guest," she announces to a classroom of seniors, pointing to me as I enter.

"Hello," I wave shyly.

"This is Mr. Buckler," she continues, "He is going to tell us about Africa."

Looking around, I feel like I'm moonlighting at a five-star educational resort. New desks and chairs gleam under the glare of bright fluorescent lights. Every square inch of wall space is covered with learning aids and inspirational quotes. At the front of the room stands a computer-activated projection unit that purrs, begging to be used. Every student has a book bag, notebook, pen, and calculator, not to mention a music player and cell phone. I've never taught in an American classroom before, but this one feels like the Star Ship Enterprise compared to its Malawian counterparts.

"Hello, everyone," I say.

"Hellooo," they moan.

"My name is Mike, and I was a Peace Corps Volunteer in Malawi."

The classroom barely stirs. A heavyset girl in the back twirls her hair and blows bubbles with her chewing gum.

"Do you mean Mali?" a frail, nerdy boy inquires, to the giggles of classmates.

"Nope, that's another country in Africa," I answer, "in West Africa, actually."

"Oh," he replies, "Sorry."

"No problem. A lot of people make that mistake."

"Where is your country located?" he asks.

"Malawi is in East Africa. Have you heard of it?"

Nothing but blank stares.

"It's a long, narrow country just south of Tanzania."

Zero recognition.

"It's the place where Madonna adopted a child."

Bingo.

"You mean, like, THE Madonna?" a Hispanic girl asks.

"Well, not THE Madonna," I explain, "She's been dead for a long time. You've seen the church paintings? I'm talking about Madonna the musician."

She and the other students suddenly perk up and nod — we're getting somewhere.

"Well, duh, of course it's that Madonna," another girl interjects, "We're not stupid, you know."

"He doesn't think we're stupid," the Hispanic girl replies, "Now, Mr. Buckler, where did Madonna adopt her beautiful child, David?"

"Excellent question," I respond, projecting a detailed map of Malawi onto the screen and pointing to the Mchinji District in the Central Region, "Madonna adopted David from somewhere in here."

"Wow, she went all the way to Africa for a kid?" an African American boy comments, "She can adopt me and my little brother in America for free."

"Me, too," I reply, "but you and I are pretty well off compared to village Malawians."

"When she came, did you meet her?" he asks.

"No, but I met a lot of other interesting people," I reply.

"Like who?"

"Let me tell you about them."

The class leans forward. A blowup of Mr. Zimbota's smiling face projects onto the screen, so lifelike that you can see the black fuzz growing out of his ears. "This is my old Headmaster and best Malawian friend," I explain with a cracking voice, before launching into a brief montage of Mr. Zimbota quotes and stories. Videos of Gift, Myson and Alfred follow, as do still images of Khwalala C.D.S.S., a village market, fields of corn, a dinner plate full of traditional Malawian fare, MP Kaliati, a witchdoctor and the girls' boarding school. For a solid fifteen minutes, the students seem genuinely interested in my presentation. They've devoured the appetizer — now it's time for the main course.

A mousy boy in the back slowly raises his hand, clutching his inhaler.

"Yes," I point at him, "do you have a question?"

"Sort of," he struggles, trying to force a question off the tip of his tongue, as the class waits.

"My cousin was a Peace Corps Volunteer," he continues, gaining momentum and courage.

"Where?" I ask.

"He worked in Romania from 2002 to 2004. He had a hard time completing projects, but he said that he learned a lot about life. What did you learn in Peace Corps?"

"Great question, David," the teacher exclaims, "I want to hear this, too."

I'm speechless. Harkening back to Malawi, where distractions were few and fleeting, I spent one-hundred weeks deep in the bush confronting the stark, unnerving mysteries of life. As I contemplated the philosophical underpinnings of my existence, there was no retreat or refuge, just an ongoing conversation with the apparition of wonderment. It was exhausting and lovely, but I haven't shared it with anyone. It's quite personal.

"In Peace Corps," I begin, "you have a lot of time to think."

"Uh-huh," David nods.

"You wonder about yourself and your place in the world," I continue, "asking yourself: Who am I? What do I believe and why? What is life all about?"

"It's like a vision quest for inner peace and perspective," the class clown blurts out, "Mr. Buckler is, like, an American Indian."

"Yes," I nod, "Something like that. But, since Malawi is in Africa, I am an African Indian."

The class laughs. Maybe my humor will distract them from delving into the deep stuff.

"What was the vision quest like?" the teacher asks, foiling my plan.

"Well, it was very long," I reply, "and at first, you unearth more questions than answers. But over time, a personal pattern of enlightenment emerges."

"What questions?" she inquires, "What answers?"

So I tell them.

"You do a lot of thinking about people," I begin.

"Sounds like a headache," the class clown quips, "There are so many types of people in the world."

"Interesting," I say, "Let's flesh that out a bit, ok?"

"Sure thing, man."

"How do people behave?" I ask him.

"We wake up and eat food. We go to the bathroom. We live."

"Who does?" I ask.

"Hmm," replies, "everyone on the planet."

"Very good," I say, "That's an important insight. What else do we all do?"

"Everything man. We pray, build stuff, die, fight, cry, and sing."

"So, what can we learn from your insight?"

"I don't know," he says scratching his head, "you tell me."

So, I do.

Nearly seven billion of us occupy the globe. We speak thousands of languages, live in myriad climates, make ends meet in countless ways and under a plethora of socioeconomic conditions, practice various cultures, and observe an assortment of religions. Sometimes, we seem more different than alike, tending toward conflict. Yet, in my travels, I have found that most people want the same basic things (e.g., family, clean food and water, shelter, safety, education, work, respect). With all of our differences, these shared aspirations unite us each and every day, in every corner of the planet.

Sharing this vast ocean of likeness, peoples of the world consciously orchestrate their destinies. By working together, embracing the ubiquity of the human condition, and realizing that divisions pale in comparison to commonalities, people can attain marvelous feats, such as stable governments and social systems, eradication of disease, masterpieces of artistic expression, and technological wonders. Conversely, dwelling upon differences, people are equally capable of wars, genocides, suffering and spoliation. Many outcomes are possible. The choices are ours.

"Well, speaking of choices, I'm choosing to call you crazy," the African American boy chimes in to a chorus of laughs, "You're a nut job."

"That's rude," the teacher scolds him, "I'll speak with you about this later."

"It's ok," I say, "I understand why he feels that way. Peace Corps is a pretty crazy experience."

"Don't let him bother you," she replies, "Please continue telling us what you learned living in Malawi. I really want to know."

"I learned that people make sense," I say, letting my words sink into the room.

I wish that I had known this from the beginning. Within the context of their everyday environments, and personal histories, people generally exhibit behaviors that seem appropriate and understandable, if not rational. As grassroots aid workers, Peace Corps Volunteers are barraged by problems that supposedly need fixing. The temptation, sadly, is to treat such maladies as functions of poor decision making and to judge the afflicted as largely responsible for their unfortunate lot in life.

Upon closer inspection, however, a holistic perspective emerges. Pixel by pixel, a portrait of village life comes into focus, each day yielding another cultural insight. Malawian men despise using condoms, for example, not because they foolishly flout the threat of HIV infection, but because condoms threaten their manhood. Friends sometimes give you inaccurate information not because they are liars, but because a wrong answer (delivered with a big smile, no less) seems kinder than a disappointing "I don't know." Ultimately, the problems around you are no less grave or disturbing, but the people seem more human, their weaknesses and strengths mirroring your own. The focus shifts from judging to empathizing and from throwing in the towel to crafting workable solutions.

"Is your name Dr. Phil?" the class clown interjects, "This stuff is too touchy-feely for me."

"I know that's a lot to process," I say, "but you asked for it."

"And we're not done, yet," the teacher interjects, "I have another question."

Half the class moans. The other half smiles.

"Shoot," I say, "I'll try to make it quick."

"Why do people in poor countries like Malawi seem so happy?" she asks, "I've always wanted to know the secret."

"The answer," I reply, "is modesty."

I've often heard people say, "Poor folks are happy. Wealthy people aren't." This certainly rings true in Malawi, where people are generally happy and positive. Dressed in rags and fighting bouts of malaria, they smile and laugh their way through each day with grace. Yet, when I travel home, Americans seem harried and bothered, operating under enormous stress loads. Why? There is nothing inherently uplifting about poverty, and there is nothing inherently miserable about wealth. What gives?

My father has a key insight. He used to tell me, "Some things in life you can control; some things you cannot. Don't worry about the latter." How would you behave if you were in tune with what the Chinese call *ch'i* (the natural energy of the Universe)? Like a surfer riding a wave, would you allow yourself the pleasures of unfettered releases, spontaneous plan changes, and freewheeling decisions? Would you be so individualistic? Would you watch the clock? Would you laugh more? Would you sleep better?

I learned in Malawi that happiness is modesty. Most poor people seem happy because they relinquish control. Accepting their lot in life as minor, extremely lucky participants, in a game designed by something greater, is liberating and relieves guilt and responsibility. Poor people freely subordinate themselves to the collective — family, tribe, faith and state, refusing to succumb to a siren song of faux personal empowerment. In short, they are listeners, collaborators, and practitioners of a holistic consciousness.

Unhappiness is narcissism. Many wealthy people believe in their own deification, existing in a delusional state of self-transcendence above and apart from others. When you are God-like, you can horde resources, flout healthy living, make war, ignore suffering, sit in judgment of everyone else, and manipulate them to follow your program. Narcissists create dangerous disconnects between what they are and what they think they should be. Their sense of control and power is a ruse, and deep down, they know it.

"Can Americans be happy like Malawians?" the teacher asks.

"Yes, I believe so," I say, "Many of us already are."

If we proceed with modesty, generous in spirit like Malawians, but rich in resources like Americans, the future is bright. Using our free will constructively, and collectively, we have the opportunity to renew our country and improve the world, helping each other and society at large. Doing that, I believe, is our purpose on Earth.

Thank you, Malawi.

* * * *

The school bell rings just as I finish. Students, jarred from philosophical daydreams, jump from their chairs and dash for the door, leaving me in their dust. A few thank me for coming and vow to pursue Peace Corps after college.

"Thanks for sharing," says the teacher.

"My pleasure," I reply, "I hope the students weren't too bored."

"No," she says, "That was pretty powerful. I would love for you to return sometime, possibly next quarter."

"That sounds great," I agree, "But, right now, I need some sleep."

"I know the feeling," she says.

"Teaching is exhausting," I sigh, heading for the door, "How do you do it?"

She tosses her hair back and laughs. We both know the secret — gourmet coffee.

Starving after the lecture, I rush home to make food. Finding corn flour in the cupboard, I cook *nsima*, garnishing it with greens, and slowly savoring each delectable handful, wondering how the Boys are doing. Then, I shower, slip into a warm bed and crack open a book — a bestseller about international development. Within seconds, my eyes become heavy, and my head bobs like a tetherball. Cameron, my former dog, appears somewhere in the depths of my subconscious. Fat and healthy, she runs across a grassy field and stops every few seconds to look back at me, like she has something to show me.

I follow her into a dense wood, and before long, we emerge into a bucolic clearing, ringed by snowcapped mountains. The air is pine fresh and everywhere I look there is radiant light. Off in the distance, alongside a gurgling stream is a grass-covered veranda where several people are engaged in lively conversation. Cameron runs to them, coming to rest in a tight chocolate ball under their feet. I try to join them, but every time I step in their direction, they move farther away. I try calling to them, but my efforts are futile — although I can see and hear them, they have no awareness of me.

As I watch them, details come into focus. Gracky, Mom, Mr. Zimbota and the Boys are laughing together, enjoying what appears to be heaven (or at least my conception of it). Dad must be elsewhere, probably helping someone fix a leaky faucet. As Mom munches on a raspberry Danish, Mr. Zimbota finishes his *nsima* lunch. They all live in the same melting-pot neighborhood, perched on a nearby butte, where the only residency requirement is being one of God's children. Africans bang their drums alongside Lutherans playing pianos and Nepalis strumming basuri. Trash gets picked up on Fridays.

Together, they reflect on how the world has changed. Since their time on Earth, environmental accords have ameliorated global warming, economic partnerships and the resulting redistribution of wealth have discouraged the onset of major wars, and most diseases have been eradicated thanks to the aggressive funding of scientific research and the equitable distribution of generic drugs. The Internet has connected people like never before, stimulating business, dispelling myths, and fostering mutual respect. Shakespeare is still the bard of choice and, for some inexplicable reason, Yanni continues to be a wildly popular musician, but those are the only things that haven't changed.

Malawi has finally risen. It's a stable democracy with a modest economy and universal health care. A revolutionary HIV vaccine has replenished entire communities, restoring families and closing orphanages. Having enjoyed the benefits of decent educations, Myson's two children (like many of their peers) are gainfully employed, one for the Ministry of Health and the other for a tourism company. Food security is an afterthought — for the last fifty years, Malawi has grown a corn surplus for its people and exported wine and cheese to the United States, which still leads the world, but only with soft power.

Marking a turning point in the war on global poverty, Peace Corps was ceremoniously decommissioned. It just wasn't needed any longer. In its place, a program sponsored by the U.S. Government selects foreigners to perform two years of community service in the United States. To toast the occasion, Gracky raises her glass of wine.

"On behalf of my dear Peace Corps grandson, I have a joke," she announces.

"Oh, very good," say the Boys, "We love jokes."

"Ok, here goes," she starts, "A corn stalk walks into a bar."

"Corn stalk cannot walk, can it?" Alfred asks.

"No, no, but it can talk," Gracky says, "To the bartender, I mean."

"Sure," Myson interjects, "I guess anything is possible."

"But the bartender speaks first," Gracky continues, "He says, 'Wanna hear a good story?'"

"What does corn stalk say back?" Gift asks, hanging off the edge of his seat.

"Come on, we want to know," Mr. Zimbota laughs, "tell us Gracky!"

"The corn stalk replies, 'Sure, I'm all ears!'"

The Malawians cannot stop laughing.

AFTERWORD

I wrote almost daily in Malawi, trying to preserve remarkable experiences that, woven together, formed a tapestry of Peace Corps service. Forgetting them would be shortsighted and tragic. It would also be a grave disservice to the people of Malawi, whom I have grown to know and love. I hope that by publishing this book, the characters that I met, and their narratives, will achieve a modicum of exposure and immortality.

As human beings, we relate to the world through stories. They help us find ourselves and communicate with one another. You may be tempted to believe that some of mine in this book are fanciful exaggerations or complete fabrications. I don't blame you. But, rest assured that what you have read is one-hundred percent "based on a true story." Sparing a sprinkle of creative license, it's the truth, as I have seen and experienced it.

Writing the book has been a joyful passion. After turning the last page, I hope that you better understand the country of Malawi and its lovely people, possess a newfound appreciation for Peace Corps, and steadfastly believe that as a country, we would do a much better job of delivering international aid if we approached the challenge as students with something to learn, not teachers with something to prove.

Very special people made this book happen.

Ralph Nader implored me to keep a journal, capturing my thoughts and adventures before they faded into oblivion. Thanks, Ralph, for yet another nugget of sage advice. You have earned my respect with an unparalleled legacy of public service and the courage to be unpopular. I listened to you, and it made all the difference.

Dave Kelleher provided much needed perspective. The brother of a Returned Peace Corps Volunteer, and no stranger to tough life decisions, he once posited an intriguing question: "Which would you regret more, missing an opportunity to serve in Peace Corps or leaving the comforts of your settled life?" This book contains the answer.

To see pictures of the people and places described herein, or donate to the Boys' college fund, visit www.FromMicrosoftToMalawi.com.

Tiwonana. Zabwino zonse.
Michael Buckler
May 2010

Rachel,

Will you marry me?

The Boys need an American mother, and I need you.

Love,

Mike

P.S. Don't answer until we get to Italy.

Breinigsville, PA USA
07 January 2011
252897BV00002B/2/P

9 780761 854012